Before
You Plan Your
Wedding . . .
Plan Your
Marriage

Dr. Greg Smalley
& Erin Smalley
With Steve Halliday

HOWARD BOOKS
A DIVISION OF SIMON & SCHUSTER
York   London   Toronto   Sydney

Our purpose at Howard Books is to:
• *Increase faith* in the hearts of growing Christians
• *Inspire holiness* in the lives of believers
• *Instill hope* in the hearts of struggling people everywhere
Because He's coming again!

Howard Books, a division of Simon & Schuster, Inc.
1230 Avenue of the Americas, New York, NY 10020
www.howardpublishing.com

Before You Plan Your Wedding . . . Plan Your Marriage © 2008
by Dr. Greg and Erin Smalley

First Howard hardcover edition January 2008

In association with the literary agency of Alive Communications, Inc.
7680 Goddard, Suite 200
Colorado Springs, CO 80920

HOWARD and colophon are registered trademarks of Simon & Schuster, Inc.

For information regarding special discounts for bulk purchases, please contact: Simon & Schuster Special Sales at 1-800-456-6798 or business@simonandschuster.com.

Edited by Steve Halliday
Jacket design by LUCAS Art & Design, Jenison, MI
Interior design by Jaime Putorti

Jacket images: Lace by GettyImages, Photodisc, Siede Preis; couple on the couch © Masterfile; wedding photo by veer.com

Manufactured in the United States of America

10 9 8 7 6 5 4 3 2 1

Library of Congress Cataloging-in-Publication Data
  Before you plan your wedding—plan your marriage / Greg and Erin Smalley with Steve Halliday.
    p.cm.
  1. Marriage. 2. Marriage—Religious aspects—Christianity. I. Smalley, Erin. II. Halliday, Steve, 1957– III. Title.
  HQ734.5674 2008
  248.8'44—dc22   2007017418

ISBN-13: 978-1-4165-4354-1
ISBN-10:   1-4165-4354-6

To Gary & Norma Smalley and Pat & Rosalie Murphy:
As our parents, thank you for showing us what it means
to have Godly, lifelong marriages.

To Gary & Carrie Oliver:
Thank you for the years of unconditional love, prayer, support,
and encouragement for our marriage.

CONTENTS

Acknowledgments   *ix*

PART ONE: BUILDING A CHRISTLIKE MARRIAGE

  1. If Only We Had Known   *3*
  2. How to Have a "10" Engagement   *21*
  3. God's Purpose for Marriage   *46*

PART TWO: HOW DO *I* STOP DANCING?

  4. Are You Expecting?   *69*
  5. Do You Want to Dance?   *93*
  6. Personal Responsibility   *126*

PART THREE: HOW DO *WE* STOP DANCING?

  7. Heart Talk   *159*
  8. Will You Forgive Me?   *184*
  9. Teamwork   *204*
 10. Putting It All Together   *223*

PART FOUR: ONENESS

 11. Leaving   *249*
 12. Cleaving   *275*

Epilogue: A Word from Erin   *305*
Appendix: Self-Test to Discover Reactions
   That Hurt Your Relationship   *313*
Notes   *317*

ACKNOWLEDGMENTS

First and foremost, we thank our Lord Jesus Christ, who fills our hearts with His amazing love.

This book could not have been completed without the help of many family members, friends, and colleagues.

Thank you to our children, Taylor, Maddy, and Garrison Smalley, for the special gift of being your parents.

Thank you to Steve Halliday, an exceptionally gifted writer, for being our collaborating author.

Thank you to Lee Hough of Alive Communications for his outstanding help in bringing this project to reality.

Thank you to our team at the Center for Relationship Enrichment— Gary Oliver, Carrie Oliver, Jan Phillips, Jackson Dunn, Ken Eichler, Judy Shoop, Judith Carson—for their support in the writing of this book.

Thank you to Howard Books and Denny Boultinghouse for their partnership and for bringing our passion for engaged couples to life.

And, finally, thank you to the Howard Books and Simon & Schuster teams who have engaged in copyediting, internal design and layout, cover design, and the myriad of details required to bring this book to press.

Part One

Building a Christlike Marriage

1

If Only We Had Known

Above all else, guard your heart,
for it is the wellspring of life.

—PROVERBS 4:23

A couple of summers ago, Erin and I were asked to take part in a wedding ceremony of a young couple we had counseled. I was to bring the message. Leading up to their wedding, I kept thinking about how people don't often remember the preacher's message, and I really wanted their day to be memorable. So, I thought long and hard about what to say—and then a brilliant idea hit. The only piece of information I needed was the type of flower the bride was going to have in her bouquet. Erin, acting as my spy, secretly discovered she was using calla lilies.

During the ceremony I talked about the beauty of the calla lilies in the bride's bouquet, and then I held up a packet of seeds (although I know lilies grow from bulbs!). "Your marriage is like this packet of seeds," I explained to the couple and their many guests. "You need some very important elements in order to grow the seeds of your relationship into a beautiful marriage bouquet."

Everything was going perfectly until I came to the last point—spending twenty minutes per day meeting your spouse's needs. Keep in mind that I was using a gardening metaphor, so to make my point, I confidently stated, "Much like fertilizer helps calla lilies grow strong and healthy, if you want a healthy marriage, you need to spend at least twenty minutes each day fertilizing each other."

The church roared with laughter. To make matters worse, I had no idea what was so funny. The metaphor had made so much sense in my head that I never looked at my words from any other perspective. I think the groom realized I was clueless, so he joked, "Can we get on with the 'I dos' so I can begin my twenty minutes of fertilizing my wife?"

I could have died.

At least I got my wish. No one will ever forget my message!

On the drive home from the reception, Erin and I talked about how much premarital training this young man and his bride-to-be had received in the months leading up to their wedding. You couldn't talk to them for more than a few minutes before it became obvious how well they knew themselves, each other, the basic building blocks of a great marriage, and where they wanted to take this new union of theirs. Erin and I were awed. We couldn't help but think, *If only we had known, before we got married, what they already know! What a difference it would have made! Oh, to have been in their shoes at the beginning!*

Now don't get us wrong; we have a great marriage today—after fifteen years of trial and error, much of it very painful! So as we watched these two become husband and wife, we marveled at how much they had already been empowered to create a strong and vibrant marriage. They had clearly been given the knowledge and the skills and the personal awareness to begin their years together on a very high note.

As we talked about how happy and confident the bride and groom looked as they strolled out of the sanctuary together, I said, "You know, I'm kind of envious of them. I wish we would have had that!" Of course, Erin nodded in enthusiastic agreement.

Which leads us to this book.

One of our major hopes is that by the time you finish absorbing the material to follow, you will be ready to stand excitedly on a platform, about to say your vows, armed with a high level of knowledge and skills and self-awareness. You simply don't need to go through everything we did in order to build a terrific marriage.

In great measure, this book contains what Erin and I wish we knew back then and lays out what we would do differently if we could do it all over. Of course, we also did a lot of things right! We want to highlight those things, too. We also draw upon our years of counseling premarital couples, tap into the most recent available research, and, finally, make use of one other unique resource:

We surveyed approximately ten thousand people regarding the most critical premarital issues so that you would get to inherit the learning of thousands of happily married couples. The collective wisdom of these couples will impart to you crucial knowledge and skills that can be applied to your premarital process. It's like getting knowledge handed down by generations of scholars. Erin and I are going to give you advice from people who have been there, done that, and learned how to have great marriages. It's like getting tomorrow's newspaper today and being able to cash in on the stock market because you already know what's going to happen.

That's important, because research conclusively shows that couples who succeed gain the knowledge they need *before* they settle into destructive patterns that often lead to divorce. In fact, you're 31 percent less likely to get divorced if you get some sort of premarital training.[1] Another study by marriage expert David Olson reports that 80 percent of the couples who did premarital training stayed together.[2] Premarital education can also reduce the stress of the prewedding period. Finally, according to marriage experts Dr. Jason Carroll and Dr. William J. Doherty, couples who participate in premarital programs experience a 30 percent increase in marital success over those who do not participate.

Such couples report improved communication, better conflict-management skills, higher dedication to one's mate, greater emphasis on the positive aspects of a relationship, and improved overall relationship quality. These benefits appear to hold for six months to three years after the program is over, and they extend to couples who enter marriage with greater risks, such as those coming from homes where parents had divorced or had high levels of conflict.³

On the other hand, if you just wing it and count on your luck and romantic attachment to make your marriage a success, your odds of succeeding are only one in four.

Such potent facts should help you to understand our vision: *To help men and women obtain the knowledge and skills to build satisfying, lifelong marriages where both people become conformed to the image of the Lord.*

Nowhere is this vision more realized than in the development of this book. We want to make a difference in your life as a couple *before* you fall into the hurtful relational patterns that too often lead to divorce.

Knowledge and Skills: Keys to Success

Erin will never forget the call she took one day at her parents' house in Phoenix, Arizona. I was on the other end of the line, euphoric with great news.

After I asked her to sit down and brace herself, I proudly announced that I had received something very exciting in the mail. I told her that she was preparing to marry a very rich man. I had received notification in the mail that *I had won the big sweepstakes!* I was in the running for a new car, a free luxury trip, or even a million bucks!

"I can imagine that you're doubting me," I said, "but before you go down that road, I should tell you that I've already called my dad and read him all the details—and he also thinks I've won!"

I ended the celebration phone call with, "Aren't you excited? I am certain that it will be the money!"

Meanwhile, Erin stood stunned on the other end of the phone. Truly, this would be anyone's greatest dream come true—entering marriage with no financial worries. Her joy, however, alternated with deep doubt. She had actually laughed out loud when I went on and on about what we would do with the money and how we would spend it and what I was going to buy her. She had worked in a psychiatric hospital during nursing school, and this call seemed eerily similar to many of the conversations she had engaged in there.

She hung up the phone thinking, *How cute and naive he is.* She probably guessed I was already putting in orders, creating house plans, and booking our luxury honeymoon.

Over the next week, I called Erin several more times to talk about our new wealth. I continued to celebrate, plan, and even share the news with many of my graduate-school friends. Finally, one of my friends encouraged me to seek legal counsel to see if this was a scam or real. Deflated, I did just that.

I made a visit to a lawyer friend—and in no time, he began giggling and laughing. He couldn't believe I would fall for this scam. "How are you going to spend all of your newly acquired wealth?" he snickered.

I left his office humiliated. Not only had I believed I was a millionaire, *everyone* knew I had believed the message of that letter, so craftily written.

That day I learned that without the proper knowledge and skills to read and understand the fine print, I could easily be led to look like a moron.

Fifteen years later, whenever Erin and I talk over this sorry incident, we still laugh at my naive thinking. In fact, however, it wasn't all that different from how we entered into marriage. We thought we understood the fine print—but in reality, we had a completely different experience than what we planned for. Without the proper knowledge and skills, we were left helpless—and, very often, humiliated.

Millions of couples have suffered a similar fate for a similar reason. And we're not talking about the death of a sweepstakes dream! What starts out as a promising adventure for many marriages often ends in the death of a relationship.

But you can avoid falling for that deceptive sweepstakes letter! You can succeed in your marriage and build a thriving relationship—so long as you get the right knowledge and the right skills. But what kinds of knowledge and skills are necessary? Where do we start? For us, that's no longer a tough question.

Make It Safe!

We often tell premarital couples that if we had only one hour to spend with them, we would use the entire time to talk about safety. Why? The reality is that you are about to go through an enormous amount of change, both good and bad. That tends to make you feel very unsafe, unsettled, unsure, nervous, even frightened. You're about to leave the single life you knew so well in exchange for a new kind of life you have no way of fully grasping. Major adjustments are sweeping in on you from a thousand directions: managing expectations, conflicts, household issues, your sexual relationship, ways to spend free time, dealing with in-laws, personality differences, moving away, leaving family, reorienting old friendships, etc.

And what naturally happens when you're trying to work through that much change that quickly? One word: conflict. This is inevitable. The presence of conflict in your first year of marriage is 100 percent natural and normal. It is virtually impossible not to bump into differences of opinions, beliefs, and behaviors as you deal with all these issues. As you endure conflict, arguments, disagreements, fights, struggles, or whatever you want to call them, you start to feel emotionally unsafe. And what happens then? Let us show you by retelling our first significant disagreement. It still makes me laugh!

We continue to debate the question even today, sixteen long years later. Did we really break up before we got engaged? And if so, who broke up with whom? Erin insists that I broke up with her; I say that we didn't break up at all.

How about if we tell you the story, and *you* decide?

We had known each other for years but started dating only after both of us had graduated from college. That in itself was a big deal, because I had a different girlfriend all through college and she had dated my roommate, so she never saw me as a potential date; I was just her brother. We liked hanging out together, and she always had fun with my family, but romance between us had never entered the picture.

We started officially dating in January. One month later, I called Erin and told her that we needed to talk. "Let's go out to dinner tomorrow night and discuss a few things," I said.

Now, my sister was already a good friend of Erin's, and she was getting engaged that very night. So before Erin and I went to the restaurant to discuss our relationship, we helped my sister's sweetie set up just the right atmosphere for him to pop the question. Here's Erin's version of what happened next:

"This all happened right around Valentine's Day. Pretty much, Greg said, 'Let's slow it down. There's just too much pressure. My mom and my sister are pressuring me.' I could agree with that, but it looked and sounded to me like we were breaking up. So when I left the restaurant, I thought that was it.

"When I got home, I found a 'secret admirer' letter that another guy had sent me. After I found out who wrote it, I started dating him. All the time, however, Greg was still functioning under the assumption that we were still 'kind of' dating. That seemed strange to me, since he didn't call and I didn't hear from him for some time. Later I learned that he had gone out of town with his dad, but he never told *me* he was going out of town. So I started dating other people and having a great time. I had accepted that 'we' weren't going to happen. I had grieved the loss of our relationship and had moved on."

The truth was, I really did have to slow it down. Both my mom and sister were completely in love with Erin; in fact, everyone was in love with Erin. They kept pestering me, "When are you going to ask her to marry you? Are you *stupid*?" They were putting enormous pressure on me to pull the trigger. But I kept saying, "Listen, I don't want to marry Erin just because you're telling me to. I want to marry her because I want to spend my life with her. And I need to make sure that this is who I believe God is calling me to be with." Everything was just going so fast!

So when we went out to dinner, I intended to say to Erin, "I really like you. In fact, I love the way this is going—I just need to slow down a little. It feels like we're moving at sixty-five miles an hour, and I want to slow it down to about forty. I want to keep moving ahead, but at a little slower pace. It's just happening too fast right now." I thought that after our conversation we would just downshift from third gear to second gear and keep right on dating.

But Erin heard something very different. Our story reminds me a little of the famous *Friends* episode, where Ross gets into trouble because he thought he and Rachel were "on a break." Well, Erin thought we were on a break.

When my sister told me that Erin had begun dating someone else, I shouted, "*What?* She's dating someone else?" I called her right away.

"Well, nice to hear from you," Erin said.

After that, it was a challenge to conquer and win her back. So I said, "I want us to date only each other."

Erin and I still debate over what really happened, but we both understand now that she filtered my words through a lens of fear. The whole conversation felt unsafe to her because she saw me as uncommitted to our relationship. Here she had been offering her heart to me, and my little speech made her feel as though I had rejected it. So, quite naturally, she took back her heart, closed it down to me, and ran.

The Biggest Factor

Your relationship is destined to take one of two paths. In fact, in every interaction between the two of you, you have a choice to make. You can either move toward creating and maintaining a safe environment, or you can fall into the trap of reacting to each other in ways that make your relational environment feel insecure and unsafe. Although many things will go into your relationship to make it into a marriage that thrills you both, the biggest factor is safety.

Why is safety so important?

The heart is the epicenter of life and relationships. Proverbs 4:2? makes this very clear, "Above all else, guard your heart, for it is the wellspring of life." When the heart feels safe, it opens. When the heart feels fear or senses a threat, it closes. Both safety and fear set in motion chain reactions that lead to very different destinations. When people feel safe, they are naturally inclined to open their hearts—and intimacy occurs naturally. Our goal in this book is to show you how to create a relationship that feels like the safest place on earth.

What Is Emotional Safety?

When you feel safe in a relationship, you naturally open your heart and reveal the real you. That's the very definition of intimacy. It's feeling free to open up and reveal who you really are, knowing that the other person will still love, accept, and value you, no matter what.

In other words, you hold your heart out to the person and say, "Here is who I am emotionally, psychologically, spiritually, and mentally. I want you to know my heart and soul. I want you to get to know who I am and appreciate who I am and value who I am. I am a very fascinating person who will take you more than one lifetime to understand! But I am not going to offer my heart to you or reveal who I really am if I don't feel safe."

You feel emotionally safe with someone when you believe that he or she will handle your heart—your deepest feelings and desires—with genuine interest, curiosity, and care.

But do you see the problem here? How many relationships can you count where you feel genuinely safe to open up and share who you really are? To how many people can you entrust your deepest thoughts and dreams?

Our son Garrison wished he had learned this concept of safety when he was younger. Garrison loves cats. They are one of his most favorite things in life. Fortunately for our son, we have a cat, Bumble; unfortunately for Garrison, Bumble will have nothing to do with him. As you can imagine, this kills him.

started when Garrison was a baby. He was so interested about Bumble from day one. Sadly, he was very rough. He never meant to hurt poor Bumble, but he would pull her around the throat, and grab her whiskers (cats hate that, by the way., Erin and I did everything we could to keep Garrison from hurting Bumble, but he would always seem to find a way.

Six years later, Bumble is still traumatized from Garrison's attacks. Worse yet, she will have nothing to do with him. The moment Garrison enters a room, Bumble darts out. This is no ordinary stroll either; I mean she tucks her tail and sprints out of the room.

Nothing that Garrison does makes a difference. We've done everything we can think of to restore that relationship, but nothing works. I've spent hours holding Bumble and Garrison in my lap so he can pet her. We've tried to "counsel" Bumble into giving Garrison another chance—stopping short of a full-blown intervention. Garrison has tried to talk her into letting him hold her. As Erin and I wrote this book at our kitchen table, one day we heard Garrison pleading with Bumble, "I just don't want you to not like me; I want you to like me. Please don't be scared of me. I will be nice to you." None of it made a bit of difference. When Garrison paused to think of some others things to say and looked away, Bumble made a break for the living-room couch. It just crushed him.

I've told Garrison over and over that Bumble doesn't feel safe with him, but he just doesn't get it. He doesn't understand why she won't just let him hold her.

You and I are no different than Bumble. When we don't feel safe, our hearts close, and we disconnect from people. Unlike Bumble, God designed us to hunger for intimacy and deep connection, to connect with others and experience relational intimacy—especially in the key human relationship, with a spouse. Yet many of us struggle with various aspects of intimacy, because it requires openness—and openness makes us vulnerable. We're not quite sure what others will say or do or how they'll use what they learn about us! This is why a lack of desire to connect—or an avoidance of intimacy in general—usually has more to do with attempting to avoid feeling hurt, humiliated, or embarrassed.

In spite of the risks, an intimate relationship offers many enormous benefits. Intimacy creates the ideal opportunity to love deeply and be loved, experience a significant sense of belonging, have a clear sense of purpose in life, have the ability to make a major difference in another's life, and have a way of fully expressing the best of who we are. And we have discovered that the foundational component of reaching this goal is to create a truly safe environment—one that is safe physically, intellectually, spiritually, and emotionally.

As we said, people are naturally inclined to be open and connect with others. Openness is the default setting for human beings. No state of being takes less energy to maintain than openness; you just have to be yourself, relaxed. Maintaining defenses, walls, force fields, and fortresses, however, takes tremendous energy. As a result, when people feel truly safe, they're free to be open and use their energy to enjoy life.

Focus on Creating Safety

Creating safety will help you to foster a climate in which you can build an open relationship that will naturally encourage growth. It will help you build a relationship in which you and your betrothed will feel cherished, honored, and alive. It's as if safety sets a soothing tone that allows you to feel relaxed.

If that sounds like paradise, maybe it's because Eden was a supremely safe place. Our relationship with God can be the safest relationship we will ever experience. God's heart is always open, His love is always available, and He always has our best interests in mind. We love how King David described how safe he felt with God:

> The LORD is my light and my salvation—
> whom shall I fear?
> The LORD is the stronghold of my life—
> of whom shall I be afraid? . . .

One thing I ask of the LORD,
  this is what I seek:
that I may dwell in the house of the LORD
  all the days of my life,
to gaze upon the beauty of the LORD
  and to seek him in his temple.
For in the day of trouble
  he will keep me safe in his dwelling;
he will hide me in the shelter of his tabernacle
  and set me high upon a rock. (Psalm 27:1, 4–5)

Before they sinned, Adam and Eve felt no fear. They enjoyed an amazingly intimate relationship with God and each other. They felt so close to each other that God described them as "united into one."[4] Nothing came between Adam and Eve—not insecurities, not sharp differences of opinion, not even clothes! They were completely open with each other—no walls, no masks, no fear. And their relationship blossomed.

Choose to Honor

Although this entire book is designed to give you tool after tool to create a safe marriage, we want to give you our very favorite way to cultivate a safe environment. This really is the foundation. It comes from one of our favorite verses. "Where your treasure is, there your heart will be also" (Matthew 6:21). We love this passage because it's basically saying your heart will be open to what you value. When two people feel valued by each other, they usually feel safe and their hearts are open. Another word for value is *honor*. Your heart will be open to what you honor.

Honor is an amazing goal for your engagement. The cumulative result of consistent honoring is like a strong, rock-solid lighthouse. By honor, we mean a simple decision to place high value, worth, and importance on the one you're going to marry by viewing him or her as a priceless gift. You just do it; it's a decision you make. Honoring gives legs to the words "I love you."

Honor is not only the first step of love, it's also the single most important principle for building an intimate relationship. The apostle Paul encouraged the early Christians to honor one another when he wrote: "Be devoted to one another in brotherly love; give preference to one another in honor" (Romans 12:10 NASB). Here's the definition of *honor* we prefer: "To give preference to someone by attaching high value to him or her."

In his research, relationship expert Dr. John Gottman found honor to be such a bedrock of a satisfying relationship that if one mate loses honor for the other, he can now predict divorce with 91 percent accuracy.[5] Without honor, you cannot attain intimacy in your relationship; in fact, it's impossible to create even a functional relationship without honor.

You and your future mate must commit yourselves to consider each other not only very valuable but one of the most valuable things in your lives, worthy of reverence, praise, and honor, without restriction. You must treat each other as treasures, and that attitude should govern all your actions and words. Whatever you highly treasure, that's where your affections, desires, and enthusiasm will lie. This creates a bedrock of safety.

Beyond pledging to honor your future mate, you can also learn to convey that honor through your words, actions, and deeds. Picture him or her as an individual personally autographed by God. Wouldn't you feel thrilled to be seen with someone who bore God's personal autograph? Wouldn't you want to have your picture taken with such a person and hang that picture in a prominent place?

Another way to take action is to list all the things you admire about each other. Take a moment and do that right now. What is it that makes you so excited to spend the rest of your life with him or her? What is it that you most appreciate? What do you value about him or her? Everyone has great qualities in some areas. Consider your partner's personality (e.g., introverted or extroverted), character traits, appearance, thinking patterns, gender differences, faith, shared values, concerns, opinions, and life goals. Maybe you most value his sense of humor, her sensitivity, his passion, her spirituality, his integrity, her attention to details, or his leadership. Whatever you value, put on your list. Post it in a highly visible place where you can see it every day. Personalize your list! The longer your list, the higher the value and honor you feel toward him or her. Let your loved one see your list and exchange lists occasionally.

Commit yourself to cultivating honor in your relationship! It will protect you from the storms that will come. The greater the honor, the safer your relationship will become.

Of course, none of us honors others perfectly. We all say or do hurtful things that dishonor the ones we really love. When you mess up like this, say, first to yourself and then out loud, "You're too valuable to treat like this. Would you forgive me?" The one you love is precious, and what you said or did to the other felt degrading and dishonoring. You honor your beloved when you see him or her—and treat him or her—as an incredible gift of God. Both of you have immeasurable value as God's unique, divine creations.

Keep Yourself Safe, Too

Understand that when you extend your heart to another person, sometimes, as a result of being human, he or she will be careless with it or will reject you.

It's brutal, and it has happened to all of us. What can we do to protect this invaluable part of ourselves, we whom God so loved that he sent His Son to die for us? Anytime you extend your heart, and he or she grabs hold of it and starts tossing it around, immediately you should say, "Excuse me. Apparently you have lost sight of how valuable I am, but I haven't—and I can't let that happen." We admit this sounds a little dorky, but you'll get the hang of it.

Of course, you can do this in a way that doesn't damage the relationship. When I extend my heart over some wall to Erin and she gets a little careless, I say, "Excuse me, honey, but I'm taking this back for right now." That's a signal to her to be a bit more careful, and it works.

This requires you to first recognize and respect your own incredible worth and value, as well as your own vulnerability. See yourself as God sees you—valuable and precious. As a result, you'll require your fiancé or fiancée to proceed with honor and care as you allow him or her into your inner sanctuary. When he or she gets distracted and forgets to treat you with honor, you respectfully inform your beloved that access to your heart is a special privilege granted by invitation only, that he or she will be asked to leave if the poor behavior continues, and that future access may be denied. Trust is earned and must be maintained and continually reestablished through respectful, honoring behavior.

Your ability to feel safe in your relationship depends more on your remembering how valuable and how vulnerable your heart is than on the other's ability to remember the same thing. The most important aspect of feeling safe is that you feel safe with you, that you are going to do what is necessary to take care of your heart—that you are willing to set boundaries when people are dishonoring you. Otherwise, you're safe only to the degree that he or she remembers—and in that case, you're helpless and have no say. One way to be safe with yourself is to never allow someone to express his or her feelings at your expense. That is never okay. If that happens, we hope that you will set an appropriate boundary, that you will say, "I would love to listen to you but not like this. If you are willing to do this another way, a way in which we both feel honored, then sign me up. But I will not sit here and allow myself to be dishonored." Why is this important? When people express their feelings at your expense (when they scream, cuss, belittle you, get angry, stonewall, and so on), what happens to your heart? Exactly, it closes. We are not saying that you don't want to listen to your fiancée. That would be bad! Instead, we are saying that it's never okay for her to dishonor you in word or action, because then your heart will close and you will disconnect from her. That's not what God desires for you in your relationship.

When you trust yourself that you will always take care of yourself, however, you can afford to give your future spouse a whole lot of freedom in your relationship. You know that he or she *is* going to forget, that he or she *is* going to have moments of untrustworthy behavior. You can live with that, however, because there's always someone taking responsibility—you. So for a time you pull back your heart and protect it. And when your loved one reestablishes honor, you can say, "Let's try this again."

A Hedge of Safety

When two people mutually commit themselves to honoring both self and each other, then the relationship begins to feel extremely safe. Both will tend to relax and open up, creating greater opportunities for deep and satisfying intimacy. If you consistently act in an honoring manner, the one you honor will be far more likely to choose to open his or her heart to you, as well. And isn't the ideal relationship one where entering into the other's presence feels like coming home to the safety of the Garden of Eden? When you make these efforts to create safety in your relationship, one day soon your home will feel like the safest place on earth.

We want to help you learn how to create a safe home environment that will enable your marriage to flourish and grow (just like the calla lily!). We want to help you focus on creating a partnership that feels like the safest place on earth. We want to help you put a hedge of protection around your relationship, one that allows you to experience the natural trial and error of two people coming together in such a way that it feels really good to both of you.

For years we worked with couples in crisis who came to us in last-ditch efforts to save their rocky marriages. We achieved a lot of success with these at-risk couples by doing just one thing: we focused on bringing some safety into their relationships. By the time they came to us, their hearts had totally closed to each other. And do you know the only way to get two closed hearts to open? They must begin to feel safe. So everything we did was designed to help these people feel safe again so that their hearts would once more open to each other.

You can benefit tremendously from their difficult learning curve. If you learn now how to make your home safe, you can build a rock-solid marriage that will bless both you and others for generations to come. Safety is the key! And everything we offer in this book is designed to help your upcoming marriage feel just a little bit safer . . . so that your hearts will stay open to each other, whatever comes your way.

Outside of a personal relationship with the Lord Jesus Christ, there is no relationship more important than marriage—and marriage requires the proper training and preparation, skill acquisition, and knowledge. After reading *Before You Plan Your Wedding . . . Plan Your Marriage*, you and your future mate will be well prepared to begin your marital journey. Our goal is to have you in top shape as you begin your life together. We are excited that you are joining us in preparing for the most important journey you will ever undertake!

Whatever the details of your story, someone proposed and someone accepted. Or perhaps you are contemplating marriage but have not yet made a formal commitment. Either way, you are reading this book because you want to have the best possible engagement and marriage. We commend you for your hope and desire, and so we say,

"Have a happy—and safe—adventure!"

COUPLE EXERCISES / HOMEWORK

Start the process of making your relationship feel like the safest place on earth by answering some basic questions:

1. On a scale of 0 to 10 (with 10 being the most safe), how safe is your relationship, for both you and your fiancée?
2. In what ways have you made it unsafe for your fiancé?
3. How do you most often damage the safety of your relational environment?
4. How do you tend to react when you feel unsafe in your relationship?

2

How to Have a "10" Engagement

I have come to the conclusion never again to think of marrying,
and for this reason, I can never be satisfied with anyone
who would be blockhead enough to have me.

—ABRAHAM LINCOLN IN A LETTER TO MRS. O. H. BROWNING,

APRIL 1, 1838

Erin and I met at Grand Canyon University in Phoenix, Arizona, soon after we both started our sophomore year. One day a good friend, David, and I were sitting on a bench in the middle of campus—a strategic location for meeting a new batch of eligible women because practically all students had to pass by that spot on their way to class.

David and I were having no luck until two beautiful girls strolled by. Before I could say anything (actually, David wiped away his drool much faster than I could mine), he informed me that he was going to ask out the girl on the left and I could have the one on the right. Unfortunately for me, Erin was the girl on the left. The girl on the right gave me only one date, which was disastrous, because I need at least two dates before someone can see beyond my idiosyncrasies.

David and Erin dated for more than two years. I got to know Erin because our social group did so many things together. Erin and I did not date each other during our years at Grand Canyon. After graduation we lost touch, but eventually we wound up on the same cruise ship together. She went as a nanny for the children of a popular Christian author, Dr. John Trent, while I went on my parents' dime—they felt bad for me after my girlfriend had dumped me. In a short time, the cruise turned into the "love boat" and I proposed about seven months later.

But it was no ordinary "take out an ad in the paper" proposal.

Erin and I had a favorite climbing spot in the foothills surrounding Phoenix. The spot sat on the peak, giving visitors a 360-degree view of the entire Phoenix valley. It was gorgeous, to say the least, and especially at sunset.

One day, a friend (not David!) and I hiked up to the spot, hauling a table, two chairs, a dozen red roses, Erin's favorite meal, a small stereo, a video camera, and other essentials. I then went back down while my friend waited until I could return with an unsuspecting Erin. When he could just see us ascending, he turned on the music and camera, lit the candle, set out our dinner, and left.

All went according to plan until Erin saw the elaborate arrangement. "Look what someone has done!" she exclaimed with a romantic tone in her voice. Then she looked at me sideways and demanded, "Why don't *you* ever think of romantic things like that?"

The enchantment had left her voice.

Since I didn't want to give away my surprise, I walked over to the table and sat down. Erin, horrified, cried out, "*Get away* from that table! What if the owners come back?"

Suddenly I knew exactly how Goldilocks must have felt. Erin tried to physically remove me from the table, and as she did so, was glancing all around for the "real" owners. Finally, I suggested that she consider the possibility that *I* was the owner and that all this was for *her*.

"Yeah, *right*," she replied, her voice dripping with sarcasm.

The deteriorating situation called for quick action. I was losing the upper hand and my perfect plan had begun to fade like the setting sun. Erin spun on her heels and was already vacating the area when I pointed out that the stereo, camera, table, chairs, plates, silverware, and glasses were all things she had seen around my house. "Either it's my stuff," I suggested, "or we're dealing with one strange thief."

Erin stopped, turned around, and took a second look. After a moment or two of stunned silence, the truth finally began to sink in. All of this really was for her!

Erin screamed with joy as she realized *I was actually romantic.*

The rest of the evening went flawlessly. We had a great dinner and a wonderful view of the sun dipping behind the valley below. At the perfect moment, I dropped down on bended knee and read a poem I'd written and had inscribed on a plaque. With tears flowing down both our cheeks, I gently slipped a diamond ring on Erin's finger and asked her to be my wife.

She accepted. And the rest is history . . . but it's not the end of the story.

Don't Feel So Bad

We've heard many wonderful marriage-proposal stories. Like you, we've also heard some bizarre proposals that make you wonder why the two people ever agreed to marry. Consider one personal ad in a local paper:

DAVID G. CONTACT ME SOON! BRING THREE
RINGS: ENGAGEMENT RING, WEDDING RING,
AND TEETHING RING. HAVE NEWS. DEBBIE.

Talk about a shotgun wedding!

An even more unusual proposal happened frequently in many ancient, northern European countries. In those days, a man would usually marry a woman from within his own community. When women were in short supply, however, or when a man saw a woman he desired (usually from another tribe), he might resort to capturing his bride-to-be by force. To kidnap a bride, a groom enlisted the help of a warrior friend, his "best man." In fact, our custom of having a best man is a relic of that two-man, strong-arm tactic—for such an important task, only the best man would do.

From this practice of abduction (which literally swept a bride off her feet) also sprang the later symbolic act of carrying the bride over the threshold of her new home. After a groom captured a bride, he disappeared with her for a while, so that her family couldn't rescue her. By the time they found the couple, the bride would already be pregnant. "Capture marriage" dominated the prehistoric world and remained legal in England even until the thirteenth century.

So if you thought *your* proposal was abnormal, we bet you don't feel so bad now!

If you want to have a great engagement period, a romantic proposal is a much better starting place than a snatch-and-grab hair dragging, but you can't let it end there. You need to do a lot more than that.

Seeding a Great Marriage

In his book *First Things First,* popular business author Stephen Covey writes about a unique tree that provides a wonderful analogy for your engagement time. You may never have heard about the Chinese bamboo tree, but as you will see, this special little plant has more to do with your engagement and its success than you might imagine.

The Chinese bamboo tree does not produce much noticeable growth for the first four years of its life. Instead, nearly all its growth takes place underground. For those first forty-eight months, you see almost nothing growing on the surface except a little bulb with a small shoot extending from it.

During these first few years the Chinese bamboo tree develops thick stems or roots, called rhizomes. Little surface growth takes place because the bamboo spends nearly all its energy sending out a network of roots that spreads out deep and wide, providing a firm base that will allow massive future growth.

If you looked at a young and frail Chinese bamboo tree during those first four years, you might think, *That is the puniest, most pathetic tree I've ever seen. It's gone several years without any noticeable growth. There must be something wrong with this tree!* You might even feel tempted to uproot the pitiful runt. But you'd make a surprising discovery if you tried.

As you took hold of that tiny tree, pulled with all your might, tugged and yanked and heaved and jerked . . . *nothing* would happen. You could struggle with everything in you and even break out in a hot sweat . . . and yet, zilch.

Do you know the beauty of the Chinese bamboo tree? Its roots grow so strong during its first four years that by its fifth year, the tree shoots up a staggering eighty feet. Eighty feet! Can you imagine? Something that on the surface had produced only a measly bulb and a tiny shoot *in one year* develops into an eighty-foot-tall tree.[1]

And you know what? The same thing can happen in your relationship during your engagement period. If you want a Chinese-bamboo-tree-like marriage, you must learn to cultivate strong roots. The right fertilized soil, plenty of water, and abundant sunlight will help you to grow those healthy roots. The key is not to get discouraged when you fail to see much external growth in your relationship. Remember: you first need *internal* growth before you can experience much *external* growth.

If you want a great marriage, then you must recognize the value of preparing the ground during your engagement time. You must spend time planting and seeding, fertilizing, watering, and weeding, even when you cannot see immediate results. When you do that, you will ultimately reap the wonderful fruits of the harvest.

The Most Dangerous Years

Don't make the same mistake Erin and I did.

I walked into my own marriage thinking, *Hey, I am the son of world-renowned Dr. Gary Smalley. Erin and I are going to have a grrreeat marriage! We are not going to be like other people, with a bunch of problems. No! We will know how to work through them before they ever occur.* It all made total sense to me. I was already on my way to earning a master's degree in counseling, and I had already joined my dad on the speaking circuit.

And yet I discovered that living in marriage is not quite so simple as all that.

Soon after the honeymoon Erin and I began managing our relational conflicts in an extremely poor way. It got so bad, just two years into our marriage, that I was convinced we were one major argument away from separation.

And then one day *the* argument happened. While I was driving, we got into a huge fight, complete with yelling. Our argument quickly escalated to the point that I had to pull off the road. Hopping mad, I drove into a parking lot in front of a health club. Neither of us considered that our windows were down or what we must have looked like to witnesses.

Did I mention that Erin was eight months pregnant at the time?

We continued to spew horrible words at each other, when a woman came out of the health club. Prior to our arrival, someone must have dropped a membership card on the ground near our car; and when the woman noticed it, she assumed it had to be Erin's. As she approached the car to let us know of the errant card, Erin finished giving me a scathing comeback. So at that moment, I yelled, "Fine, just walk home!"

This lady heard my angry words, looked directly at Erin's bulging tummy, and gave me a look that would freeze the sun's core. Appalled at my brutishness and apparently shriveled heart, she tenderly helped Erin out of the car.

I'll never forget that woman's look of total disgust. In that moment, I was convinced my wife and I were not going to make it. *Something* had to change. We needed help! As we discovered so painfully that day, the first two years of marriage for many newlyweds are difficult.

According to Dr. David Olson, the first year of marriage is the most dangerous in terms of the likelihood of divorce, followed by the second year of marriage.[2] Furthermore, a variety of studies suggest that the primary seeds of marital distress and divorce are already present at the moment an unprepared couple says, "I do." These studies show that premarital variables can predict which couples will do well and which will not—with accuracies of 80 to 94 percent.[3]

Despite the story we just told you, today Erin and I have a great marriage that is night-and-day different from the one we endured in those first few years. Although our relationship is far from perfect, we have worked hard to cultivate a marriage that thrills both of us. We still face conflict (it's usually Erin's fault!) and have to work through difficult issues, but we wouldn't trade our marriage for anything.

You can make the commitment today to do the work now that will pay off during your early years of married life. Don't sacrifice the time you need for your relationship by focusing on things that have little long-term relational value (i.e., planning your wedding).

The truth is, if you want a great engagement, you can have it—it really is your choice. But you must be intentional about the choices you make. Begin by laying a solid foundation *now* for a great marriage. You'll never regret it!

The Foundations of a Great Engagement

Over the past several years, we have surveyed ten thousand seminar attendees to ask them about their engagement time. We focused on two central questions:

+ What was the best part of your engagement?
+ What was the worst part of your engagement?

Some of their answers may surprise you! But if you're out to have a great engagement, you'll do well to listen carefully to their insights. Let's look first at their answers to question number one.

The Best of Times

In general, people felt the best part of their engagement could be traced to how they *focused their attention totally on each other*. Either they were enjoying a spiritual experience together, doing fun things, or talking about their relationship—and as a result, deepening their knowledge about each other.

As one person wrote, "the rest of the world didn't exist." These couples were completely involved with each other—the world of one revolved around the other. See if you can relate to a sampling of what these couples said they most cherished about their engagement time:

✦ We realized we were best friends committed to each other for a lifetime.

✦ We fell deeper in love as we learned more about each other.

✦ We were so incredibly in love, we put much more effort into pleasing each other in every way.

✦ We tried to learn not only how to build a relationship together, but how to strengthen our relationship with the Lord as well.

✦ It was a time of security—we could enjoy each other because we had won the prize and could relax—we no longer wasted energy on the hunt.

✦ We had an unwritten book before us, one that we would write together and fill with the most wonderful hopes and dreams.

These couples identified the following four components of their engagements as "the best."

They built a vibrant spiritual relationship with each other. The successful couples we surveyed took the time to weave God firmly into their relationships, long before they spoke their wedding vows. As one man put it,

"We made sure the Lord was going to be part of our engagement as well as part of our marriage."

These couples told us that they spent time together in God's Word, often through reading aloud a daily devotion. They had a strong, consistent prayer life, both together and individually. They went to church together. They made sure they were "equally yoked"—that is, that they shared a common commitment to Christ and had similar ideas on how to serve Him. They thoroughly discussed their spiritual beliefs. They made growing spiritually together just as important as growing together emotionally.

As these couples made such attempts to build a vibrant spiritual life together, they also tended to experience joyful emotions for each other—those warm, fuzzy feelings we all like so much, such as excitement, giddiness, euphoria, and "the spark."

How do you rate your spiritual relationship with each other? Do you pray together regularly concerning the needs in your relationship or your personal lives? Do you discuss the things that you are learning from your personal devotions or from the latest service you attended at church?

No matter how you rate your current spiritual relationship, don't get discouraged. You *can* have a vibrant mutual spirituality before you say your "I dos." If you could do only one thing to enhance your spiritual relationship, we would encourage you, without hesitation, to learn to pray together. Of all things, why prayer? Relationships benefit in amazing ways when couples pray together.

In 1999 The Barna Group came out with a study that showed born-again Christians are more likely than others to experience divorce.[4] This shocking figure made us wonder what is going on. Then we found a Gallup poll done in 1997 by the National Association of Marriage Enhancement, in Phoenix, Arizona. It showed the divorce rate among couples who go to church regularly is one out of two, whereas for those who pray together regularly, the divorce rate is one out of 1,152.[5] That's a divorce rate of less than 1 percent!

Could it be that prayer is the missing link in keeping couples together? It's obvious that just because a couple is Christian, doesn't mean the partners won't get divorced; nor does it predict relational satisfaction. But could prayer increase relational satisfaction, thereby decreasing a couple's chance for divorce?

I became extremely fascinated with this possibility. At one of our large marriage seminars, I surveyed more than one thousand married individuals about their prayer lives. What I found blew me away. Twenty-nine percent of the couples never prayed together, while 16 percent prayed together daily. That makes us sad. The rest split evenly between praying together weekly and monthly.

But do you know the really amazing finding? We discovered that on a scale of 1 to 10 (with 10 being the best), the couples who prayed together every day rated their relational satisfaction an 8, while those who never prayed together rated their relational satisfaction a 5. You don't have to be a researcher to see that's a huge difference!

This study shows what many couples already understand: it is prayer that makes two people one and binds two hearts together with the heart of God. James, the brother of Jesus, wrote, "Draw near to God and He will draw near to you" (James 4:8 NASB).

Prayer, like no other resource in the universe, intertwines the heart of God and the hearts of two people coming to Him in prayer. Prayer holds a couple together and causes each anniversary to be a joyful occasion that builds a stronger, more invincible union between husband and wife.

Although praying together is central to a great relationship, many couples are reluctant to spend the time sharing their intimate thoughts and concerns with their fiancées/fiancés. Don't let busyness rob you of the closeness and intimacy of prayer! In addition to increasing your relational satisfaction, prayer has many other benefits as well:

+ God ordained that couples pray together. 1 Peter 3:7 says, "Husbands, in the same way be considerate as you live with your wives, and treat them with respect as the weaker partner and as heirs with you of the gracious gift of life, so that nothing will hinder your prayers." The interesting thing about the word *prayers* is that the original Greek literally means "your prayers together." This is not a warning to the husband that *his* prayers will be hindered, but rather a warning to the husband that his prayers *together* with his wife will be hindered if he fails to honor her as he should.

✦ You will be following Christ's example: "Jesus often withdrew to lonely places and prayed" (Luke 5:16).

✦ It creates emotional and spiritual safety in the relationship by strengthening the bond between the two of you.

✦ It encourages openness between you two as you learn how you both think about spiritual issues.

✦ It makes it easier for you to discern God's will as a couple.

✦ It invites God's power into your relationship. Jesus promises in Matthew 18:20, "Where two or three are gathered together in my name, there am I in the midst of them" (KJV). *Nothing* is so powerful as inviting Christ into the relationship through the act of praying together.

✦ It decreases the conflict in your relationship as you develop more humility, increases your patience with each other, and helps you to see things from God's point of view.

✦ It strengthens unity. When a man and woman join to seek out the Lord's will for their future marriage, unity is renewed, restored, and rebuilt.

✦ It lays the foundation for a strong spiritual legacy for any children you may have, and their children, for generations to come.

So how can you develop a lifestyle of prayer as a couple, even before you walk down the aisle? Here are a few suggestions:

✦ Make an intentional decision to regularly pray together. Start every day with each other in prayer. In just a few minutes, you can unite spiritually for the tasks and challenges ahead. You can share your hopes and find mutual comfort and support in seeking God together. The enemy does not want you to discover the treasure of prayer as a couple! One of his strategies is to keep you and your future spouse from praying together by keeping you busy. Instead of worrying about all the wedding plans, take courage and suggest that you begin praying together.

✦ Be each other's prayer partner. Tremendous power is available when you do this. The Bible says two are better than one. There are times in your prayer life when you need others to pray with you and pray for you. Who better than the one who knows you best? Jesus said, "I tell you that if two of you on earth agree about anything you ask for, it will be done for you by my Father in heaven" (Matthew 18:19).

✦ Invest in books on prayer and study the prayers of the Bible. Read them aloud to each other. Discuss them. Try out their principles together. See what works for you and what doesn't. Use your study to actually pray together, not merely to learn about praying together.

Wasn't it Ben Franklin who once said, "An ounce of prevention is worth a pound of cure"? Whoever said it, it's still great advice. Satan works hard to destroy marriages. It is time for us to do some preventive maintenance to prevent the all-too-common disintegration of Christian homes.

They spent significant time together. In a survey of my own, I spent a year polling about ten thousand couples regarding their time together before they got married. "If you could give only one piece of advice to not-yet-married couples," I asked, "what would it be?" I wanted to understand the most critical elements of a new relationship.

One answer came through loud and clear: *spend time together.* Time together revolved around two important issues: doing things together and making the relationship a top priority. These individuals gave undivided attention to each other, spent a lot of "alone together time," put each other first, and desired to be together. Listen to how some couples talked about spending time together:

+ We looked forward to being together.
+ We spent hours and hours together.
+ We loved the time we had together, just the two of us: romance, adventures together, and communication.
+ We remember the thrill of constantly being in close contact.
+ We enjoyed getting wrapped up in the actual relationship rather than the wedding.

And what did they do together? What does time together mean? It can mean ministry together, sharing common interests, trips, meals, coffee-shop talks, trying new things (such as ballroom dancing), beach walks, parties—you name it. The couples we surveyed listed a lot of things, including:

+ **Places:** Long walks on the beach, sitting on the couch together, listening to radio, walks in the park, studying together, traveling to beautiful places, enjoying the sunrise on the front porch, camping trips, taking lots of pictures.
+ **Physical:** Holding hands, standing or sitting side by side, warm hugs, making out, doing unexpected things.
+ **Things:** Calling each other every night to say goodnight, hot meals cooked together, combining our households and obtaining new possessions together. Dr. John Gottman found that couples who bought a major appliance together—such as a washing machine, refrigerator, oven, dryer, etc.—stayed married longer than couples who made no such purchase. He be-

lieves that couples who make such a long-term investment are sending the message, "Let's buy something that will last twenty to thirty years, because we are still going to be together."[6]

They got to know each other on a deeper level. As we said, it's crucial for you to spend time with each other. But should you direct all this time toward any specified goal? The ten thousand couples we surveyed certainly thought so. Second on their list was "getting to know each other on a deep level."

Happily engaged couples increase their knowledge of each other. If you want to have a great marriage, you must develop a large fund of knowledge. You must learn his or her likes, dislikes, personality quirks—everything. Every husband and wife ought to earn a PhD in each other during their engagement and first year of marriage.

In the excellent book *The Seven Principles for Making Marriage Work,* John Gottman and Nan Silver suggest that successful marriages require husbands and wives to know each other and to periodically update their knowledge. Gottman and Silver found that husbands who developed a "map" of their wives' worlds, who made it their business to know their wives' psychological worlds, wound up in the 33 percent whose marital satisfaction remained high when a couple made the transition to parenthood.[7]

Tellingly, a lack of knowledge about each other led to some of the worst times in the engagement period for many couples. One person declared a personal frustration: "I found out late in the engagement that he really didn't like shopping, and I had thought for several years that he loved to shop." If you don't get to deeply know your spouse, you may well discover that differences in your backgrounds and circumstances can deeply undermine your marriage.

The most satisfied couples talked to each other with openness, without the pressure of living together, became best friends, and discovered multiple aspects of their betrothed. That takes a lot of talking! So what did engaged couples talk about?

Our ten thousand couples discussed all areas of expectations and touchy subjects, such as finances, religion, careers, sex, children, family, holidays, and the honeymoon. They learned about friends, family histories, and personal memories. They discussed how their family backgrounds were both similar and different. They spoke about personal interests, habits, hidden routines, medical issues, and true character. They also had conversations about the mundane, sharing with each other as much as they could remember of their lives, from birth to the present.

These couples made it a point to talk about their respective needs. They wanted to know a partner's thoughts about the future, about every dream in his or her heart. They spoke of fears, excitements, goals, hopes, and dreams. They discussed the roles that each expected to play in the relationship and how that might impact their life together. They tried to set goals and a direction for the future and planned future living arrangements.

One person advised, "Discuss every decision, every vision, and do those things together. If along the way you find you're uninterested or unwilling to experience these activities together—or if you have no desire to develop such an interest—then you are not a match." Such a growing knowledge base produces confidence and assures both people that they have each chosen "the right one."

We believe that asking questions is so important during the engagement time that we want to suggest several resources that contain specific questions you can ask each other. Among the best are these:

+ Bobb and Cheryl Biehl, *Pre-Marriage Questions: Getting to "Really Know" Your Life-Mate-to-Be*
+ Jeffrey Hoffman, *Are We Compatible?: Questions for Couples*
+ Todd Outcalt, *Before You Say "I Do": Important Questions for Couples to Ask Before Marriage*
+ Bob Phillips, *How Can I Be Sure?: Questions to Ask Before You Get Married*

+ Sidney Smith, *Before Saying Yes to Marriage: 101 Questions to Ask Yourself*
+ H. Norman Wright, *101 Questions to Ask Before You Get Engaged*

Ask questions about personality differences, family histories, relational needs, deepest thoughts, wants, beliefs, areas of sensitivity, trust, retirement, fears, interests, pets, television, holidays, space, children, taxes, secrets, savings, travel, romance, dreams, hopes, exes, friends, love, cleaning, cooking, parenthood, snoring, commitment, ethics, careers, in-laws, education, money, religion, values—and that's just to get you started!

They did some premarital counseling/preparation. Premarital counseling came just below the top three components just discussed in terms of the best things couples did during their engagement time. We simply cannot emphasize this point enough. Seek out a good Christian counselor and meet with him or her regularly to discuss your future life and marriage together. Furthermore, "read, read, and read"—devour positive, uplifting books on relationships.

A very low percentage of couples in the United States experience any kind of in-depth marriage preparation program. Couples typically spend a great deal of time preparing for the wedding ceremony, which lasts only an hour or so, and very little time preparing for the marriage, which is intended to last a lifetime. One reason couples avoid talking about the marriage in depth is fear that exposure of their differences will break off the engagement. It is critical, however, to explore the differences and deal with them *before* marriage so that they do not carry over into marriage.

Some approaches to premarital counseling are clearly more effective than others. One study found that although lectures may produce attitude change about family topics, large lecture courses for groups of couples are not an effective way of helping couples prepare for marriage. In general, the lectures disappoint rather than excite.[8]

The most useful program includes (1) a premarital inventory that assesses the couple's strengths and areas of potential growth, and the discussion of the results of this assessment with a trained counselor; (2) participation in some kind of small discussion group in which couples express feelings and concerns with each other; and (3) training in communication and problem-solving skills.

Researchers have developed inventories (e.g., PREPARE) that can be taken before marriage and can predict one's chances of marital success or failure with 80 to 85 percent accuracy.[9] Love is not enough to make a successful marriage! Although almost everyone who marries is in love, about 43 percent of all marriages end in divorce.[10] Don't let yours be one of them!

Finally, get advice from happily married older couples. Seek out some trusted mentors and observe, observe, and observe! Talk to others and include your friends in your wedding plans. Research supports the importance of friends as a source for finding a compatible mate.[11] Furthermore, research shows that friends' approval and positive perceptions are good predictors of positive marital outcomes.[12]

In terms of doing things together, you must also understand a very important difference between men and women. When defining intimacy— a deep emotional connection—most men and women do not see eye to eye, according to renowned sociolinguist Dr. Deborah Tannen. She insists that men and women define intimacy very differently.

Women usually view intimacy as "deep talking" or connecting through words. This is why Erin usually does not feel intimate when we watch TV or do something together. Instead, she feels a deep connection—she senses intimacy growing between us—when we communicate at a deep level, sharing our feelings and needs.

On the other hand, men usually view intimacy as "doing things" or connecting through activity (for example, TV, board games, wrestling, basketball).[13] This is why I do not feel intimate when we are merely talking. Get me talking while I'm playing Ping-Pong or basketball, of course, and that's a different story! Then I feel connected because of the combination of action and words.

You're probably like most couples—you want to deepen the intimacy or connection you feel between each other. You want to develop a closer friendship with each other. If that's your desire, *the key is to make sure that both of you get your intimacy needs met.*

Since most guys crave activity over talk, and most women prefer deep conversation to action, the engagement time must contain both deep conversation and activity. It's important to create times in which you both feel that your unique intimacy needs have been met.

And here's the really cool thing: did you notice that the top four answers our surveyed couples gave about what they liked best about their engagement time all involved spending time together (activity) and getting to know each other on a deeper level (meaningful conversation)? Isn't that beautiful? When both her needs and his needs get addressed, you're in for a delightful time.

The Worst of Times

While you can learn the most from the positive experiences of those who have gone before, you can also learn from their mistakes and regrets. In general, the majority of things these surveyed couples didn't like—in other words, the worst parts of their engagement—were the issues that kept them from spending time together or spending the wrong kind of time together and so suffering a lack of knowledge about each other. Let's take a closer look at "the worst" part of the engagement, starting with the most frequent answer.

They were apart during the engagement. Couples can get separated at this time for several reasons: military service, school, jobs, geographically distant homes, etc. The point is, the more you can be together, the better it is, and the more you are apart, the worse it tends to be.

I can speak from personal experience here, because I came home from school just two days before our wedding. I left most of the details of planning to Erin, and she rightly felt that, basically, I just showed up for the ceremony. I had opted for a reunion-syndrome mode of relating, and therefore I didn't know how to deal with the realities of our relationship.

Couples who fall into the reunion syndrome are so often separated geographically that when they're together, it feels like a celebration. It has a special-occasion or party feel to it. Couples in the reunion mode often don't get into deep conflict or experience many negative circumstances, simply because they're not together enough. This style of relating creates a false relationship heavily loaded on the positive and celebration side—until they get married.

As one man we surveyed wrote, "At the time, I was in the navy, and the ship I was stationed on, the USS *Carl Vinson* (CVN-70), was on a six-month Western Pacific and Persian Gulf deployment. Because of my absence and the separation, she was forced to make 98 percent of the plans and preparations herself—and that made me feel bad."

I can relate! Erin and I had a difficult engagement time, primarily because I moved to Denver to attend graduate school just two weeks after we got engaged. Being separated for the duration of our engagement was *not* one of our better decisions. Today, Erin and I both encourage engaged couples not to separate for long periods of time. When we were on the plane heading to our honeymoon, Erin leaned over and said to me, "I feel like I'm going to be sleeping with a stranger tonight." She was totally right. We *were* strangers. We had been separated for nine months, with several weekend reunions. At first I got mad at her for saying such a thing. Now, however, I can understand and appreciate the truth of her comment.

Planning the wedding/honeymoon was difficult. Why should planning the wedding or honeymoon be so difficult for so many couples? The reasons are legion—among them: too many people want input into the wedding plans or want to make plans without the input of the future bride or groom; one partner (usually the man) doesn't want to spend time planning the arrangements; the sheer number of decisions that have to be made (setting a date, whom to invite, wedding location, inside vs. outside, big vs. small, formal vs. informal, choosing china and crystal patterns, flowers, music, minister, furniture, etc.); trying to get everything done for the wedding while keeping everyone happy.

So much can happen! We heard one story about a crazed man who held up a bakery on the day of one couple's wedding. He wanted to kill himself and the owners, who had made the couple's wedding cake. The man held them hostage for five hours until he fell asleep. The baker then escaped and took the cake to the wedding, three hours late. The couple compassionately asked him to stay for the remainder of the reception!

They lacked knowledge about each other or did not have enough time to get to know each other. If you don't spend time getting to know each other before you're married, don't expect things to change much once you become husband and wife. Once you're married, circumstances can change, you get busy, or other things get in the way, so you'll *never* really get to know each other. As one person put it, "By the time we were married, we still didn't really know each other. After two years of marriage, with one child and another on the way, we still don't know each other or how to communicate. We are so busy that I don't know if we will ever get to know one another."

They had premarital sex. Many couples expressed deep regret over the compromises they made physically and sexually in their engagement relationship. We surveyed one group from Austin, Texas, a nice Bible Belt city. I assumed that this group of happily married Christians must surely have a lower premarital-sex experience than other groups. I was mistaken. Nearly 80 percent reported that they engaged in premarital sex.

It's no wonder that this issue is one of the most difficult parts of the engagement!

If you want a great engagement, set appropriate physical boundaries, get into accountability groups or same-sex friendships, do more group things, and have less time alone at night. The real question becomes how to find the proper limits to show affection (no touching at all is very hard, because we are touchy-feely people). How far is too far? How do you put on the brakes?

If you are already living together, we strongly recommend that you live apart for the remainder of your engagement, not just for moral reasons, but because research has shown the negative results of living together prior to marriage. One study discovered that cohabiting couples are less satisfied than married spouses with their partnerships, are not as close to their parents, are less committed to each other, and, if they eventually marry, have higher chances of divorce.[14]

Let's make it clear: *don't spend time engaged in premarital sex!* Why not? When you save sex for marriage, as the days of strife and stress arrive, you'll be able to recapture your friendship skills. Build the excitement for your wedding night and honeymoon! Stay committed to God's commandment of waiting to have intimacy until after you are married. Seek God for strength.

Research shows a strong relationship between premarital sexual intercourse and one's values and higher marital quality.[15] A prominent poll conducted by the University of Chicago revealed that adults who report the highest levels of sexual satisfaction were those who preserved sexual relations until marriage.[16]

Take the Time You Need

This engagement time is a crucial period for your future marriage. During the next few weeks and months you will be constructing the foundation on which you will build your entire marriage. So whatever you do, don't make the big mistake I made early on in our engagement. Don't devalue this precious time!

Almost as soon as Erin said yes to my proposal, I blurted out, "How quickly can we get married?" It's not as though I didn't have time to ask the question more thoughtfully. In fact, it took us about three hours to carry down all the stuff I had taken up the mountain (obviously, I hadn't thought through *that* part of my plan). To make matters worse, back at my home we had a house full of guests waiting to celebrate our engagement. It took us so long to get back that many people began to wonder if Erin had refused or if I'd kidnapped her, like the ancient Europeans. I jokingly entered the party shouting, "Relax . . . it took some persuading, but she finally consented!"

While I loved the idea of marriage, I hated the whole concept of being engaged for any significant length of time. I didn't want to wait nine whole months to be married. Instead, I wanted a quick engagement; I couldn't wait to start our new life together. I had very little desire to delay my gratification. At one point, I even suggested that Erin and I go to Las Vegas and book a quickie wedding at the Little White Wedding Chapel.

Luckily for me, Erin had much better sense than I did. She encouraged me to slow down, be patient, and use the time of our engagement to deepen our relationship.

I didn't know it then, but research is very clear about couples who date only a short time before getting married. One study showed that people who marry after brief courtships may make premature commitments; they have too little time to filter negative information regarding their spouses or to establish constructive conflict-resolution patterns.[17] Furthermore, shorter dating periods may not allow individuals to screen out incompatible partners. They may also allow individuals too little chance to experience some troublesome differences prior to marriage.

And what happens to couples who don't know each other well when problems inevitably surface after marriage? Their problems quickly escalate and intensify and cause significant difficulties.[18] On the flip side, the better acquainted the individuals in a couple are before marriage, the higher their marital quality.[19]

Why is this time together so important? It's key because what you do now will impact your future marital relationship in countless ways—some good and some bad. The good news is that *you* dictate how your engagement time will affect your marriage. Is your premarital time going to have a positive or negative influence on your marriage? The key is to understand a central truth about a great engagement—a truth that might surprise you.

Begin with the End in Mind

How can you have a great engagement? The final piece of the puzzle we want to highlight is the necessity of developing a clear picture of what you want to accomplish during your engagement.

If you want to increase your chances of having what we would consider a successful engagement, it's imperative that you visualize what needs to happen. In other words, you must *begin with the end in mind.* According to bestselling author Stephen Covey in his book *The 7 Habits of Highly Effective People:*

> *Begin today with the image or picture of the end of your life as your frame of reference or the criterion by which everything else is examined. Each part of your life—today's behavior, tomorrow's behavior, next week's behavior, next month's behavior—can be examined in the context of the whole, of what really matters most to you. By keeping that end clearly in mind, you can make certain that whatever you do on any particular day does not violate the criteria you have defined as supremely important, and that each day of your life contributes in a meaningful way to the vision you have of your life as a whole. To begin with the end in mind means to start with a clear understanding of your destination. It means to know where you're going so that you better understand where you are now and so that the steps you take are always in the right direction.[20]*

Ask yourself, "What is our ultimate goal during our engagement time?" Perhaps you want to deepen the intimacy or connection you feel with each other. Or maybe you want to spend more time together or increase your knowledge of your mate-to-be or get to know the in-laws or plan a "killer" wedding or get counseling to deal with past issues or learn how to manage conflict or meet important relational needs or foster a healthy spiritual relationship. Whatever your goal(s), your premarital success depends upon your ability to see the end clearly in your mind. To help you do this, we'd like to end this chapter by inviting you to take a few moments to take the following self-test.

COUPLE EXERCISES/HOMEWORK

Self-Test

1. All things being possible, what kind of engagement would you like? (Please rank.)

Engagement								*Extraordinary*		
From Hell				*Average*				*Engagement*		
0	*1*	*2*	*3*	*4*	*5*	*6*	*7*	*8*	*9*	*10*

2. In order to strengthen your future marital relationship, what things would you like to see accomplished during your engagement?

3. What would need to happen over the course of your engagement to bring to reality your answer to question 1? What would you need to do? What would your fiancée/fiancé need to do? What would your parents, future in-laws, and friends need to do?

3

God's Purpose for Marriage

I can honestly say that I never thought about God's purpose for marriage when we got engaged," Erin admits. "I was a newer Christian; I'd been a believer only for about three years and hadn't truly begun my spiritual development and growth.

"I had been dating one guy right before Greg, and I remember thinking, *Okay, which one do you want me to pick, God? Do I stay with my Catholic upbringing and go in this direction, or do I step into this new world?*

"But I had never even thought about the purpose of marriage. I just took the plunge."

Today, both Erin and I can look back and see God's sovereign hand in bringing us together. We recognize how well our personalities mesh and how much fun we have together. And we constantly thank God that He knew all of this back then, while we remained oblivious to what He was up to.

Our marriage, including both its pains and its joys, has encouraged us to grow and become more like Christ. But at the beginning, neither of us had a clear idea of what we were entering into. And that reminds me of a story.

One of our favorite memories comes from our predating days. My parents owned a home on the Lake Taneycomo River, not far from the Kanakuk sports camps that attract thousands of young campers each summer. Erin and I came up with this great idea to put on wet suits and jump into this nasty river—as cold as ice, with cow dung and other assorted debris floating in it—about half a mile upriver from the campers. We swam down to a bank near them, crawled up to some bushes, and then hid. When the campers got close, we popped up and scared the crud out of them. Looking back, I can't believe we got in that water, but we had great fun.

I tell you this story because we entered marriage much like we entered the river—obliviously. We put on our wet suits to protect us from the cold, then ran and jumped in, and that was about it. Without a second thought, we flung ourselves into all the muck, the cow dung, and the unseen microbials.

Marriage, of course, proved a lot harder than scaring campers. And over the last fifteen years, we've greatly cleaned up our "river." But just imagine how much smoother things would have gone for us if we had entered marriage knowing its true purpose! Imagine plunging into a cool, refreshing river deliciously free of cow dung, unseen microbials, and other floating debris.

Well, here's the good news: you don't have to imagine it at all, because in this chapter, we want to give you what we so sorely lacked. We want to help you both see and understand God's purpose for marriage. Believe us, the difference it will make to your upcoming union is nothing short of profound.

The Place to Begin

Many couples start sowing seeds of unsafety in their relationship when they imagine that marriage is all about helping each other be happy. They sincerely believe that happiness is the goal and purpose of marriage. Even Christians make this mistake—and it is one huge cause for so much *un*happiness in their relationships.

In fact, God's preeminent goal for your upcoming marriage is not your mutual happiness at all. It really isn't! That will surely come if you cooperate with God's real purpose for your marriage. But, in fact, He wants so much more than mere happiness for you: He wants joy; He wants impact; He wants significance and spiritual power and a compelling attractiveness that turns people's heads.

In other words, He wants to use your marriage to help you become more like His Son. That's the goal of marriage, to help you become more like Christ. Purpose is the place to begin!

If Erin and I had known, going into marriage, that it wasn't intended to be the answer to all our problems and the antidote to all our fears and weaknesses and deficits, we both could have saved ourselves a lot of pain and matured a lot faster than we did. It helps enormously just to know that God designed marriage—with its joys and its trials, its ups and its downs, its good times and its bad times—to help us grow to be more like Christ. When you realize ahead of time that the process will not always be pain free and easy (and that it's not supposed to be), then when the rough times come, they don't feel quite so threatening.

Knowing the true purpose of marriage also helps in a big way to make your marriage much safer. It vastly increases your chances of creating a satisfying and fulfilling relationship. And it has the power to change even bad things, the things that otherwise could threaten your marriage, into things that will actually make it stronger, better, and more solid.

How About You?

Do you have goals for your marriage? What do you hope to accomplish and experience with your future mate?

As I said, we never gave these questions much thought when we were getting married. Erin and I had stars in our eyes. We were in love. We imagined that our relationship was going to be pure magic. We were going to be that one-in-a-million couple who could say their marriage is total bliss.

The hope didn't last long.

If you are like us, on some level, either consciously or unconsciously, you are about to walk into your marriage with each of you having different hopes and dreams. And although we often remain unaware of these expectations (see chapter 4), they nevertheless shape the way we live and relate to our spouses.

God's purpose for marriage is very different than we expected. Many couples enter marriage with a host of romanticized ideas about love and marriage. With great excitement they anticipate a spouse who will be all that they ever dreamed of in a mate. They feel thrilled that God has finally brought someone who will meet all their romantic and emotional needs.

Be honest, now; until this moment, has your goal in marriage been to find happiness? Maybe you long to be whole or complete; to have a large home, perfect kids, and a family that everyone looks up to; to live securely and comfortably; to have someone at your side to drive away the loneliness, rejection, pain, sadness, or abandonment that torments you. Maybe you just want to satisfy your hormones or fulfill your sexual desires, or have a spouse who will love you the way you always wanted to be loved. To use a popular phrase, you want to find your soul mate.

But we have to tell you, if any of these goals describe your understanding of the purpose of your upcoming marriage, then you're in trouble. Big trouble! If grabbing happiness or finding a soul mate is your objective, then you're setting yourself up for many years of hurt and frustration—because what happens when you are *not* happy? What will an absence of happiness mean for your union? We can predict your questions, because we've heard them time and again:

+ Did I marry the wrong person?
+ Is there something wrong with me or with my mate?
+ Is my true soul mate still out there somewhere?

✦ If I'm not happy with this person, then shouldn't I look for someone who will make me happy?

Shortly after the wedding, most of us begin to see faults and chinks in the armor that we overlooked before the ceremony. Or we simply become disappointed. When our kids were young, Erin and I encountered an ongoing frustration in our relationship. Anytime I traveled, Erin would let our children sleep in bed with her. The problem? When I returned home, I would find my three kids in bed with my wife. This would then go on for the next several days.

I finally decided to have a talk with the children. I explained that while it was okay to sleep with Mommy when I was gone, the night before I returned home, they should not sleep with Mommy. They reluctantly agreed.

Several weeks later, after my next trip, Erin and the children picked me up in the terminal (back in the good old days when you could still greet people at the gate). Since the plane was late, the whole family had come into the terminal to wait for the plane's arrival, along with hundreds of others waiting for their arriving passengers.

As I entered the waiting area, my son, Garrison, saw me and came running, shouting at the top of his lungs, "Hi, Dad! I've got some good news!"

I waved back and asked loudly, "What's the good news?"

"The good news is," he yelled, "nobody slept with Mommy while you were away!"

If only you could have seen the looks.

Your future spouse *will* let you down. Suddenly you realize that this new husband or wife needs some serious work. In fact, it appears he or she is far from being able to fully meet your needs. You begin to see that—horrors!—instead of being sold on *your* ideas of marriage, this individual entered into the union with his or her own goals, along with his or her own list of needs and expectations.

You know what happens then, don't you? Your goal of happiness or expecting your spouse to be your soul mate causes you to try changing your spouse into the person you want him or her to be. You buy into the myth that if your spouse could change in one or two key ways, your marriage would be great.

Isn't it interesting that God never mentions any of these goals in the Bible? Nowhere does He talk about happiness, soul mates, a large home, perfect kids, security, comfort, companionship, sex, or even love as the purpose for marriage. Instead, He tends to say things like this:

> *Wives, submit to your husbands as to the Lord. . . .*
> *Husbands, love your wives, just as Christ loved the church and gave himself up for her. (Ephesians 5:22, 25)*

God created mankind and life on planet Earth, including marriage, with something far more wonderful in mind than simply providing a place where we can get our needs met and find happiness. C. S. Lewis said it well:

> *This is the whole of Christianity. There is nothing else. It is so easy to get muddled about that. It is easy to think that the Church has a lot of different objectives—education, building, missions, holding services. The Church exists for nothing else but to draw men into Christ, to make them little Christs. If they are not doing that, all the cathedrals, clergy, missions, sermons, even the Bible itself, are simply a waste of time. God became Man for no other purpose. It is even doubtful, you know, whether the whole universe was created for any other purpose. It says in the Bible that the whole universe was made for Christ and that everything is to be gathered together in Him.*[1]

God uses marriage to accomplish a very important goal—to help us become like Christ. As Paul so clearly understood, "Those God foreknew he also predestined to be *conformed to the likeness of his Son*, that he might be the firstborn among many brothers (Romans 8:29). If you miss out on this, your marriage is destined for pain and frustration. But if you "get it"—especially now as you prepare to enter the company of the hitched—then you will be so far ahead of the pack that you'll be experiencing what you really want in your marriage long before Erin and I did in ours.

The Real Test

As you prepare to enter the holy state of matrimony, rather than asking yourself, *How will my needs be met?* ask, *Does my life show evidence of Christ's character?* Marriage is not the answer to meeting life's needs. It never was designed to do that. Christ is the answer. In God's infinite wisdom He knew that our greatest relational needs would be met as we become like His son. As with everything else He created, God wants to use marriage to direct us toward Himself. God uses the challenges and the joys of marriage to help shape and mold us into the image of Jesus—and that's been His goal from the beginning:

> God said, "Let us make man in our image, in our likeness, and let them rule over the fish of the sea and the birds of the air, over the livestock, over all the earth, and over all the creatures that move along the ground."
> So God created man in his own image,
> in the image of God he created him;
> male and female he created them. (Genesis 1:26–27)

This seems so simple: a great marriage is the outcome of becoming Christlike. So, the real question is, how do we know if we are becoming like Jesus? Is the answer church attendance, tithing, time in the Word, frequency and duration of prayer, learning Bible doctrine, or abstaining from sin? These are important, but Christ makes it very clear about how we know if our lives are being transformed, in John 13:34–35: "A new command I give you: Love one another. As I have loved you, so you must love one another. By this all men will know that you are my disciples, if you love one another." As you both become Christlike, the evidence will be your ability to love each other as Christ loves you.

A Christlike love in your marriage begins by putting into practice what Jesus Christ called the greatest commandment: " 'You must love the Lord your God with all your heart, all your soul, all your mind, and all your strength.' The second is equally important: 'Love your neighbor as yourself' " (Mark 12:29–31 NLT).

By now you may be wondering, *how can I live out the greatest commandment?* It really boils down to three important components. Each of these three components is as important as the others. Neglect any one of the three, and you'll soon be heading for trouble in your engagement and future marriage. When you pay special attention to all three, however, you'll vastly increase your chances of strengthening and deepening the special relationship you're building.

Plug In to the True Power Source

At certain times in our lives, we run headlong into an inescapable fact: *life is not fulfilling.* It's actually often unfair and exhausting. We can never take in enough "life" from enough people, places, or things to keep our lives filled and overflowing with the contentment we want so much.

Focusing on people and places and things does not deliver the positive emotions we want. Instead, it saddles us with the very negative emotions we've tried all our lives to avoid. When we depend on a person, place, or thing for "life," we wind up with hurt feelings, worry, anxiety, fear, unrest, uncertainty, and confusion.

Nevertheless, we all sometimes look to people, places, and things to provide us with what we need. We're all selfish; we all want others to cooperate in meeting our needs right now. My dad discovered this the hard way.

"Why won't this boat work!" echoed across the lake as my dad yelled and stomped his foot. Now it was official: he was completely frustrated and totally embarrassed. Dad had bragged about his new boat, how wonderful it was, what a great time we'd have on the lake, and now the only thing that came to his mind was the proverb: "Pride cometh before a fall."

A missionary family was staying with us—seven of them altogether. In addition to room and board, Dad promised them an enjoyable adventure out on the lake aboard the brand-new boat that he'd recently purchased.

The next day, we packed a picnic lunch, loaded fishing gear, water skis, and anything else that could be used for water fun. Dad and I then herded this entire family onto our boat. The best part was that this was to be the missionary family's first time on a lake boat. It was going to be the perfect day. Dad should have known better!

With everyone aboard, anticipation brewing, excitement in the air, I pushed away from the dock and then took my seat behind my father the Skipper. I guess that made me Gilligan!

"Let's go have some fun!" Dad yelled. The entire boat erupted in screams and whistles of joy and happiness.

Trying to ham it up even more, Dad told the young kids to give him an official count down.

Five . . . Four . . . Three . . . Two . . . One . . . Blast-off!

We flew away from the dock like a rocket ship. The best part was hearing the five-year-old boy say to his father, "This is the coolest boat on the lake!"

Dad was in heaven. But then something happened.

Why are we losing speed? Dad thought. Worse yet, why had the engine stopped?

"Daddy," cried the young boy, "What's wrong, why are we slowing down? I want to go faster!"

"Don't worry, everyone," Dad said, "I'll have this fixed in a second."

After turning the ignition key several times, the engine roared back to life. And once again we were off.

And then it happened again. The engine died. What was going on?

This pattern of the engine starting and the engine stopping went on for the next fifteen minutes. Dad checked the engine, gas level, oil, and any other thing he could possibly think of. As soon as he'd get the engine running, it would die. Finally he screamed out of total frustration. I'm sure he wanted to sink that stupid boat right where it sat floating, but with the missionary family aboard, he figured his salvation was at stake if something happened to one of them.

And that's when I said, "Yeah, Dad, what is this cord for? Because any time the motor is running and I pull it, the engine stops." And then I started laughing.

I'm sure this is how Abraham possibly could have placed his son Isaac on the altar to sacrifice him. Like me, I'm sure Isaac had done something to completely irritate his father.

The cord that I was pulling every time Dad got the boat running was the emergency engine kill. My father had been ready to blow up his boat, while all along it had been me playing a practical joke. At least I thought it was funny!

For a boat, or anything electrical to function as it was designed, it needs to be connected to a power source. If human relationships are to function as they were designed, they, too, need to be connected to the relational power Source. And there is only one power in the universe that provides the perfect and unlimited Source that makes a marriage work.

God!

He wants to be the first and foremost one to meet your needs. In fact, He's the only one who really can do so. He's the only power Source that fits you. That's how you were designed, and there's no getting around it.

God is the ultimate Source of relationships. Galatians 2:20 describes this real Source for lasting fulfillment: "I am crucified with Christ: nevertheless I live, yet not I, but Christ liveth in me: and the life which I now live in the flesh I live by the faith of the Son of God, who loved me, and gave himself for me" (KJV). Christ alone can fill you to overflowing, because God designed you to be wired to his heavenly 220-volt (Galatians 2:20, get it?) current, not our earthly 110 stuff. Galatians 1:10 says, "Am I now trying to win the approval of men, or of God? Or am I trying to please men? If I were still trying to please men, I would not be a servant of Christ."

Matthew 6:33 also clearly shows us our Source of life: "Seek first his kingdom and his righteousness, and all these things will be given to you as well." When you put God first in your life, He promises to meet all your needs. When you look to Christ to be your main Source of life, He becomes number one for you. In other words, He's the highest priority in your life. When you focus on Jesus Christ as the sole Source of your life, an amazing thing happens. Because He loves you and actually possesses the wisdom, love, peace, and joy you've always wanted, He alone can fill you to the fullest. And that's exactly what He promises to do for all His children:

> *I pray that out of his glorious riches he may strengthen you with power through his Spirit in your inner being, so that Christ may dwell in your hearts through faith. And I pray that you, being rooted and established in love, may have power, together with all the saints, to grasp how wide and long and high and deep is the love of Christ, and to know this love that surpasses knowledge*—that you may be filled to the measure of all the fullness of God.
>
> *Now to him who is able to do immeasurably more than all we ask or imagine, according to his power that is at work within us, to him be glory in the church and in Christ Jesus throughout all generations, for ever and ever! Amen. (Ephesians 3:16–21)*

Can you be any more filled than full? Absolutely not!

If you ever start to feel worry, fear, hurt, or any other negative emotion, you should thank God for them. Then you should pray and ask forgiveness for trying to plug in to something that is less than God. Finally, ask Him alone to fill your life. Psalm 62:5–8 says, "Find rest, O my soul, in God alone; my hope comes from him. He alone is my rock and my salvation; he is my fortress, I will not be shaken. My salvation and my honor depend on God; he is my mighty rock, my refuge. Trust in him at all times, O people; pour out your hearts to him, for God is our refuge."

We are to wait and hope in God alone. He's our rock, our salvation, our rear guard, our hiding place. He's everything we'll ever need! Nothing on this earth compares to knowing Him.

> *Whatever was to my profit I now consider loss for the sake of Christ.*
> *What is more, I consider everything a loss compared to the surpassing*
> *greatness of knowing Christ Jesus my Lord, for whose sake I have lost*
> *all things. I consider them rubbish, that I may gain Christ and be*
> *found in him, not having a righteousness of my own that comes from*
> *the law, but that which is through faith in Christ—the righteousness*
> *that comes from God and is by faith. (Philippians 3:7–9)*

God placed deep within you an affinity for a connectedness with Him because "he is a God who is passionate about his relationship with you" (Exodus 34:14 NLT). It is in that relationship—that intimate connection with God—that you and I find meaning, purpose, significance, completeness, and a relational sense of belonging. Why? Because the almighty God of the universe created us in His image and likeness with the express purpose of our knowing and connecting to Him so intimately that we become more and more like Him. Ponder the following verses:

- ✦ We, who with unveiled faces all reflect the Lord's glory, are being transformed into his likeness with ever-increasing glory, which comes from the Lord, who is the Spirit. (2 Corinthians 3:18)
- ✦ He chose us in him before the creation of the world to be holy and blameless in his sight. In love he predestined us to

be adopted as his sons through Jesus Christ, in accordance with his pleasure and will. (Ephesians 1:4–5)

✦ His divine power has given us everything we need for life and godliness through our knowledge of him who called us by his own glory and goodness. (2 Peter 1:3)

Everything starts with God. That's how He designed it. The Lord created you to depend completely upon Him—heart, soul, mind, strength. He fills you up in ways that nothing else can. He created you; He redeems you; He will glorify you. You will never find ultimate satisfaction except in a vital, dynamic relationship with Him.

And how did God design you to relate to Him? Clear back in the creation story we hear Him say, "Let us make people in our own image, to be like ourselves" (Genesis 1:26 NLT). God gave you certain characteristics that mimic His own so that you could communicate with Him effectively and relate to Him deeply. He desires to interact with you on a warmly personal basis, to build loving relationships with you, to enjoy sweet fellowship with you.

Yet He did not create you as an independent being designed to grow and develop and mature apart from Him. You might say that God is no deist—He did not design humans so that they would grow interested in something else and just wander away from Him.

God designed you to need Him, to remain incomplete without Him. When Matthew 5:48 tells you to, "Be perfect [or complete] . . . as your heavenly Father is perfect," it reminds you that you are designed incomplete. God didn't intend for you to function without Him. He is the completer. He is omni-everything; you and I are omni-nothing. He compensates for all our limitations, and only through a vital connection with Him can we transcend our limits. Without Him we find ourselves relegated to a life of unnecessary frustration and difficulty.

It's not about whether you have a relationship with God; it's about whether you act in ways that enhance and bring life to that relationship, or whether you do things that hinder and bring death to it. Christ wants you to have life in all its fullness: "I have come that they may have life, and have it to the full" (John 10:10).

God made you for a relationship with Himself. The best thing you can ever do for yourself—and for your upcoming marriage—is to develop your personal connection to God through a dynamic faith in Christ, so that you learn how to love God "with all your heart, all your soul, all your mind, and all your strength" (Mark 12:30 NLT).

If you are going to experience a meaningful and lasting marriage, it will be because your relational nature has been connected to God's relational nature. That is the way God designed it from the very beginning.

Seek a Balanced Life

Do you want harmony in your personal life? If so, you'll get it only by paying balanced attention to all four parts of who you are. Who are you?

In the greatest commandment, Jesus taught us to love God with all our heart, soul, mind, and strength. In this single sentence, Jesus summarizes the four key areas that make up our entire being: we are to love with our emotions (heart), our spiritual being (soul), our intellect (mind), and our physical body (strength). In other words, Jesus encouraged us to love God as whole persons.

What difference does it make if we are balanced or not? The answer may surprise you. To understand, picture yourself as a large battery. You have two terminals on top of your head for charging yourself and several more on the sides where others can plug in to meet their own electrical needs.

Clearly, it's important for you to keep the top terminals well maintained and firmly connected to your power Source: God Himself. When you do that—when God's love continuously recharges you—then you can pass His love on to others around you, including your future mate. You could even wear a sign: Plug in to me! I'm here to share my love with you.

On the other hand, what would happen if you allowed impurities and the junk of life—things like fear, anger, resentment, or other damaging emotions—to corrode your terminals? Soon they'd cut your power supply line to God.

Or what would happen if you became so busy caring for others that you forgot to connect regularly to your heavenly Source of power and wisdom? You know the answer! You would very quickly become a dead battery, one devoid of all power. And of what use is a dead battery to anyone?

A balanced life can profoundly change people for the better and enable them to enjoy successful, happy relationships—with God and with one another.

Christ was a master at personal balance and taking care of his whole person:

✦ Emotionally:
- Jesus, knowing that they intended to come and make him king by force, withdrew again to a mountain by himself. (John 6:15)
- [Jesus] said to them, "My soul is overwhelmed with sorrow to the point of death. Stay here and keep watch with me." (Matthew 26:38)

✦ Spiritually:
- Jesus often withdrew to lonely places and prayed. (Luke 5:16)
- After he had dismissed them, he went up on a mountainside by himself to pray. (Matthew 14:23)

✦ Mentally:
- The child grew and became strong; he was filled with wisdom. (Luke 2:40)
- Jesus grew both in wisdom and stature, and in favor with God and men. (Luke 2:52)

✦ Physically:

* Because so many people were coming and going that they did not even have a chance to eat, he said to them, "Come with me by yourselves to a quiet place and get some rest." (Mark 6:31)

Christ grew up and matured *as a whole man*. His body grew. His mind grew. His heart for God grew. His relationships with people grew.

The Bible is also clear about the importance of taking good care of yourself. "No one hates his own body but lovingly cares for it, just as Christ cares for his body, which is the church" (Ephesians 5:29 NLT). Paul doesn't denounce those who feed and care for their bodies; he commends them. He also tells his young protégé, Timothy, to "Stop drinking only water, and use a little wine because of your stomach and your frequent illnesses" (1 Timothy 5:23).

It's only when you allow your cup to be filled that you can fill the cup of others. If you have nothing in your cup, you can't give anything away. In fact, healthy balance sets you up to give generously. If you take seriously God's direction to "be filled with the Spirit" (Ephesians 5:18), you don't have to worry that God will drive you to give until nothing's left. And you don't have to wait to give until somebody else does something for you. If you take care of yourself, you can act from a position of wholeness, not neediness. And that sets you up for relationship success, especially in your relationship with your future wife or husband.

Love Others As Yourself

Do you want true fulfillment in life? If so, then you have no option but to open your heart to receive God's love, and then to open your heart to others to fill them with the same love God has showered upon you. When you love God with every part of your being, He fills you to overflowing with His amazing love and energy—and out of that overflow, you give to others.

This is the balanced life, the only kind of life worth living.

We want to give you one of the most important statements we can make for a successful marriage: *Living a balanced life and taking good care of yourself is always in the best interest of all parties involved.* Now do you see why? When you love yourself as God commanded and take good care of your heart, soul, mind, and body, it's best for your future spouse and others because you can't give what you don't have. If you are empty, you have nothing to give them. But if you fill up and then give from your fullness, and then refill, and then give again from fullness, you will always have plenty of God's love to give. That is living out the greatest commandment.

The strongest objection to spending time taking care of yourself is that it's selfish. So, how do you guard against selfishness? By keeping in mind that if you don't take care of yourself—if you don't go to God and receive the love He so freely gives—then you will have no overflow to offer to others. Without an overflow, you will find it very difficult to care for others and almost impossible to obey Jesus's command to love your neighbor as yourself.

In all your relationships—especially with your future mate—you should strive to be continuously filled and poured out in a never-ending cycle of receiving and giving God's love. This is the very essence of a balanced life.

By keeping your heart open and full of God's love, by loving your fiancée/fiancé, you love yourself.

Safety and Fulfillment

When you look to others to be the source of your fulfillment—even when those people are as great as your future bride or groom!—you run into significant relational problems. When you mistakenly look to another person to fill you up, you place a burden on that person and on the relationship that neither can bear. It makes the relationship patently unsafe. God intends for us to live on and share out of *His* abundance, not on our limited resources or out of those of our mate-to-be. Everybody has needs; that's a given. We all need certain things to survive, and if we don't get them, we die.

One of those universal human needs is food. When we feel hungry, our bodies are telling us that it's time to eat. We're not telling you anything new here! But we do want to make the point that you had better be sure of the source you choose to meet your legitimate needs. Consider the following note that someone left in a company lunchroom:

> *Whoever used the milk in the small plastic container that was in the refrigerator yesterday, please do NOT own up to it. I would find it forever difficult to meet your gaze across a cafeteria table whilst having a discussion about java applets or brand identity. Just be aware that that milk was EXPRESSLY for my son, if you get my drift. I will label these things from now on, but if you found your coffee tasted just a little bit special, you might think of calling your mom and telling her you love her.*

How do you plan to meet your legitimate needs in your home? Where will you look to find fulfillment within your marriage? How you answer those simple questions—and how you live out your answers—will either make your home very safe or extremely unsafe.

What happens, for example, if I believe that Erin's job is to meet my needs? If I take the view that my well-being is at stake unless she does what I want her to do, then I will create a totally unsafe environment for her. And it's not hard to see why.

Anytime I approach Erin with this "you must meet my needs" mindset, she will start to see me as a kind of enormous vacuum cleaner. She might not grasp it at a conscious level, but at some unconscious level she'll be thinking, *It's not safe to come alongside you, because every time I do, I feel this awful sucking sensation.*

If, on the other hand, I really get that she's my assistant and that as an adult *I'm* responsible for my own well-being, then she will feel very safe around me. When she knows that I have learned how to plug in to God as my true Source—physically, spiritually, emotionally, and mentally—she can relax and not worry that I'll suck the life out of her. So it feels totally safe to her when I say, "Hey, if you're willing, this is what I'd love from you. If you want to do this, that would be great. Still, you know that the buck stops with me. *I'm* responsible for me. And so whether you agree to do this or not, the job has to get done, and that's my responsibility." That creates incredible safety.

In the early years of our marriage, there were plenty of times when Erin would want to immediately talk about her day as soon as I walked in the door. Her hope was that I would listen and validate her feelings—especially if something negative or hurtful had happened. However, there were many times when I wasn't in a place to listen to her. Maybe I was in a bad mood or I felt exhausted or my mind was on something else. The typical pattern was that I would sit down and watch TV or immediately tell her how to "fix" her feelings. As you can imagine, this was not what Erin wanted (she wanted me to validate her feelings), and if I wasn't willing or able, this usually led to a fight or hurt feelings.

The reality is that Erin is 100 percent responsible for validating her own emotions. I am her assistant in this process. I have an amazing opportunity to care for her feelings. My desire is to help validate how she feels, but I'm not ultimately responsible for doing this. If I'm not available for whatever reason, Erin has a choice. She can either get upset, shut down, try to get me to listen to her, or validate her own feelings. Since she is ultimately responsible, she always has the option of caring for how she feels herself: she can take her emotions to the Lord, she can call a friend, she can ask if I'd be willing to do this later, and so on. When I see that Erin knows how to validate her own emotions *and does that job,* she feels so safe to me. I know that she isn't going to manipulate me to get her feelings validated. When she assumes responsibility for her emotions, this actually makes it easier for me to come alongside of her because I know she's in control and I can just be her assistant. On my side of the equation, since I'm 100 percent responsible for me, I want to do everything I can to be at a place to validate her feelings.

Think of the analogy of a company. If I'm the CEO, I have a main executive assistant who is my first and foremost helper. I turn to that person to provide me with most of the assistance I need. But I also have a whole corporation of people to help me accomplish the firm's goals. In a similar way, you want to learn to see your future spouse as your go-to person, your primary and foremost assistant. You also need other people in your life, friends and family and others. In fact, you'll need lots of other places to turn for help. There will be days when your spouse won't be available, so you need backups.

"There are times I know it's better to bounce things off my friends before I speak to Greg," Erin says, "to process issues that might be sensitive between us."

We both like it when the other can meet some need of ours, but we work hard to make sure we never start thinking of the other as our source. We want to create a safe home environment, and that means understanding that *God* meets our legitimate needs, not each other. And it's the responsibility of each of us to go to Him for what we need.

COUPLE EXERCISES/HOMEWORK

1. What is the purpose of marriage?
2. In what ways have you bought into the idea of "happiness," finding a "soul-mate," or having someone "complete" you as the goal of marriage?
3. How would you define God's purpose for your marriage? How are God's purpose for marriage and your purpose for marriage different? How are they the same?
4. List several goals that you have for your marriage? In other words, what do you hope to accomplish and experience with your future mate?
5. How do you anticipate that God will use your marriage to make you more like Christ?
6. How does your life right now show evidence of Christ's character?
7. What types of things do you "plug" in to in order to feel fulfilled in life (e.g., school, job, shopping, food, people, buying things, ministry, etc.)?

Part Two

How Do *I* Stop Dancing?

4

Are You Expecting?

There is hardly any activity, any enterprise, which is started with such tremendous hopes and expectations and which fails so regularly as love.

—ERICH FROMM

During our engagement, when I was in Denver and Erin hadn't yet joined me, I would often go out with a married friend named John. John's wife, Julie, didn't much care for our excursions, because she expected her husband to be with her all the time. But since I was still single, I would pick up John and we'd go off to see movies, play video games, visit Sam's Club for free food, go to a local Chinese buffet, and finally attend our one graduate class for the day.

Eventually Julie had to sit both of us down and say to me, "Look, John is a married man. I can't *wait* for Erin to get here, so you'll be a married man, too."

Soon enough, Julie got her wish. And once Erin and I got married and she joined me in Denver, my new wife expected that my Nintendo playing would stop.

But it didn't.

John and I would wait until our wives went to sleep, and then get up at midnight and meet in my living room to play video games. That way, we figured, they wouldn't get mad at us. Late one night while we played,

Erin heard some commotion, got up, and walked into the living room. She didn't have her contacts in, so she couldn't see clearly what was happening. Bleary-eyed, she asked me, "What are you doing?"

Before I could answer, John took a dive between the coffee table and the couch. "Uh, I just couldn't sleep," I replied, "so I started playing a video game."

"*What?*" she asked. "What are you doing?"

John started snickering.

"Who's there with you?" she demanded.

"Just John." Our secret out, John popped up to say hi.

"You are *so* weird," Erin said to me, and then went back to bed.

Erin got a phone call the next morning from Julie. "Just in case you don't know," she reported, "our husbands were up last night. I noticed that John's clothes had moved from where he took them off when he went to bed." She was angry. Our little stunt didn't anger Erin, but it did annoy her. She thought of the whole thing as stupid. But the episode did lead to another conference meeting.

One day soon afterward, John and I came home to play video games—and we couldn't find the gaming unit. I discovered later that Erin had hidden it in the bottom of the hamper.

"My expectation was that video games were going to stop when we got married," Erin said, "because we were going to have deep, meaningful conversations instead."

She paused, then added, "*Ha!*"

It Applies to Everyone

Don't let the title of this chapter mislead you. We are not talking about pregnancy! This isn't a chapter on having a shotgun wedding. Whether you're male or female, the question, "Are you expecting?" applies to everyone. And as you may already have guessed, the answer is . . .

Yes, you are!

We all enter into marriage "expecting." All of us have expectations—

lots of them. Some we are consciously aware of, while many others lurk silently in the dark. Expectations are always there, hovering in the background of our daily experiences. Whether we are attuned to them or oblivious to them, our expectations come into play in a multitude of ways.

One explanation for the nation's high divorce rate and the current prevalence of marital dissatisfaction is that Americans have high and unrealistic expectations of marriage. They expect a spouse to simultaneously be a friend, a confidant(e), a fulfilling sex partner, a counselor, and a parent.[1]

We won't be talking in this chapter about unmet expectations that result from a partner's failure to follow through on a promise. Those are quite legitimate. Rather, we are referring to undeclared expectations brought into the relationship, based on a personal set of relational ideals. The focus here is on the way you think things are supposed to be in your relationship.

To get an idea of where we're going, consider the following abbreviated list of expectations that we compiled from couples who attended a Seattle, Washington, seminar. As you read through the list, think about the problems that could arise when these expectations are not met or are unfulfilled.

- ✦ We'll call each other during the day to see what the other is doing.
- ✦ Do not call me at work.
- ✦ Call every day to say, "I love you."
- ✦ Put the toilet seat down.
- ✦ Never forget important dates—birthdays and others.
- ✦ Keep up your physical appearance.
- ✦ Do not talk with others about home problems.
- ✦ He cleans the car and mows the lawn.
- ✦ She keeps the house clean.
- ✦ Whoever cooks, the other cleans.

✦ Sex anytime of the day is okay.
✦ He will fix everything in the house.
✦ No yelling.
✦ Family devotions after dinner.
✦ The wife takes care of the finances.
✦ Do not discuss weight problems.
✦ Spend time volunteering at church and in the community.
✦ He should give me time to exercise.
✦ Never work on Sunday.
✦ We will tithe to the church.
✦ Defend me when your mother and sister criticize me.
✦ Call your in-laws Mom and Dad, not by their first names.
✦ Keep moms and dads out of spousal conflict.

As Erin and I realized, traditional courtship provides partners with idealized views of each other. This makes early marriage a period of difficult and sometimes severe adjustment for couples, because after the wedding they discover the unpleasant realities that have been masked during the dating and engagement period.[2]

Furthermore, successful couples do not go into marriage starry-eyed and naive. They don't sugarcoat the challenges of marriage, and they recognize that the relationship will not always be perfectly smooth. Couples who succeed know that if they work together, they can create and maintain a strong marriage. Thus, it's crucial to have realistic expectations about the very real challenges of marriage.[3]

So—what are *your* expectations for your upcoming marriage? The key is to think through what you expect and how it will affect your relationship. Another way of looking at expectations is to think about what you anticipate happening in your marriage, what you believe and assume will happen, what you hope and wish will take place, and the standards that must be maintained for you to feel satisfied. Your answers to these will uncover your relational expectations.

Why Is It Important to Explore Expectations?

Why do you need to investigate your expectations? To answer this question, I would like to tell you about one of my most embarrassing experiences growing up.

In high school I fell in love with a girl from another school whom I'll call Crystal. We attended the same church youth group. I really wanted to ask Crystal out, but I could never muster up the courage. One day, my break finally came. She was having a birthday party to which she invited a bunch of her school and church friends—including yours truly. I remember feeling nervous to be at Crystal's home and around people I didn't know.

At the party, things went fairly smoothly . . . at first. I made sure that I personally asked Crystal where I should place her present so she could see firsthand the impressive size of the gift. I had rehearsed a few funny lines that I used on her right off the bat, and she even chuckled at one of them. Things looked promising!

And then a call went out to gather us together to watch her open the gifts.

At the time, I was outside horsing around with some of my church friends. We didn't hear the announcement until Crystal's dad yelled for us to come in. The problem was, he raised his voice just loud enough to draw everyone's attention to the goofballs playing outside. Seeing all these unfamiliar kids staring at us made me feel very uncomfortable and self-conscious. As I quickly started to walk through the massive sliding glass door, I tried to keep my eye on Crystal. She was watching me! I was in luck.

Unfortunately, I should have chosen to keep my eye on the glass door.

What I thought was an open door turned out to be very closed. I hit that door like it wasn't even there. *Crash!* The sound alone humiliated me, but to make matters worse, the impact knocked me flat on my back. I stood up to a chorus of laughter. Initially, I hoped that not everyone had noticed. Wrong! They had all noticed—especially Crystal. She was shaking her head and rolling her eyes.

I never did get a date with Crystal.

The point of the story is that marital expectations are a lot like that sliding glass door I so gracefully slammed into. If you don't specifically look for them, you won't see them, and that's how they can bring much pain, frustration, and disappointment to your relationship.

Expectations are a very common source of stress. They frequently create all sorts of mischief, including emotional distress, relationship conflicts, communication breakdowns, misunderstandings, distrust, and a wide range of other problems. Expectations produce stress in two main ways:

> They are usually unconscious and therefore hidden from our view.
>
> They are frequently untrue, unrealistic, or otherwise misleading.[4]

When we consciously or unconsciously harbor expectations that are too high, we set ourselves up for feeling frustrated, angry, and personally demoralized.

Furthermore, we all enter marriage assuming that certain events will transpire and our relationship will develop in a certain way. These expectations often remain unspoken, even after we get married. Because our spouse is unaware of them, often they are not fulfilled.

What if a wife is used to big birthday celebrations and elaborate Christmas decorations, and the husband isn't? What if the husband expects his wife will make breakfast for him (that was mine), and she doesn't even like breakfast? What if the wife expects the husband to mow the lawn and care for the yard (that was Erin's), and he'd rather play video games?

Though hints of these differences may appear in courtship, often the huge gulf does not yawn wide until after marriage, when the two are thrust together for sixteen hours a day. If your expectations differ, conflict will result! While most of these expectations are desires—ideal situations—rather than necessities, they still play an important part in marital happiness.[5]

Realistic versus Unrealistic Expectations

What do you feel is realistically obtainable from your relationship? That's the key question. Notice that this is different than an ideal expectation, something that you would like to be true of your relationship under ideal circumstances.

One research study looked at the difference in relational expectations between engaged couples and recently married couples (married an average of 2.4 years). The researchers discovered that the engaged couples had higher levels of expectations than the married couples. In other words, the engaged individuals, when contemplating what they expected from their upcoming marriages, tended to have higher expectations than their married counterparts.[6]

This means that if you want to continue to feel satisfied with your relationship, you will have to do some reevaluation of your expectations after you get married. Otherwise, the relatively high and idealistic relationship expectations you have right now will contribute to a significant drop in relational satisfaction after your honeymoon period ends.

Remember, expectations come in many packages—from what you wish your spouse were like to what you hope to get for a gift. If you don't identify and then talk about the expectation, then you run the risk of developing frustration and disappointment in your relationship. Take Lisa, for example.

Lisa's birthday came and went; her husband, Bill, had apparently forgotten to buy her anything. That night while in bed, she decided to bring up the incident.

"Well, for your last birthday," Bill began, "I bought you a very nice hockey stick, *which you never use.* So, I decided not to buy you anything more until you do."

Lisa, understandably upset, held back her tears and sank into the pillows.

Months passed, and finally Bill's birthday came. He and Lisa got all dressed up and went out for a beautiful meal. Afterward, Lisa presented him with a birthday gift, then gave him a little peck on the cheek and a big smile. Intrigued, Bill enthusiastically unwrapped it . . . to find a certificate for a burial plot.

Unlike Lisa and Bill, you should aim to alter and lower your relational expectations through effective communication. Notice we said alter *and* lower. We want to help you lower unrealistically high marital expectations without deflating your optimism for the future of your union.

The Engagement Dilemma

You need high expectations . . . at first! Hey, we all develop high expectations for our relationships. Why wouldn't we? Why would you want to marry someone if you did not expect the relationship would give birth to a wonderful future?

In fact, high expectations solidify a person's commitment to his or her relationship. Expectation of a high level of relational satisfaction builds positive momentum by removing much of the uncertainty regarding marriage.

This, however, creates an "engagement dilemma." Dr. Ronald Sabatelli, who has spent years studying relational expectations, notes that the engagement dilemma "is one created by the contradiction between needing to believe, prior to marriage, that one's marriage will be extraordinary and the likelihood that such high expectations will contribute to some disillusionment with the relationship once marriage occurs."[7]

In essence, most premarital couples believe that they are participating in a very special relationship. It's this very enthusiasm and excitement that helps a couple to resolve any reluctance about marriage. This is where you create high expectations. Still, when you believe that you are in a special relationship, take a look at what can happen. You will tend to . . .

+ ignore flaws in each other;
+ deny the possibility of any future marital conflicts;
+ place each other on pedestals;
+ give unqualified attention and admiration to your future marital partner.[8]

We want to help you maintain hopefulness within your relationship. On the other hand, we don't want that relational optimism to be so lofty that your towering expectations set you up for disappointment and failure.

In other words, we don't want you to be like we were.

Gremlins Called Marital Myths

When we got married, in many ways I expected the fairy tale. Raised on reruns of *Leave It to Beaver*, *Bewitched*, *I Love Lucy*, *Father Knows Best*, and *Ozzie & Harriet*, I was convinced that marriage would be a "happily ever after" event. Those shows made me believe that life was wonderful, that Erin could meet all my needs, that children were icing on the cake, and that marriage would solve all my problems. After all, my TV told me that Ward and June Cleaver illustrated the way things really were in marriage!

If you watch late-night TV, enjoy classic movies, listen to love songs, or read romantic novels, then you also may have an image of the perfect marriage. Unfortunately, many myths surrounding marriage—the ones that give couples unrealistic expectations, the ones that ensure disappointment and frustration for those who look for a Cinderella-like happily-ever-after storybook marriage—largely originate in popular sources of entertainment.

Many media images and popular portrayals of marriage are likely to foster unrealistic beliefs. Eternal romantic love, for example, is central to contemporary notions of marriage.[9] These extremely high romantic beliefs also reflect unrealistic standards for a marital relationship. Overly high romantic beliefs are based on notions that love is always sexually and emotionally stimulating, mysterious, and all-encompassing.[10]

I really bought into one myth about marriage that has to do with the honeymoon night. I had watched so many movies and TV programs that portrayed an unbelievable night of passion and perfection that, as a result, I went into my honeymoon with sky-high expectations.

After a great wedding ceremony and reception, Erin and I spent our first night in a hotel by Los Angeles International Airport, a beautiful facility overlooking the ocean. We had a suite, with a main living area and a bedroom. As an average guy, I couldn't have cared less about the living area. I had an interest in only *one* room.

Night had fallen by the time we arrived. So the moment we got to our room, I was eager to do what I'd seen in the movies and on TV. And things were going just perfectly—until Erin said she heard a noise.

"It wasn't me!" I instantly proclaimed.

"No," Erin replied, giggling, "I didn't mean that kind of noise. I think someone is in the main room."

"What are you talking about?" I asked.

"I think there is someone in the living room," she whispered, "Go see!"

That last statement was not something I longed to hear: *"Go see."* It meant I had to act all brave and courageous, when in reality the noise scared me. Without thinking, I jumped out of bed and burst into the living room—instantly prompting a loud shriek.

It turned out our maid had entered the suite to tidy up, without realizing some guests were rather busy in the bedroom.

And do you know the worst part? I couldn't tell if she screamed because I had startled her, or because she saw me buck naked. Unfortunately, I'll never know.

You can imagine how the experience put a damper on our first night!

My expectation of a passionate, private sexual encounter lay shattered on the living-room floor.

Of course, Erin and I are not alone in having our first night together go awry. One study found that 32 percent of newlyweds did not have sex on their wedding night. The main reason? They said they were too exhausted.[11]

In another study, the average number of times a couple made love each day on their honeymoon was 2.28. On the other end of the spectrum, 3 percent reported that they did not make love at all on their honeymoon.[12]

When asked if their partner met their expectations when they slept together for the first time, 13 percent said no, while 87 percent reported yes.[13] Finally, in a survey that we conducted in 1997, 62 percent of the couples surveyed reported that they did not experience any conflict during their honeymoon; 34 percent reported experiencing "some" conflict; and 3 percent reported experiencing "frequent" conflict.

So many people marry for all the wrong reasons. They're deceived by a few gremlins called marriage myths that leave them disappointed, disillusioned, and, all too often, divorced. Consider just a few of the more popular marital myths.

Myth # 1: If you fight or argue, then you must have a bad relationship.

REALITY: Conflict happens in every marriage. Fighting fair and for the relationship, and not just to win, can actually increase the health of a marriage.

Myth # 2: My mate always knows how to meet my needs and will meet all my needs without my having to verbalize them.

REALITY: Regardless of a spouse's intelligence or personal strengths, no individual has the ability to read a partner's mind. Needs for security, affection, emotional support, encouragement, or physical assistance often must be verbalized in clear language, sometimes repeatedly. If the need is something the spouse can realistically provide, she must first know the need exists.

I've heard people say, "Why should I have to tell my mate what I expect? She should know." This is belief in mind reading, and it destroys helpful communication patterns. Some take this misperception a step further and feel that something is wrong with the relationship if she needs to ask. Or worse, "if she asks and I respond, then it won't be meaningful." The belief that spouses should be able to read each other's minds often is based on the assumption that mind reading reflects the degree of love and intimacy in the relationship. Yet spouses' attempts at mind reading often result in misperceptions, misunderstandings, and escalation of conflict.[14]

Myth #3: My mate will make me whole.
REALITY: Spouses complement each other; they do not complete each other.

Myth #4: This person will bring me happiness.
REALITY: We can't expect our spouse to be our one source of happiness. Our personal happiness must come from within ourselves. Marriage can complement our own individual happiness, but it can't be the primary source. Only God can be our source for joy.

Myth #5: Love is forever, without work; once decided, always committed.
REALITY: A good marriage doesn't just happen. It takes nurturing and work.

Myth #6: The honeymoon will last forever and everything will be rosy after the wedding vows.

REALITY: If you've already read this far, you know our story—so how could you still believe this one?

Myth #7: We'll have sex every night.
REALITY: Virtually all relationships experience peaks and valleys. Sometimes, the realities of married life will cloud over romantic feelings. Scott Peck, in his book *The Road Less Traveled*, states, "Every couple falls in love; every couple falls out of love."[15] Just because the feelings of love are not always present, it doesn't necessarily indicate a lack of love. Love may often involve feelings, but it also requires a continual choice.

Problems with Expectations

So what's the problem if you carry some unstated wishes, hopes, desires, rules, standards, or anticipations into your marriage, and they don't take place in your relationship? Of course, there isn't just *one* problem; there could be a host of them. Take a little time to ponder nine of the most common.

1. *A mismatch in expectations can lead to conflict.* For the most part, it's not that your fiancée/fiancé's expectations are outrageous, but that they might fuel some conflict if they don't match your own. Furthermore, spouses may perceive differences in their preferences, habits, expectations, and opinions as insults or evidence of being unloved.[16]

2. *Unreasonable expectations usually lead to conflict.* Studies show that it's more likely that relationships will develop problems when expectations are unreasonable.[17] In other words, conflict is more likely to occur if you act on unrealistic or unreasonable expectations. And what is an unrealistic expectation? Who decides if it's unrealistic? Most of the time, unrealistic

expectations are based on inaccurate beliefs. For example, "conflict or arguments are inherently destructive to relationships." That belief is untrue, but if one partner holds it, then he or she will look at an arguing spouse in a very negative light.

3. *Unexpressed expectations can lead to conflict.* As we've said, one of the main problems with expectations is that spouses often do not talk about what they expect from each other. Many times a person is not even aware that a spouse's expectation exists.

When we got married, for example, Erin always expected that we would move back to Phoenix after I finished my course work at Denver Seminary. To her, that was the plan, and her expectation never changed. She expected that we would live in the house my parents owned on a golf course . . . and then they sold the house.

"I felt like, 'Uh, that was *my* house!'" Erin says. It caused her a great deal of consternation. Now, we had never talked about going back to Phoenix; she just assumed we would. Her family lived there, and she just expected we would return there after our two years at seminary. Her parents had the same expectation—and it never happened. In fact, over the years, we continued to move farther away. Not until five years after our wedding did we actually discuss the fact that we weren't going back.

4. *Expectations can distort our perception.* Expectations can be powerful filters, distorting our perception of what really goes on in the relationship. Many of the expectations that caused Erin and I so many problems revolved around money.

When we were about to be married, I looked at all the interest Erin was paying on a school loan and said to her, "Hey, paying all this interest is just stupid. Let's just pay it off." I had saved up enough to pay off the loan, so that's what we did. And I expected that we'd work to build back the amount of savings I had used to get rid of the loan— which really meant that she'd work to build it, since I was in school and she was the only one working. For years it bothered me that she didn't seem to be interested in actively building up our savings. Do you know the real problem? I never clearly verbalized how big of a deal it was to me. So I would watch Erin spend money on something I didn't think was essential and think, *Well, that hundred dollars could have gone right into rebuilding our savings!* I perceived Erin as something of a spendthrift, all because of an expectation that I had never made clear.

5. *Unmet expectations can lead to negative emotions.* Unmet expectations can lead to negative emotions such as disappointment, anger, and frustration. Many of our moods and emotions are intimately tied to our expectations. And when your spouse fails to live up to your expectations, you can easily feel annoyed, disappointed, angry, or sad.

   I often tell couples that when you experience these negative emotions within your marital relationship, first try to identify the expectation that did not get met. This allows you to take responsibility for your expectations and determine if the expectation is reasonable or unreasonable.

6. *Unmet expectations can have a snowball effect.* When an expectation is not met, it can trigger a deeper issue or hurt. The greater and longer-held the expectation, the deeper the hurt it can trigger—even if the expectation is merely *in danger of* being unmet.

   My brother had always expected that at my wedding he would be the one to reach inside his coat pocket, pull out the ring, and hand it to me. But on the day of the ceremony, the priest who officiated asked me for the ring.

"I don't have it," I replied. "My brother has it."

So unbeknownst to either Erin or me, the priest went to my brother and said, "Hey, I need the ring beforehand."

"Why?" Michael asked.

"That's just how we do it," the priest replied.

"*Uh uh,*" Michael declared. "I've always wanted to hand it to my brother."

"Well, I need it," repeated the priest.

"Bottom line?" Michael answered. "You're not getting it. And so when it comes time for the ring exchange, it's up to you how you handle it, but I'm telling you right now, I'm holding on to it. *I'm* giving it to him."

We didn't know any of this was going on; the whole big deal was going on behind our backs. Everything turned out fine in the end and the priest handled everything great, but it could have snowballed into one huge, horrible mess. In the same way that Michael's deep desire got triggered, imagine the countless issues in your future marriage that can escalate into fights. Issues like sex, finances, communication, children, jobs, time together, household chores, all have the potential of snowballing into nasty arguments when they go unfilled.

7. *Unfulfilled expectations often turn into demands.* When expectations go unfulfilled, very often they eventually evolve into demands. You go from wishing or hoping something will happen in your relationship to demanding it or insisting that it take place—and a demanding environment ultimately causes your mate to feel controlled and places him or her on the defensive.

8. *Unshared expectations limit teamwork.* You simply can't work together as a team if you don't share your expectations. How can your spouse fulfill an expectation if he or she doesn't even know it exists? This blocks your unity or oneness.

When we got married, Erin expected that I would take care of her emotionally, physically, mentally, and financially. "The ironic thing is," she says, "that I was so independent. I thought getting married meant that independence was about to go away. I expected that, suddenly, I wouldn't be independent anymore; instead, Greg would take care of me. So every time he didn't do that—I can think of times when I would leave to get in the car, find ice or snow on my windows, expect that Greg would take care of that for me . . . and meanwhile, he stayed upstairs, safe and warm in bed—I got madder and madder and more and more discouraged. Those expectations certainly didn't help us to grow in unity!"

9. *Unrealistic expectations give away your responsibility.* You are 100 percent responsible for your own level of happiness. When you nurture unrealistic expectations, you give the responsibility for your happiness away to another person, which also gives that person tremendous power over you. You become dependent upon that person for your happiness.

In a sense, you are saying, "I feel satisfied only if this person fulfills my expectations." Unfortunately, the reverse is also true: "I am unhappy so long as this person does not fulfill my expectations." Since your spouse *will* let you down, your attempt to control or manipulate him or her into making you happy (your unrealistic expectation) fails—and you end up feeling miserable and helpless to do anything about it.

Steps to Dealing with Expectations

Now let's turn our focus to some specific steps you can take to deal with your relational expectations.

1. *Claim them.* First, assume total responsibility for your own happiness. Understand that people cannot fulfill your life or make you happy. Regardless of your dreams or excitement about your upcoming marriage, your future spouse is not responsible for making you happy or your honeymoon a success according to your criteria.

2. *Feel them.* Recognize the feelings connected with unmet expectations—emotions such as disappointment, frustration, hurt, and fear. How can you tell if you have an unmet expectation? *Disappointment.* When you feel disappointment in your relationship, then most likely some expectation hasn't been met. When expectations get met, partners feel satisfied, happy, fulfilled, gratified, contented, respected, cared for, and loved. On the other hand, when expectations are not met or are in conflict, other less-pleasant emotions emerge. These feelings are an indication that expectations are not meshing.

   It is important to understand what you're feeling, validate the feeling, and then move to uncover the expectation on which it is based. In some cases, your partner won't even know of the expectation; in fact, the only indication of its existence is its emotional effect.

3. *Recognize them.* Once you're aware of the feelings associated with unmet or unfulfilled expectations, then you can gain the awareness necessary to make the needed adjustment. Awareness answers questions like: What was I expecting should happen? What was I wishing or hoping would take place?

What were my assumptions about my partner and his or her behavior?

Push yourself to take a hard look at your expectations. The point of these questions is to consider whether the answers to the questions are realistic, productive, and workable. It's not that they are true or false, or right or wrong; instead, the answers are preferences, likes, or disbeliefs. We want to help you to identify the distortions, enabling you to change your way of thinking.

4. *Understand them.* Where are the expectations coming from? Do they have their source in dreams, wishes, assumptions, hopes, standards, your family of origin, past relationships, TV, culture, or somewhere else?

5. *Evaluate them.* Are your expectations reasonable or unreasonable? Are they realistic or unrealistic? Challenge your expectations within yourself. Evaluation means that you determine if the expectations seem to be supported by objective reality.

Other important questions to ask yourself include these: Is it objectively true that my mate should act that way? Is this expectation essential to the attainment of any specific goal I have for our marriage? Does this expectation affect my future spouse's perception of me? Does this expectation help me achieve the kind of emotional responses I want for my spouse and me in marriage?

If you answer no to these questions, it's very possible that this expectation is unrealistic. If any demand or expectation is valid, then address the expectation in a new manner, such as: "I would appreciate it if you would . . ." or "I would really prefer that you . . ."

6. *Express them.* Remember, the ultimate goal of expectations is to

make them clear. In other words, make your unspoken desires spoken. Clearly express your expectations.

Sharing your expectations allows you to define a mutual vision of how you want your future marriage to be. The best part is that when you express your expectations, you allow your partner to decide if he or she can satisfy that need. He or she gets the opportunity to decide if the expectation can be met most of the time, some of the time, or none of the time.

Before I see clients in a counseling session, I have them sign an informed consent form. This form outlines important information, like who the counselor is, his or her degrees and credentials, what type of agency he or she works for, the basic values and beliefs of the organization, some risks of therapy, limits of confidentiality, counseling fee, how to reach the counselor after hours, name of supervisor if he or she has one, cancellation policy, etc. This allows the client to understand many aspects of therapy, both covert and overt, so he or she can make an informed decision on whether or not to proceed with therapy. A counselor can do therapy with someone only if that person consents to doing it; the information assists him or her in making an informed consent.

Sharing your expectations *before* frustration, disappointment, or conflict sets in is like getting your mate's informed consent. It allows him or her to say either "I can" or "I can't" meet your expectations. And it works great.

Expectations and Safety

What are your expectations about sex, cooking breakfast, where you're going to live, where you'll go for the holidays? When the power goes out, who's going to find the circuit-breaker box and get the power back on?

The more you and your future spouse make your expectations explicit, the safer your marriage will feel. You'll create an appropriate expectation by putting it out there so that your partner can let you know what he or she is or is not willing to do. Then it becomes a healthy expectation. Both of you will know what it is and can say, "Yes, this is what I really want."

To add a level of safety to your union, you should begin now to generate a list of expectations, think through the items on that list, and then walk through them together. "Are you going to handle the checkbook, or am I? Are we going to work off of a budget? And if so, who will create it? Will we be at my parents' place for Christmas, or yours? Will we live close by family or far away? Will we buy a house or rent?"

We encourage you to go through exactly this kind of process, in which you both verbalize your expectations and try to move them from unrealistic to realistic. Give the other person a chance to shape what is appropriate. Do your best to shed light on and give air to the expectations that, until now, may have remained buried.

Expectations Discussed = Problems Avoided

Right after I asked Erin's father for her hand in marriage, but before we actually got engaged, her mother said to me, "Don't you have religious issues to work out?"

You see, while I grew up in a Southern Baptist home, Erin grew up in a Catholic home. We had never made church a big deal, because we shared a common faith and trust in Jesus Christ. But during the months of our engagement, Erin called me in Denver one day and said, "I don't know if I can do this. I don't know that I can leave my faith and my church."

Because I knew Erin's heart, I didn't react. I just said, "Okay, well, let's just keep praying about it and talking about it."

We knew we both believed the same thing. We were both saved and wanted to follow Christ and become like Him. And we decided together that we could find some church that would meet our mutual needs.

On the first or second night of our honeymoon, as we were lying in bed, we started talking about where we wanted to go to church when we returned home. Erin talked about what she wanted out of church, and I described what I wanted. We never made denomination or style of worship the issue. We just said, "Here's what you want; here's what I want. We want basically the same thing. Let's just find it."

I remember thinking, *Hey, if we can find that in a Catholic church, what do I care? If we can find that in a Baptist church or someplace else, what difference does it make?*

So when we got home, we searched until we found the particular dynamics we wanted. And because each of us knew the expectations of the other, the whole process went smoothly, happily, and well.

Let your expectations work *for* you, not against you!

COUPLE EXERCISES/HOMEWORK

Changing Your Unfulfilled Expectations

In his excellent book *So You're Getting Married,* Dr. H. Norman Wright provides a great exercise for couples to deal with expectations.[18] When your expectations go unmet, how will the problem be resolved? How can you change your expectations of your future spouse? Spend some time working through the following three assignments:

1. Collect a list of your expectations for your marriage and mate in the following areas:
    + sexual relationship
    + handling finances
    + social life or friends
    + matters of recreation or how to spend leisure time
    + household tasks
    + marital roles
    + religious matters
    + demonstration of affection
    + ways of dealing with in-laws
    + goals, philosophy of life, career decisions
    + making major decisions

2. Ask yourself the following questions for each expectation:
    + Is this expectation supported by objective reality? Is it objectively true that he or she should act this way?
    + Am I hurt in any way if this expectation is not fulfilled?
    + Is this expectation essential to the attainment of any specific goal I have for my marriage?
    + What does this expectation do to my future spouse's perception of me?

✦ Does this expectation help me achieve the kind of emotional responses I want for my spouse and me in marriage?

If you answered no to the first question and to at least two others, it's very possible that this expectation is unrealistic. If any demand or expectation is valid, then approach your fiancée/fiancé in a new manner, such as: "I would appreciate it if you would . . ." or, "I would really prefer that you . . ."

3. Have your partner review the list and make one of the following statements about each expectation:

✦ "I can meet this expectation most of the time, and I appreciate knowing about this. Can you tell me why this is important to you?"

✦ "I can meet this expectation some of the time, and I appreciate knowing about this. Can you tell me why this is important to you? How can I share with you when I cannot meet this so it would be acceptable to you?"

✦ "This expectation would be difficult for me to meet for these reasons. Can you tell me why this is so important to you? How will this affect you? How can some adjustments be worked out?

5

Do You Want to Dance?

Marriage is like an electric battery—it makes you dance, but you can't let go.

—AUTHOR UNKNOWN

I can almost taste the irony. I make my living teaching about relationships at the university level. I also travel quite a bit around the country, instructing others on how to improve their marriages. And why is that so ironic? It is, you see, because just two years into my own marriage, I doubted that Erin and I were going to make it. *I don't think she wants to be around me any longer,* I thought.

And I wasn't far from wrong.

What went so haywire, you may be wondering? It had everything to do with a destructive dance in which we found ourselves stuck.

Every time that Erin and I tried to manage our differences or work through our conflicts, we wound up spinning in a vicious cycle. We simply could not understand why our discussions so often ended in explosions. We seemed to act out the very same script, time after time. We tried everything to break free of this dance. But nothing worked. It seemed as though the harder we tried to stop dancing, the more we danced. And so we felt utterly stuck.

When we couldn't take it any longer, we finally found a counselor. Although our marriage therapist offered us a lot of great advice, we never seemed to get to the root of our conflict. He taught us how to communicate better, how to set up rules for fair fighting, even how to better understand each other's love language—all great stuff! Erin and I would do great with our issues in his office, but once back home, we would quickly slip back into the old, ugly patterns.

It felt to me as though our counselor was simply rearranging the deck chairs on the Titanic. We seemed to be dealing merely with surface issues—things to make our marriage "ship" look pretty. But all the while, our relationship was sinking, and we couldn't figure out why. We failed to understand what was tearing holes in the bottom of our marriage. We had no understanding of the iceberg that was driving our conflicts.

So for the next seven years, Erin and I continued to spin around. Our habits didn't change for the better until we finally understood that we had become mired in a destructive relationship dance. We remained stuck until we got a handle on our unique relationship dance and recognized that certain identifiable "buttons" set us off, starting us on yet another futile round of accusations, attacks, rationalizations, and silent treatments.

In this chapter, we want to help you to begin to identify your own Fear Dance, so that you don't have to endure the same kind of heartbreak that plagued us for so long. And make no mistake, you and your future spouse already have such a dance! It may not seem as destructive as ours was, but it's there in some form. Perhaps you'll see what we mean if we describe ours in a little more detail.

Meet Our Fear Dance

My doctoral studies kept me extremely busy. By then I had a wife, young daughter, classes and exams, a dissertation to write, an internship to prepare for, and a part-time job. So you can imagine that, many times, Erin didn't feel like a priority. The issue caused us to dance more than once (a *lot* more). It usually went something like this:

> *Erin:* "You are too busy! You never seem to have time for Taylor and me. If this is what it's going to be like, being the wife of a psychologist, I'm not sure it's worth it."

Greg: "Here we go again! I'll be sure to grab a suitcase and get ready for the guilt trip."

Erin: "*That's* real mature. I was just trying to have an adult conversation. Adults are supposed to be able to talk."

Greg: "Conversation? All you're doing is criticizing me for trying to be successful in school. What do you want me to do, flunk out? Quit? Stay home and tend to your every need?"

Erin: "That's not what I'm saying! I just don't feel like a top priority. Everything else seems to take precedence over me and Taylor."

Greg: "*Every*thing? Didn't you and I go out to dinner yesterday when I should have been studying for my test? You *are* a priority. The problem is that your expectations are too high. I can't possibly go to school, work, and be home whenever you want. That's impossible!"

And so it went. After one of these heated exchanges, I really wanted to make up for the nasty things I had said. I wanted to do something nice for my bride. As I thought about what to do, the typical stuff like flowers, a card, candy, or sex (I only wish *that* one would work!) didn't seem to be enough. I needed something that would take real effort, that would make a huge statement about my love for Erin and how she really was a priority for me. Whatever it was, it would need to cost me more than money alone; it needed to cost me time, my most precious commodity.

And then it hit me! Erin had recently spilled something on our couch and had mentioned how much she hated the stains it left on two cushions. What a great opportunity! If I cleaned the cushions and removed the stains, not only would Erin love that she once more owned a beautiful couch, but she would be blown away by the time and effort it took me to accomplish such a time-consuming feat. Piece of cake, right?

Wrong!

Erin doesn't let me near our washing machine for a very good reason. In my ignorance, I simply unzipped the cushions and removed the covers. I then placed the soiled covers in the washing machine and let technology do the rest.

After the buzzer went off, I inspected the covers and congratulated myself on my genius. With no stain in sight, I proceeded to place the covers in the dryer.

How I wish I had read the fine print on those irritating tags they place on the underside of the cushions! They would have presented a strongly worded caution about how to dry the covers. They may, in fact, have warned me about a certain little thing called shrinkage. Perhaps they might have encouraged me to get them dry-cleaned.

Helpful information *before* I washed and dried them on my own!

Of course, when I tried putting the covers back on the cushions, they seemed to fit much more snugly than I remembered. When I stood back to glory in my cleverness, our couch no longer looked like a couch. Instead of being flat on top, the cushions slanted to a point—like three garish mountain peaks.

I was dead meat.

When Erin came home, she found me sprawled across the couch, watching TV. But she's no dummy, and it didn't take long for her to notice that our cushions looked . . . well, *very* odd.

"Before you say anything," I begged, "I just want you to know that I tried to do something nice for you."

"Greg," she said in that motherly voice, "*what* have you done?"

I could keep going, but I'm sure you get my point. I doubt I have to lay out for you the ugly details of our dance. And besides, our dance isn't terribly different from the one that keeps most couples hopping.

A man and his wife were having some problems at home and decided to give each other the silent treatment. But then the man realized that he needed his wife to wake him at 5:00 a.m. the next day for an early-morning business flight. Loath to be the first to break the silence (and thereby *lose*), he wrote on a piece of paper, "Please wake me at 5:00 a.m." He left it where he knew she would find it.

The next morning the man woke up, only to discover it was 9:00 a.m.

and he had missed his flight. Furious, he was about to confront his wife and demand to know why she hadn't awakened him, when he noticed another little piece of paper by the bed.

"It is 5:00 a.m.," the paper said. "Wake up."

In fact, *all* couples dance in some way or another. Some couples dance in an obvious, overt manner, while others dance in a more subtle way that might be easy to miss. But regardless of the kind of dance, it destroys relationships.

And you are no exception.

You Dance, Too

Do you ever wonder why you do and say certain things that you wish you didn't, things that seem so out of character with who you'd like to be? What drives your arguments with your fiancée/fiancé? What lies at the heart of your fights?

It's simple, really: your "buttons" get pushed. Your future mate does or says something that hits you wrong, and immediately you either want to go after that person or distance yourself from him or her. We all get our buttons pushed throughout the day, multiple times.

For Erin and me, the problem was that no one ever told us that we had buttons and that those buttons were going to get pushed continuously in our marriage. Both our dance and yours look like this:

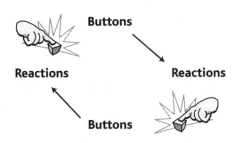

In general, the dance works like this: when someone pushes your buttons, you don't like the resulting feeling, so you react in some way to deal with that unwanted feeling. Usually, however, the way you react pushes your fiancée/faincé's button. Since she doesn't like how that feels, she reacts in some way, hoping her reaction will make her feel better.

Unfortunately, the dance never gets you what you really want. Your reactions push your partner's original button (or a new one), and thus you continue to spin around until you either escalate out of control or withdraw. Erin and I do this, and you and your future spouse do, as well. It's universal.

What Do We Mean by Buttons?

We all have buttons, and it doesn't matter if you don't like it or are oblivious to it. You have them, we have them, all of us have them. No one likes how it feels when the buttons get pushed; usually, it sends a very painful message. Ponder the following list of some of the most common buttons:

BUTTON	WHAT THAT BUTTON SAYS TO ME
Rejected	My fiancée doesn't want me; my fiancée doesn't need me; I am not necessary in this relationship; my fiancée does not desire me; I feel unwanted.
Abandoned	I will be alone; my fiancé will ultimately leave me; I will be left alone to care for myself; my fiancé won't be committed to me for life; I will be deserted.
Disconnected	We will become emotionally detached or separated.
Like a failure	I am not successful at being a future husband/wife; I will not perform right or correctly; I will not live up to expectations; I will fall short in my relationship; I am not good enough.
Helpless or powerless	I cannot do anything to change my fiancée or my situation; I do not possess the power, resources, capacity, or ability to get what I want; I will be controlled by my fiancée.
Defective	Something is wrong with me; I'm the problem.

Inadequate	I am not capable; I am incompetent.
Inferior	Everyone else is better than I am; I am less valuable or important than others.
Invalidated	Who I am, what I think, what I do, or how I feel is not valued.
Unloved	My fiancé doesn't love me anymore; my fiancé has no affection or desire for me; my relationship lacks warm attachment, admiration, enthusiasm, or devotion; I feel as if we are just future roommates—there are no romantic feelings between us.
Worthless/ devalued	I am useless; I have no value to my fiancée.
Don't measure up	I am never able to meet my fiancé's expectations of me; I am not good enough as a fiancé.
Unaccepted	My fiancée does not accept me; my partner is not pleased with me; my fiancée does not approve of me.
Judged	I am always being unfairly judged or misjudged; my fiancé forms faulty or negative opinions about me; I am always being evaluated; my fiancé does not approve of me.
Ignored	My fiancée will not pay attention to me; I will be unknown in my marriage; I feel neglected.
Unimportant	I am not important to my fiancé; I am irrelevant, insignificant, or of little priority to my fiancé.
Intimacy	I am afraid of opening up emotionally to my fiancée; I will be hurt emotionally if I allow my fiancée past my "walls."
Misunderstood	My fiancée/fiancé will fail to understand me correctly; she/he will get the wrong idea or impression about me; I will be misinterpreted or misread.
Misportrayed	My fiancée has an inaccurate perception of me; I am misrepresented or represented in a false way; I am described in a negative or untrue manner; my fiancée paints a wrong picture of me; my fiancée has negative beliefs about me.
Disrespected	People will not respect me; my fiancé disregards me; there is a feeling of contempt toward me; people show no esteem, reverence, admiration, or high opinion toward me; my fiancé has little regard for me.

What We Do When Our Buttons Get Pushed

Most of us, consciously or unconsciously, fall into well-worn patterns of reacting when someone pushes our buttons. We don't like the message we hear about ourselves, and we'll do anything to soothe our hurt. We'll do or say whatever it takes to avoid the unwanted feelings.

When we react, we are capable of doing many things—and none of them helps us get to where we want to be. The chart below shows some of the most common ways we react when someone pushes our buttons.

REACTION	WHAT THAT REACTION LOOKS LIKE
Withdrawal	You avoid others or alienate yourself, without resolution; you sulk or use the silent treatment.
Escalation	Your emotions spiral out of control; you argue, raise your voice, fly into a rage.
Belittling or sarcasm	You devalue or dishonor someone with words or actions; you call your fiancée names or take potshots at her.
Negative beliefs	You believe your fiancé is far worse than he really is; you see your fiancé in a negative light or attribute negative motives to him.
Blaming	You place responsibility on others, not accepting fault; you're convinced the problem is your fiancée's fault.
Exaggeration	You make overstatements or embellish the truth.
Tantrums	You have a fit of bad temper.
Denial	You refuse to admit the truth or accept reality.
Invalidation	You devalue your fiancé; you do not appreciate who your partner-to-be is, what he feels or thinks or does.
Defensiveness	Instead of listening, you defend yourself by providing an explanation.
Clinginess	You develop a strong emotional attachment or dependence on your fiancée.
Passive aggression	You display negative emotions, resentment, and aggression in passive ways, such as procrastination and stubbornness.

Care taking	You become responsible for others by giving physical or emotional care and support to the point you are doing everything for your fiancé, and he does nothing to care for himself.
Acting out	You engage in negative behaviors like drug or alcohol abuse, sexual affairs, excessive shopping, or overeating.
Overfunctioning	You do what others should be doing for themselves, and you take responsibility for them.
Fix-it mode	You focus almost exclusively on what is needed to solve the problem.
Complaining	You express unhappiness or make accusations.
Aggression or abuse	You become verbally or physically aggressive, possibly abusive.
Manipulation	You control your fiancée for your own advantage.
Anger and rage	You display strong feelings of displeasure or violent and uncontrolled emotions.
Catastrophize	You use dramatic, exaggerated expressions to depict the relationship as in danger or as though it has failed.
Numbing out	You become devoid of emotion, or you have no regard for your fiancé's needs or troubles.

What Do You Want?

Such reactions are nothing more than strategies we employ to get what we want. Usually they are the opposite of our buttons or fears. The opposite of trapped, for example, is freedom; the opposite of failure is success; the opposite of helplessness is power; the opposite of inadequacy is competency.

These strategies represent our deepest heart's cry. It's like the words of James 4:1: "What causes fights and quarrels among you? Don't they come from your desires that battle within you?" Isn't that verse amazing? James says it's our deepest wants and desires that cause fights and quarrels. That means that when we can discover and claim these wants and desires, then we will know how to break the cycle of the Fear Dance and move toward a new dance—the dance of love, the very thing for which God created us.

What is it you want most? Consider this list of common wants and desires:

DESIRE	WHAT THAT DESIRE MEANS TO ME
Acceptance	I want to be warmly received without condition.
Grace	I want something good (i.e., forgiveness) that I don't deserve.
Connection	I want to be united to others.
Companion-ship	I want deep, intimate relationships.
Success	I want to achieve or accomplish something.
Self-determina-tion	I want to have independence and free will.
Understanding	I want to be known.
Love	I want to feel attractive to others.
Validation	I want to be valued for who I am.
Competence	I want to have skills and abilities that bring success.
Respect	I want to be admired and esteemed.
Worth	I want to feel important.
Honor	I want to feel like a priceless treasure.
Commitment	I want to have unconditional security in relationships.
Significance	I want to have meaning and purpose.
Attention	I want to be noticed.
Comfort	I want to feel a sense of well-being.
Support	I want to be cared for.
Approval	I want to be liked and accepted.
Wanted	I want to be sought after.
Safety	I want to feel protected and secure.
Affection	I want to feel fondness and warmth.

Trust	I want to have faith in others.
Hope	I want confidence that I will get what I love and desire.
Joy	I want to feel satisfied and happy.

The very fact that couples engage in the Fear Dance shows us that both partners want something. I, for example, want to feel successful and avoid failure. Erin wants to feel valued for who she is, for her feelings, and for what she thinks. When we start our own Fear Dance, we labor under the illusion that by reacting in unhealthy ways, we'll get what we really want. But it never works out that way. Take a look at a graphic of our Fear Dance:

Fear Dance

Think about your own relationship. You want to connect, but you fear you're not attractive enough (or competent enough or smart enough or whatever). You want to be accepted, but you fear you're not good enough. You want respect, but you fear the other person will look down on you. You want to control your situation, but you fear you are power-less.

Do you see how your fears actually reflect your wants? When you believe your wants won't be fulfilled, you feel fear:

YOU WANT ...	SO YOU FEAR ...
Acceptance	Rejection
Grace	Judgment
Connection	Disconnection
Companionship	Loneliness
Success	Failure
Self-determination	Powerlessness
Understanding	Being misunderstood
Love	Being scorned
Validation	Being invalidated
Competence	Feeling defective
Respect	Inferiority
Worth	Worthlessness
Honor	Feeling devalued
Dignity	Humiliation
Commitment	Abandonment
Significance	Feeling unimportant
Attention	Feeling ignored
Support	Neglect
Approval	Condemnation
Wanted	Feeling unwanted
Safety	Danger
Affection	Feeling disliked
Trust	Mistrust
Hope	Despair
Joy	Unhappiness

How Your Fear Buttons Work

Let's put these pieces—fears, reactions, and wants—together. One of the most powerful things about actually seeing your Fear Dance is that you begin to understand that the very things you do in reaction to your buttons getting pushed, in turn, trigger your partner's buttons. Remember, no one person is to blame for a Fear Dance, but rather both partners help create this crazy cycle, which effectively stifles feelings of safety in your relationship.

As Erin and I look back, we see the Fear Dance playing out in every major argument of our marriage. We recognized the pattern early on, but we didn't know how to break it.

My greatest fear is the fear of failure. If I feel I'm failing—or even if I feel I'm at risk for failure—I deal with that feeling by turning to certain unhealthy reactions (like defending myself, trying to fix the problem, rationalizing my behavior, or minimizing Erin's feelings). These things usually push Erin's buttons. Her main button is feeling invalidated. She wants me to value her feelings. But when I'm defending myself, I'm not valuing anything of hers. I'm so focused on me that she feels invalidated. She reacts by criticizing, escalating, blaming, or using sarcasm. In the end, both of our hearts close up and we disconnect. At that stage, you have two people in a marriage who feel completely alone—and loneliness is the kiss of death to a marriage.

Fight or Flight

When someone pushes our fear buttons, we react, either with fight or flight. We fight when we go after someone by getting angry, escalating, using sarcasm, throwing tantrums, defending ourselves, invalidating the other, trying to fix the problem, or complaining. We flee when we move away or pull back by withdrawing, stuffing our feelings, indulging in negative beliefs, or engaging in denial, passive aggressiveness, manipulation, numbing out, stonewalling, or shutting down. Every reaction will be some version of either a fight or a flight.

The hormone adrenaline courses through our bodies in times of danger or in moments when we don't feel safe, helping us get ready to respond and protect ourselves. As the hormones surge through our bodies, our hearts begin to beat faster, and we begin to breathe more rapidly to get oxygen and blood to the lungs, brain, and muscles. Other physiological sensations may include shaking, trembling, and excessive perspiration. Some people feel as though they are going to be sick.

Here's the thing: while the fight-or-flight response is great for survival, it is lousy for promoting intimate connections.

So—which style do you tend to favor: fight or flight?

FIGHT	FLIGHT
• Defensiveness	• Withdrawal
• Anger	• Negative beliefs
• Fix-it mode	• Shutdown
• Escalation	• Isolation
• Criticism	• Passive aggression

The Four Deadliest Reactions

Let's briefly address the four most destructive reactions. None is helpful, but watch out for the last one!

Withdrawal

Many men and women (although usually it's the man) withdraw whenever a conflict erupts. They do not want to discuss it, they do not want to mention it; they simply leave, either physically or emotionally.

When a person's heartbeat rises above about a hundred beats per minute (seventy is normal), he or she goes into fight-or-flight mode. The reason why men tend to withdraw more often than women is that during a conflict, a man's heart rate naturally rises above a hundred much faster than a woman's. And the moment they enter into fight-or-flight mode, men usually choose "flight" or withdraw to get away or to end the argument.

Habitual withdrawal as a way to deal with conflict is a high predictor of divorce, and it's not hard to see why. If spouses withdraw from a conflict, they don't ever solve it. They might try to work out the problem separately or attempt to return the relationship to the status quo, but they never solve anything. And in time, that often leads to divorce.

Withdrawal only delays the inevitable. When we avoid conflict, we merely brush the hurt under the rugs of our souls. Eventually the mound of hurt gets so big that it starts spilling out the sides—and what seeps out often looks a lot like anger, bitterness, depression, drug and alcohol abuse, eating disorders, or worse.

Escalation

When some men and women face conflict, they escalate; that is, they increase the intensity and volume of their conflict. It's probably safe to say that these couples fight rather than just argue. Couples who escalate during conflict tend to yell and scream at each other. The fight spirals out of control.

This reaction is all about adrenaline and has little to do with rational thinking. How can you think rationally when you're screaming at the top of your lungs? It also tends to make arguments vicious. When the blood starts boiling, partners say things they do not mean but cannot take back. Such arguments end up looking like a war zone—but neither side ever wins.

Belittling

This reaction leaves a sour taste in the mouth. Recognize any of the following?

✦ "Any similarity between you and a human is purely coincidental."

✦ "Calling you 'stupid' would be an insult to stupid people."

+ "Do you want people to accept you as you are, or do you want them to like you?"
+ "Go ahead, tell me everything you know. That'll take only ten seconds."
+ "You're not stupid; you're possessed by a retarded ghost."
+ "You're the kind of man someone would use as a blueprint to build an idiot."
+ "How did you get here? Did someone leave your cage open?"
+ "I'm busy now. Can I ignore you some other time?"

Hurtful remarks stick. And who wants to hang on to a relationship in which one is constantly belittled? When we belittle our life partner, we devalue and dishonor him or her. We put ourselves above them and look down on them, as if they hold an inferior position to us. This, too, kills relationships.

Negative Beliefs

Erin and I consider this reaction the most brutal of all. By negative beliefs, we mean accepting as true something that is far more negative than the reality.

If a husband believes his wife is purposely ruining their relationship, for example, he'll notice and focus on everything she does that appears negative. At the same time, he'll neglect or reinterpret all the contrary evidence. If he sees her doing something positive, he'll say to himself, "She's doing that only so she can spend more time on herself. She is *so* selfish!" Both positive and negative events may occur throughout the day, but either he doesn't see the good or he interprets it as chance or as manipulation. He continues to focus on the negative, which becomes his evidence. He'll point friends to his jar of evidence and say, "Do you *see* what I'm living with?" And his friends likely will agree: "Ughh—you're right."

Do you see how destructive this reaction can be? Imagine a wife who sees her husband as mean-spirited and unloving. She interprets all of his behavior through that negative filter. Therefore, nothing her husband does will measure up, because she's already tried and convicted him. Suppose that one day he brings home flowers, just to encourage her. When he knocks to surprise her and she opens the door, she starts sobbing. Confused, he asks the reason for her tears. "I've had a horrible day at home, the kids are still screaming, the dishwasher broke," she says, "and now you come home *drunk!*"

These four reactions can damage your relationship—and if you don't start taking steps *now* to change them, they can destroy your upcoming marriage. Not sure how seriously your reactions may have hurt your relationship? Take the quiz on page 313 to see to what extent these reactions have invaded your relationship.

Marital Conflict Can Make Us More Like Christ

As the old saying has it, when life gives you lemons, make lemonade. "It is difficult to make people miserable while they feel worthy of themselves," said Abraham Lincoln.

The apostle Paul often went on "treasure hunts" and encouraged his believing friends to do the same. That's why he told his Roman brothers, "And not only this, but we also exult in our tribulations, knowing that tribulation brings about perseverance; and perseverance, proven character; and proven character, hope; and hope does not disappoint" (Romans 5:3–5 NASB). The apostle James spoke essentially the same message when he wrote, "Consider it pure joy, my brothers, whenever you face trials of many kinds, because you know that the testing of your faith develops perseverance. Perseverance must finish its work so that you may be mature and complete, not lacking anything" (James 1:2–4).

What does this mean for your upcoming marriage? It means that when you encounter a trial—and it may happen sooner than you think!—try hard to understand what God may be attempting to teach you through it.

First and foremost, God is going to use the coming difficulties in our marriage to help us become more like Jesus. Suffering is what makes us "mature" or "complete." Remember, Jesus Himself was made perfect through His suffering. "In bringing many sons to glory, it was fitting that God, for whom and through whom everything exists, should make the author of their salvation perfect through suffering" (Hebrews 2:10). If trials were an important part of Jesus's own preparation for His divine mission, then how much more crucial are they for us and for our marriage? It is through trials that we are shaped into the image of Christ. Consider these two verses:

> In this [inheritance] you greatly rejoice, though now for a little while you may have had to suffer grief in all kinds of trials. These have come so that your faith—of greater worth than gold, which perishes even though refined by fire—may be proved genuine and may result in praise, glory and honor when Jesus Christ is revealed. (1 Peter 1:6–7)

> Endure hardship as discipline; . . . God disciplines us for our good, that we may share in his holiness, . . . it produces a harvest of righteousness and peace for those who have been trained by it. (Hebrews 12:7, 10, 11)

The amazing "treasure" found in every experience of pain, heartache, and disappointment is that God uses these challenges to refine our character and strengthen our faith. Again, God's most important goal for us is that we become conformed to the image of his Son.

How can we treasure-hunt the trials in our marriage? A psychologist once gave a group of couples on the brink of divorce a single assignment. "Go home," he told them, "and write all of the positive things that your partner does throughout the week. Write nothing else. Do it as a competition. I'll reward the winner."

Seventy percent of the couples who complied and went on this treasure hunt reported a significant improvement in their level of marital satisfaction. They thanked the psychologist and praised his efforts, but he explained that *they* had done the work. Their marriages began to improve when they started to change their perception of the other and began focusing on the positive. Once they felt better about their relationships, they started to act differently within their relationships. The exercise had a real snowball effect.

Positive thinking is largely a choice. By thinking rightly and positively, you can begin to change a bad situation into a good one. I love the apostle Paul's take on this idea: "Whatever is true, whatever is noble, whatever is right, whatever is pure, whatever is lovely, whatever is admirable—if anything is excellent or praiseworthy—think about such things" (Philippians 4:8).

Whenever someone asks me for an autograph, I always write the reference "Philippians 4:8" next to my name. That verse offers one of my favorite pieces of marriage advice, and it has nothing explicitly to do with marriage. When we focus on the positive, when we let our minds dwell on the true and the noble and the right and the pure and the lovely and the admirable—when we concentrate on things excellent and praiseworthy—we set ourselves up for success, in marriage and elsewhere. This is not a Pollyanna fantasy, as some have scoffed. The practice is thoroughly biblical and powerfully shapes the way you and I relate to others. And that includes your future mate.

A woman came in to see a divorce lawyer, determined to dump her husband. She hated her mate and told the attorney she wanted to hurt him as much as possible.

"I can help you with that," the lawyer said. "Here's what you do. Go home, and be incredibly nice to your husband for three months. Compliment him on his appearance, on his intelligence, on his ability to run a home. Make him feel as though you're still head over heels for him. And then, when he least expects it, serve him with divorce papers. You'll cut out his heart."

The woman loved the diabolical idea and went home to put it into practice. When the divorce lawyer didn't hear from his prospective client for more than four months, he called her to see how their plan was working.

"Are you ready to divorce him now?" the attorney asked.

"*Divorce* him?" the woman asked incredulously. "Why on earth would I want to divorce him? I'm married to the most wonderful man in the whole world!"

Don't underestimate the power of positive thinking! A more potent skill is hard to find.

Adopting God's Goal = Joy

God will not only use the coming difficulties in your marriage to help you become more like Jesus, but He also uses the pain we encounter to teach us JOY. There is one statement that I hear over and over from parents as they talk about their child's upcoming marriage that makes me cringe: "I just want my son or daughter to be *HAPPY.*" I can't stand that word because it is not only far from reality but, more important, it is a world away from God's desire for marriage. Many couples want to avoid the challenges of marriage because they mistakenly believe that God's ultimate goal for them is happiness and they've assumed that marriage was designed primarily to make them "happy." Sadly, millions of couples have bought this lie. The problem is that happiness is a feeling based solely on what *happens* to us. Therefore, when someone's marriage makes him unhappy, he concludes that what he needs is a different marriage—one that will make him happy. The truth is that God doesn't want us to be happy, he wants us to be full of joy—his joy. Happiness also implies the absence of pain. The truth is we live in a fallen world. Even when we are walking in line with God's will, we are going to experience many trials and tribulations—even a difficult marriage. Your expectation should be that your marriage will have wonderful times and painful valleys. If your goal in marriage is to find happiness, you will naturally avoid and resist opportunities for suffering. But if you share God's values and crave *godliness,* then you will genuinely find joy in the difficulties that marriage will bring. *Joy* comes from trusting in God's love and sovereignty. It is an *inner peace* not connected to current circumstance (Philippians 4:4–9). Even in the most painful marital difficulties, we can still experience great joy, so long as we trust God, believing that He will not give us more than we can handle and that He will use the trial to strengthen our faith. Best of all, joy comes from trusting that God intends to use the trial to conform us into the image of His son. It is this very promise that allows you to *rejoice* when you encounter the opportunities for growth afforded by suffering.

As you get ready to walk down the aisle, do not forget this one thing: *the primary purpose of marriage is to glorify God.* It is His design for man and woman. It has been His created purpose from the beginning of time, His way of illustrating His love for the world. Marriage brings glory to God.

Commit today that yours will, as well.

What's the Real Problem?

Returning to the issue of your buttons, they are not, in and of themselves, the real problem. The problem is how you choose to deal with them. Erin and I typically explain to worried individuals, "Some of the ways you're dealing with your buttons right now are problematic. I'd say they're red flags. I'd also say that if you keep doing things this way, over the course of years you're going to put your marriage at risk."

Would you like to know the truth? The buttons that will set you off in your marriage are present right now, during your engagement—and were there even when you began dating. But when those buttons got pushed in the early days, you didn't normally respond in problematic ways. And even if you did react in an unhealthy fashion, your fiancé's rose-colored lenses made your unpleasant response seem not quite so negative or overwhelming. If you don't learn *now* how to recognize the particular steps of your own Fear Dance and deal with them in a productive way, you're in for a rough time.

You want to know the real problem with the dance? When you start reacting, you become an adversary with your future spouse, which makes your relationship feel unsafe. And when you feel unsafe, your heart closes, and you disconnect from the relationship.

None of us like fear, but as an emotion, fear can be a very useful source of information. By acknowledging and discussing your fear, you can actually open the door to intimacy. On a personal level, the key is learning to recognize and understand the fear and what is going on for you emotionally. On a relational level, it's being willing to be vulnerable enough to share your fears with your future spouse. That opens the door to a deep experience of caring, compassion, understanding, and love—in other words, intimacy.

That's the dance. It hurts. It's universal, in one form or another. You're dancing right now, even if you don't realize it.

But here's the best news: we can teach you to recognize it, stop it, and recover from its hurtful effects. And that's just what we'd like to do next.

COUPLE EXERCISES/HOMEWORK

Identifying Your Dance

The Fear Dance Test

1. Describe a recent conflict or negative situation with your fiancée/fiancé—something that really "pushed your buttons." For the purpose of this exercise, be sure that you and your future spouse write down the *same conflict.*

2. What were the BUTTONS that got pushed during the conflict? Another way to look at BUTTONS is this: How did what happened during the conflict make you feel about *yourself*? And *what message* did you receive? That is, as a result of the above conflict I felt _____, and to me that meant I feared/thought _____ would happen/was happening. Check all that apply, but "star" the most important feelings.

MALE'S ANSWERS √	"AS A RESULT OF THE CONFLICT, I FELT . . ."	WHAT THAT FEELING MEANS TO ME	FEMALE'S ANSWERS √
	Rejected	I will be discarded; I will be seen as useless; my fiancée/fiancé doesn't need me; I am not necessary in this relationship; she/he doesn't desire intimacy with me.	
	Unwanted	My fiancée/fiancé doesn't want me; she/he will not choose me; she/he is staying in the engagement out of duty, obligation, or because it's the "right" thing to do.	
	Abandoned	I will be alone; my fiancée/fiancé will ultimately leave me; she/he won't be committed to me for life.	

	Disconnected	We will become emotionally detached or separated; there are walls or barriers between us in the relationship.	
	Like a failure	I am not successful as a fiancée/fiancé; I will not perform right or correctly; I will fall short in my relationship; I won't make the grade.	
	Helpless or powerless	I cannot do anything to change my fiancée/fiancé or my situation; I do not possess the power, resources, capacity, or ability to get what I want.	
	Controlled	I will be controlled; my fiancée/fiancé will exercise authority over me; I will be made to "submit"; my fiancée/fiancé will restrain me; I will be treated like a child or my fiancée/fiancé will act like my parent.	
	Defective	Something is wrong with me; I'm the problem; I am unlovable.	
	Inadequate	I am not capable; I am incompetent.	
	Inferior	Everyone else is better than I am; I am less valuable or important than others.	
	Invalidated	Who I am, what I think, what I do, or how I feel is not valued.	
	Unloved	My fiancée/fiancé doesn't love me anymore; she/he has no affection or desire for me; my relationship lacks warm attachment, admiration, enthusiasm, or devotion.	
	Dissatisfied	I will not experience satisfaction within the relationship; I will exist in misery for the rest of my life; I am not pleased within my relationship; I feel no joy in my relationship.	

	Taken advantage of	I will be cheated by my fiancée/fiancé; she/he will take advantage of me; she/he will withhold something I need; I will feel like a "doormat"; I won't get what I want.	
	Worthless or devalued	I am useless; my fiancée/fiancé fails to recognize my value and worth; I feel cheapened, less than, or undervalued in the relationship; I have little or no value to my fiancée/fiancé; she/he does not see me as priceless.	
	Not good enough/ Don't measure up	Nothing I do is ever acceptable, satisfactory, or sufficient for my fiancée/fiancé; there will always be more "hoops" to jump through; I will never be able to meet her or his expectations of me; my efforts will never be enough.	
	Unaccepted	My fiancée/fiancé does not accept me; my partner is not pleased with me; she/he does not approve of me.	
	Judged	I am always being unfairly judged or misjudged; my fiancée/fiancé forms faulty or negative opinions about me; I am always being evaluated; she or he does not approve of me.	
	Humiliated	This relationship is extremely destructive to my self-respect or dignity.	
	Ignored	My fiancée/fiancé will not pay attention to me; I feel neglected.	
	Unimportant	I am not important to my fiancée/fiancé; I am irrelevant, insignificant, or of little priority to her or him.	
	Useless	I am of no use in this relationship; I am ineffective; I am not needed.	

	Intimacy	I am afraid of opening up emotion-ally; I will be hurt emotionally if I allow my fiancée/fiancé past my "walls."	
	Misunderstood	My fiancée/fiancé will fail to un-derstand me correctly; she/he will get the wrong idea or impression about me; I will be misinterpreted or misread.	
	Misportrayed	My fiancée/fiancé has an inaccu-rate portrayal of me; I am misrepre-sented or represented in a false way; I am described in a negative or untrue manner; she/he paints a wrong picture of me; she/he has negative beliefs about me.	
	Disrespected	I will be insulted; my fiancée/ fiancé does not admire me; she/he will have a low opinion of me; I will be disregarded; my fiancée/ fiancé does not respect me; she/he does not look up to me.	
	Out of control	My marriage will be wild, unruly, or hectic; my fiancée/fiancé will be un-manageable or uncontrollable; things will feel disorganized or in disorder.	
	Alone	I will be by myself or on my own; I will be without help or assistance; I will be lonely; I will be isolated.	
	Insignificant	I will be irrelevant to my fiancée/ fiancé; I will be of no consequence; I am immaterial, not worth men-tioning, trivial in her or his eyes; I am of minor importance to my fiancée/fiancé.	
	Unknown	My fiancée will not know me; it's like I'm a stranger; I will be nameless or anonymous to my fiancée/fiancé; I will be unfamiliar to her or him.	

Boring	There will be no passion in our marriage; my fiancée/fiancé perceives me as dull and dreary; our relationship is uninteresting; my fiancée/fiancé will believe that she/he knows everything there is to know about me; I feel as if we are just roommates—there will be no romantic feelings between us.	
Disappointment	I will be a let-down in the marriage; my fiancée/fiancé will be disappointed and disillusioned by me.	
Phony	My fiancée/fiancé will see me as fake or not genuine and will believe that I'm a fraud, pretender, or an imposter; it will be perceived that I'm not who I say I am; I will be viewed as a hypocrite.	
Unfair	My fiancée/fiancé will treat me unfairly and want me to do things she/he is unwilling to do (there is a double standard); I will be asked to do things that are unreasonable or excessive; my fiancée/fiancé treats me differently than others; I won't be treated equally.	
Dishonesty	Our relationship will lack truth, honesty, or trustworthiness; my fiancée/fiancé willfully perverts truth in order to deceive, cheat, or defraud me; she/he will mislead me or give a false appearance.	
Betrayed	My fiancée/fiancé will be disloyal or unfaithful; she/he has given up on the relationship; I'll be let down; my fiancée/fiancé will share or reveal private information with others.	

		I do not know what is going on in the relationship; I do not have the necessary information; I'm in the dark; I'm clueless; things feel secretive, hidden, or undisclosed; I'll appear ignorant or uniformed.	
	Unaware		
	Other:		

3. What do you *do* when your buttons get pushed? (Your buttons are the items you checked from question 2.) How do you react when you feel those ways? Identify your common coping strategies to deal with those buttons or feelings. Check all that apply—but "star" the most important reactions or coping behaviors.

MALE'S ANSWERS √	REACTIONS— WHAT ONE DOES	EXPLANATION	FEMALE'S ANSWERS √
	Withdraw	I avoid others or alienate myself without resolution; I am distant; I sulk or use the silent treatment.	
	Stonewall	I turn into a stone wall by not responding to my fiancée/fiancé.	
	Escalate	My emotions spiral out of control; I argue, raise my voice, or fly into a rage.	
	Emotionally shut down	I detach emotionally and close my heart toward my fiancée/fiancé; I numb out; I become devoid of emotion; I have no regard for others' needs or troubles.	
	Pacify	I try to soothe, calm down, or placate my fiancée/fiancé; I try to get her/him not to feel negative emotions.	
	Earn-it mode	I try to do more to earn others' love and care.	
	Belittle	I devalue or dishonor someone with words or actions; I call my fiancée/fiancé names, use insults, ridicule, take potshots, or mock her or him.	

	Negative beliefs	I believe my fiancée/fiancé is far worse than is really the case; I see her or him in a negative light or attribute negative motives to him or her; I see my future mate through a negative lens.	
	Arrogance	I posture myself as superior to, better than, or wiser than my fiancée/fiancé.	
	Blame	I place responsibility on others, not accepting fault; I'm convinced the problem is the other's fault.	
	Innocent victim	I see my fiancée/fiancé as an attacking monster and myself as put upon, unfairly accused, mistreated, or unappreciated.	
	Control	I hold back, restrain, oppress, or dominate; I "rule over" my fiancée/fiancé; I talk over or prevent my fiancée/fiancé from having a chance to explain her or his position, opinions, or feelings.	
	Dishonesty	I lie about, fail to reveal, give out false impressions, or I falsify my thoughts, feelings, habits, likes, dislikes, personal history, daily activities, or plans for the future.	
	Withhold	I withhold my affections, feelings, intimacy, or love from my fiancée/fiancé.	
	Demand	I try to force my fiancée/fiancé to do something, usually with implied threat of punishment if I'm refused.	
	Annoying behavior	I use irritating habits or activities to infuriate, annoy, upset, or to get on my fiancée's/fiancé's nerves.	
	Provoke	I intentionally aggravate, hassle, goad, or irritate my fiancée/fiancé.	
	Isolate	I shut down; I go into seclusion or into my "cave."	
	Exaggerate	I make overstatements or embellish the truth; I make statements using "I always" or "I never."	

	Tantrums	I have a fit of bad temper; I become irritable, crabby, or grumpy.	
	Denial	I refuse to admit the truth or reality.	
	Invalidate	I devalue my fiancée/fiancé; I do not appreciate who my mate-to-be is, what she/he feels or thinks or does.	
	Distress-maintaining thoughts	I replay the argument over and over; I don't stop thinking about the conflict or what my fiancée/fiancé does that frustrates or hurts me.	
	Independence	I become independent (separate from my fiancée/fiancé) in my attitude, behavior, and decision making.	
	Rewrite history	I recast my earlier times together in a negative light; my recall of previous disappointments and slights becomes dramatically enhanced.	
	Defensiveness	Instead of listening, I defend myself by providing an explanation; I make excuses for my actions.	
	Clinginess	I develop a strong emotional attachment or dependence on my fiancée/fiancé; I hold tight to my fiancée/fiancé.	
	Passive-aggressive behavior	I display negative emotions, resentment, and aggression in passive ways, such as procrastination, forgetfulness, and stubbornness.	
	Avoidance	I get involved in activities to avoid my fiancée/fiancé.	
	Care-take	I become responsible for others by giving physical or emotional care and support to the point I am doing everything, and my future partner does little to care for herself or himself.	
	Pessimism	I become negative, distrustful, cynical, and skeptical in my view of my fiancée/fiancé and of marriage.	

	Act-out	I engage in negative behaviors like drug or alcohol abuse, premarital affairs, excessive shopping, or overeating.	
	Fix-it mode	I focus almost exclusively on what is needed to solve or fix the problem.	
	Complain	I express unhappiness or make accusations.	
	Criticize	I pass judgment, condemn, or point out faults; I attack my fiancée's/fiancé's personality or character.	
	Strike out	I lash out in anger, become verbally, or physically aggressive or abusive.	
	Manipulation	I control, influence, or maneuver my fiancée/fiancé for my own advantage.	
	Anger or rage	I display strong feelings of displeasure or violent and uncontrolled emotions.	
	Catastrophize	I use dramatic, exaggerated expressions to depict that the relationship is in danger or that it has failed.	
	Pursue the truth	I try to determine what really happened or who is telling the truth.	
	Judge	I negatively criticize, evaluate, form an opinion, or conclude something about my fiancée/fiancé.	
	Selfishness	I become more concerned with me and my interests, feelings, wants, or desires.	
	Lecture	I sermonize, talk down to, scold, or reprimand my fiancée/fiancé.	
	Cross-complain	I meet my fiancée's/fiancé's complaint (or criticism) with an immediate complaint of my own, totally ignoring what she/he has said.	
	Whine	I express myself by using a childish, high-pitched nasal tone and stress one syllable toward the end of the sentence.	
	Negative body language	I give a false smile, shift from side to side, or fold my arms across my chest.	

	Humor	I use humor as a way of not dealing with the issue at hand.	
	Sarcasm	I use negative or hostile humor, hurtful words, belittling comments, cutting remarks, or demeaning statements.	
	Minimize	I assert that my fiancée/fiancé is over-reacting to an issue; I intentionally underestimate, downplay, or soft-pedal the issue or her or his feelings.	
	Rationalize	I attempt to make my actions seem reasonable; I try to attribute my behavior to credible motives; I try to provide believable but untrue reasons for my conduct.	
	Yes, but . . .	I start out agreeing (yes) but I end up disagreeing (but).	
	Indifference	I become cold, smug, and show no concern for my fiancée/fiancé or future marriage.	
	Dump on	I emotionally "vomit," unload, or dump on my fiancée/fiancé.	
	Abdicate	I give away responsibilities; I deny responsibilities.	
	Self-depreciate	I run myself down or become very critical of myself.	
	Mind read	I make assumptions about my fiancée's/fiancé's private feelings, behaviors, or motives.	
	Repeat yourself	I repeat my own position over and over instead of understanding my fiancée's/fiancé's position.	
	Right/Wrong	I argue about who is right and who is wrong; I debate whose position is the correct or right one.	
	Self-abandonment	I desert myself; I neglect me; I take care of everyone except me.	

	Righteous indig-nation	I believe that I deserve to be angry, re-sentful, or annoyed with my fiancée/fiancé because of what she/he did.	
	Stubborn	I will not budge from my position; I become inflexible or persistent.	
	Righteousness	I make it a moral issue or argue about issues of morality or righteousness.	
	Play dumb	I pretend not to understand or know what my fiancée/fiancé is talking about.	
	Nag	I badger, pester, or harass my fiancée/fiancé to do something I want.	
	Other:		

4. Now it's your turn to diagram your personal Fear Dance. Turn to the blank chart called "Your Fear Dance" below. Fill in the feelings you marked in question 2 (e.g., rejected, un-wanted, like a failure, etc.) on the blank lines under "Male's [or Female's] Buttons." Have your fiancée/fiancé fill in the other section based on her or his responses. Then fill in the coping strategies you marked in question 3 (e.g., withdrawal, stonewall, escalate, etc.) on the blank lines under "Male's [or Female's] Reactions." Again, have your fiancée/fiancé fill in the other section based on her or his responses.

Your Fear Dance

Male's Buttons

Female's Reactions

Male's Reactions

Female's Buttons

6

Personal Responsibility

A woman marries a man expecting he will change, but he doesn't. A man marries a woman expecting that she won't change, and she does.

—AUTHOR UNKNOWN

Somewhere around AD 30, a Jewish preacher and former carpenter named Jesus gave us the first step in breaking the Fear Dance. It is one of our favorite verses because it champions such "in your face" advice:

> *Why do you look at the speck of sawdust in your brother's eye and pay no attention to the plank in your own eye? How can you say to your brother, "Let me take the speck out of your eye," when all the time there is a plank in your own eye? You hypocrite,* first take the plank out of your own eye, *then you will see clearly to remove the speck from your brother's eye." (Matthew 7:3–5)*

Isn't that *awesome*? How many of us would be bold enough to call powerful religious leaders hypocrites? Very few, but Jesus was. And I am so thankful, because His encouragement saved my marriage.

For many years, when I tried to break out of the Fear Dance, I was convinced that Erin was both the problem and the solution. When we would go in for counseling, I loved to point my finger at Erin and talk about her issues. It's so much more fun to talk about others! I literally kept a running list of all the things she needed to change so that we could have a great marriage. I was willing to "help her grow," of course, because I loved her so much.

Yeah, right!

I had no idea that this approach kept me dependent upon Erin for my happiness and served only to make things worse. I felt like the poor guy who died and went to heaven. As the guy stood in a massive group, God gave two simple instructions: "I want the men to make two lines, one line for the men who dominated their wives on earth, and the other for the men who were dominated by their wives. Also, I want all the women to go with Saint Peter."

With that, the women exited, leaving two lines of men. The line of men who had been dominated by their wives was one hundred miles long, while the line of men who had dominated their wives included only one man.

God became angry at such a pitiful sight and said, "You husbands should be ashamed of yourselves! I created you in My image—and you were *all* whipped by your mates? Look at the only one of my sons that stood up and made Me proud! Learn from him. Tell them, My son, how did you manage to be the only one in this line?"

"I don't know," the man replied meekly, "my wife told me to stand here."

I felt exactly like this man for many years in my own marriage. And I'm not talking about feeling dominated by Erin! She did no such thing. Instead, I felt like I was standing in a long line with a whole bunch of others who also depended totally on their mates. It wasn't because Erin tried to control me, but because I gave her total control over my life. Let me show you how it happened.

A Strange Dance

One of the strangest Fear Dances we ever had took place early one morning. Erin and I had been feeling disconnected because I had been very busy at work and had been traveling a lot for my job. The morning started off pretty innocently (they always do!).

"What time are you going to leave to take the girls to school?" Erin asked.

"What are you talking about?" I replied, confused. "I told you yesterday that I have an early meeting. I have to leave for the office right now if I'm going to make it."

"You never said anything about an early-morning meeting!"

"I certainly did. Is it possible you forgot?"

"Is it possible that you forgot to mention the meeting to me?"

I'm pretty sure both of us were asking rhetorical questions by this point! I then proceeded to withdraw and left for work. Later that day I called home and, as you might imagine, heard a very cold and distant wife on the other end of the line.

"I just called to remind you about tonight," I said, tentatively.

"What's tonight?" Erin asked with frigid indifference.

"Yeah, *right!* Stop kidding. Are you going to be ready by 5:00 p.m.?"

"Greg, I'm *not* kidding. What's happening at 5:00 p.m.?"

"The dinner we are going to on the *Branson Belle* [a dinner cruise on a massive old-time–looking riverboat]."

"You've said nothing about a dinner on the *Branson Belle.*"

"You're just trying to get me back for this morning!"

"No, I'm not! I really have heard nothing about this dinner. *This* is what I'm talking about. You're not communicating with me! You are too busy with your own life. I'm just an inconvenient afterthought."

Erin and I proceeded to dance around this issue for a few more sentences until I hung up the phone, completely frustrated. I ended up at the dinner alone and had to enjoy a delicious prime-rib dinner, with all the trimmings, without her. *That will teach her a lesson,* I rationalized.

When I returned home later that night, all the lights were out. I silently crept into bed. Looking back, I do remember feeling a little strange as I fell asleep, but nothing to feel alarmed about.

I couldn't have been more wrong!

Around 1:30 a.m., I woke up with a terrible stomachache. My entire body was tingling and my lips had swollen to such a degree that I could barely form words.

"Erin," I stammered, "Thomething ith wrong with me. I thhhhink I'm dying."

While I wasn't really dying, I was having an allergic reaction to the prime rib. I know what you're thinking: *divine justice!* I know Erin cracked a smile when she realized what was happening to me.

To make a long story short, Erin rushed me to the hospital, and they gave me a healthy dose of epinephrine to combat the allergic reaction. Erin joked that since my entire family knew we had been in a fight (they were at the dinner), they would have accused her of killing me had I died from the reaction.

At least I would have had the last laugh!

The next day, however, Erin and I talked about what had happened. Take one guess about who each of us wanted to talk about? *Exactly*—the other!

Erin wanted to talk about my failure to mention my early meeting and the dinner. I wanted to talk about how critical and harsh she was. I wanted to focus on how little grace she seemed to extend to me. I wanted to talk about her side of the dance—her reactions that I didn't like.

You know the problem, don't you? So long as I remained convinced that the solution to my marriage problems depended upon Erin changing, I was left completely powerless. Since I couldn't control Erin (or anyone else, for that matter), to the extent that my well-being remained dependent on her changing, I gave my power to her. And since I had no real ability to control Erin's thoughts, feelings, and behavior, any attempt to do so was totally futile.

You're Responsible for Your Buttons

When I blame Erin for how I feel or behave, I am giving her power to determine my worth, identity, adequacy, lovability, etc. And I let her determine how I should act ("I couldn't help myself because you ____" or "if you just would have ____, then I would have ____").

But the Bible speaks much to the contrary. It insists that each of us will be held fully accountable before the Lord for what we do or don't do. Just ask Adam. When he and his wife were caught red-handed with the forbidden fruit, he tried to blame Eve for his choices: "The woman you put here with me—she gave me some fruit from the tree, and I ate it" (Genesis 3:12). In the same way that blaming Eve for his poor choices didn't work for Adam, it will never work for us.

Therefore, your ultimate goal must be to *take full personal responsibility for your feelings, actions, and responses.*

Notice several Scripture verses that highlight personal responsibility:

+ Search *me*, O God, and know *my* heart. (Psalm 139:23)
+ When Peter saw him, he asked, "Lord, what about him?" Jesus answered, "If I want him to remain alive until I return, what is that to you? *You* must follow me." (John 21:21–22)
+ If it is possible, as far as it depends on *you*, live at peace with everyone. (Romans 12:18)
+ Each one should carry his *own* load. (Galatians 6:5)

We trust that you see the key part in each one of these verses: *you.* You always have the option to take personal responsibility for how you react when your fear buttons get pushed.

By nature, most of us want to blame those who upset us. We work hard to try to get our fiancé to change how he treats us. We attempt in many unhealthy ways to manipulate our loved ones, to force them to quit pushing our buttons. But what usually happens when we take this approach? It succeeds only in pushing our loved one's own fear buttons, which in turn perpetuates and accelerates the deadly cycle. We wind up feeling hurt, abused, estranged, and lonely—and our relationship takes a turn for the worse.

If you want to break the pattern of the Fear Dance, the first step is to take personal responsibility for your own buttons. This means that you refuse to focus on what the other person has done.

Too many of us think, *If only my fiancée would say this* or *If only my fiancé would do that,* rather than thinking, *I can't change him, but I can change how I react to him,* or *I can't control what she does, but I can control what I do.* Personal responsibility requires that you take a hard look at your own side of the equation. You might say to yourself, *You know what? This person just pushed my fear button. Normally I would withdraw and run away, even though that never solves anything. But I'm not going to do that this time. This time I'm going to take responsibility for how I act, rather than trying to manipulate this person into acting toward me in a certain way.*

We've all heard the phrase "personal responsibility," but very few of us have been taught how to put this life-changing concept into action relationally. The process begins with accepting a very important job.

Step One: Accept the Job

Personal responsibility is not optional. You have no choice. In fact, it's your job! Jesus made this clear in what we call "the greatest commandment." When asked to name the greatest of all God's mandates, He gave a simple answer: " 'Love the Lord your God with all your heart and with all your soul and with all your mind and with all your strength.' The second is this: 'Love your neighbor as yourself' " (Mark 12:29–31).

Notice something important in these verses. Many of us have been taught that there are three commandments here: Love God, others, and self. Right? Upon closer review, however, we see there are really only two commands and one assumption. You know the two commandments: Love God, and love others. The assumption is that we already love ourselves. "As you love yourself" is not a command; Jesus assumes it's already happening, because God designed us to do that job all along.

What job? you may be wondering. Your job is to become the man or woman God created and called you to be. Loving yourself means being conformed to the image of the Lord—becoming Christlike. This is your job, and the key is to understand who is responsible for this job. Is it your fiancé? No. The answer is, *you* are 100 percent responsible for your own personal journey. If God is the "owner" of you, then He has appointed you as the "manager" of you. This is the goal. This is the job. Accept it!

Step Two: Identify What You Can Control, and Surrender All Else

The power we've been talking about is not power over others, but power over your personal well-being. It's the power to shape the kind of person you are. Nobody else has control over that!

Another benefit to taking personal responsibility is that it leads to true peace and serenity. Are you familiar with the Serenity Prayer? The key to serenity, or peace, is putting your efforts and energy into trying to control only those things that you can control—like yourself, for instance. You sacrifice your peace the moment you try to control things that you cannot control—like your fiancée, your friends, your boss, and the world.

To take personal responsibility is to live out the Serenity Prayer: "God grant me the serenity to accept the things I cannot change, courage to change the things I can, and the wisdom to know the difference."[1]

Notice the first part of the prayer: "accept the things I cannot change." What can you not change? Everything but your own self! You have no ability to control whether someone pushes your buttons. You can't change your future spouse. You will totally waste your time if you focus on your fiancé. As you've probably already discovered, trying to manipulate your loved one doesn't work. Blaming him or her only keeps you stuck.

The second part of the Serenity Prayer is the key here: "change the things I can." What can you control? Yourself. Period! When you find yourself spinning around in the Fear Dance, the first place to look is on your side of the dance. You first have to notice your own "stuff." You live out Matthew 7:5 when you first take the log out of your own eye. Only then will you see clearly to focus on the speck in your future mate's eye. What does this look like? Look at the following diagram:

Personal Responsibility: "I have control over . . ."

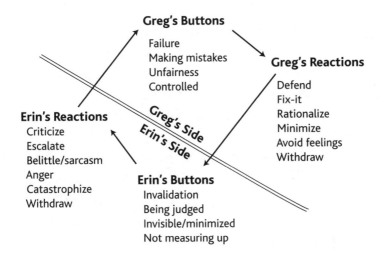

You take personal responsibility by first dividing your stuff from the other person's stuff. Again, you can change only what is on your side of the dance (your buttons and your reactions). The "wisdom to know the difference" means that you stay focused on your side of the equation.

As you look at the dance card, what do you notice that you have control over? First, you can take responsibility for reactions (notice that it's circled). You have a choice whether you react or respond to others. There is a difference. While reactions tend to have a knee-jerk element, a response is your choice, whether to get angry, defend yourself, criticize, escalate, or withdraw. It's your choice! You choose if you are going to respond to your future mate by being patient, kind, loving, humble, giving, honoring, and tender.

Second, although you cannot keep people from pushing your buttons (never make that your goal), you can do something once your buttons get pushed (notice that this is also circled). You have the option to care about how you feel and to attend to your buttons.

So, let's make this practical. What do you do when your buttons get pushed?

Step Three: Manage Your Buttons

Do you remember the old TV show from the '70s *The Incredible Hulk*? Probably not, but surely you remember the movie *The Hulk* that came out in 2003. Either way, do you remember the scientist who would turn into the Hulk? (This would make a good trivia question.) His name was Bruce Banner. Some people say it was David Banner, but that was only in the comic book, in case you were wondering!

And how would you describe Dr. Banner? He was easygoing, mild-mannered, relaxed, laid back, and mellow—a pretty safe person to be around. What would happen to turn him into the Hulk? Most people say anger. But anger is always a reaction. The truth about anger is that it's not generally a primary emotion. Anger is a secondary emotion that is purposeful and goal directed. Behind almost all expressions of anger are deeper feelings like fear, hurt, sadness, frustration, etc. We often choose anger to hide these feelings in order to avoid something or to get someone to do something. We may want to avoid things like getting emotionally close, getting hurt, having someone see that we are frightened or feeling frustrated. Or perhaps we get angry to get someone to behave, our coworkers to work harder, or to make our loved ones remember how much we don't like it when they are late.

People frequently do not even realize that there really are deeper feelings underneath their displays of anger. We are often unable to face the truth of how hurt, frightened, or frustrated we are. We often unconsciously choose anger instead. We may even believe that anger is our natural response because the split second between the deeper feeling and the anger occurs so fast it's as if the first true feeling didn't even occur. Thus, we either try to hide our fear, hurt, or frustration behind a show of power, or we use anger to intimidate people into doing what we want them to do. Either way the use of anger is fundamentally a *reaction*. We can learn how we use anger by asking ourselves two great questions, "what am I trying to accomplish with my anger?" and/or "what am I hoping will occur if I get angry?" The answer will frequently reveal what we are really trying to accomplish with our anger.

So what really turned Dr. Banner into the Hulk? Something frightened him. Either he would feel threatened, or someone he cared about was being threatened. You could accurately say that someone pushed his emotional fear buttons.

And how would you describe the Hulk? Please don't say, "green." Let's go deeper. He was full of rage, and he would try to destroy people. He would bonk them on the head or throw them through a window. The bottom line was that he wasn't safe to be around.

This is the point we're trying to make: when our fear buttons get pushed, we become the Hulk. If you're a lady, you become the "Hulkette." Just imagine a cute little pink bow on top of your head and a strip of cloth around your chest (this is a Christian book, for crying out loud!).

Maybe you're thinking, *Come on, guys! I don't bonk people on the head or throw them through windows. I don't become the Hulk!*

Remember, all your reactions are either a "fight" or a "flight." The Hulk certainly was more the fighting type. If you are more of the flighting type, however—you withdraw, shut down, get passive-aggressive, stuff how you feel; and you are still unsafe. These types of reactions, although subtle and passive, are just as destructive to a future marriage as the fight reactions.

The point is, we are unsafe when in reaction mode. It's not hard for me to think of the many times I've done some terrible things by reacting to Erin. I have screamed at her, used cuss words, punched walls, stormed off in a huff, and the list goes on. Beyond the relational damage I inflict, I risk losing my integrity—and the day will come when I will stand before the Lord to give an account of my choices and behaviors. *All* my choices and behaviors (see Matthew 12:36; Romans 14:12).

I wish I had understood how to break the dance earlier in our marriage! I'm convinced that it would have saved us a lot of pain and heartache. Although God has used our painful experiences, as He will yours, we're thrilled that you can create a much healthier dance in your upcoming marriage than we did.

If reacting when our buttons get pushed doesn't get us where we want to be relationally, then what can we do? Allow us to recount a funny story (at least, it's funny *now*) to use as a backdrop for explaining how to break out of the dance.

Breaking Out of the Dance

A number of years ago, our family had to use an unfamiliar airport as we got ready to leave town on vacation. Because Murphy's Law reigns supreme anytime you are trying to hustle to an airport, as soon as we started driving, I noticed we were almost out of gas.

"Erin!" I yelled, "you never got gas!"

"I thought you were going to do that!"

And our dance started to build momentum.

As I pulled into the gas station, I noted how many motorcycles had gathered. They seemed to be everywhere! It looked like a biker convention, with every shape and size of motorcycle known to man.

"Are we having a Hells Angels convention?" I asked Erin.

"Remember that Branson is hosting something for bikers who are raising money for some charity," she explained. Bikers and charity seemed like a contradiction to me, but who was I to judge?

As I weaved in and out of bikers, I felt as though I were driving through an obstacle course. I finally found a spot and pulled right behind a beautiful motorcycle hitched to a small trailer (with matching colors). I must admit it looked impressive—and expensive.

After topping off the tank, I whistled at the rising cost of fuel and how much I had just spent to fill our vehicle. Either that distracted me, or it was my three kids fighting in the back seat, because as I pulled away from the gas pump, I felt a strange bump. Instantly the beautiful (and expensive) motorcycle in front of me toppled over.

"That can't be good," I said to Erin. "Someone is going to be very upset."

It hadn't dawned on me yet that *I* had knocked over the bike. When I got out to see why the motorcycle had fallen, I noticed that I had rammed the trailer with my SUV.

I stood there for several seconds, in complete disbelief. I quickly scanned the parking lot to see if anyone had noticed my blunder. Since I didn't see any Hells Angels running my way, I figured, "no harm, no foul." I could simply right the fallen bike and we'd be on our way!

Well, let me tell you that those bikes are insanely heavy. I couldn't budge the thing. I instantly started to bead up with sweat. I would have to go in and confess to someone what I had done—someone, I hoped, who wasn't packing heat.

Talk about feeling like a complete failure!

Scores of my buttons flashed inside my head as I walked into the gas station. I felt as if I had just tripped an alarm inside my skull.

"Uh—does anyone own a new, red Honda Gold Wing with matching trailer?" I timidly asked.

And just my luck, this hulk of a man said, "Why?"

"You're not going to like this," I stammered, "But my *pregnant wife* . . ." (I'm just kidding) ". . . but I accidentally knocked it over."

I can't tell you what he said in reaction to my confession—mainly because I've blocked it out, or possibly because I had never heard some of the words he used. Thank goodness the man's wife (or *woman* as he called her) helped calm him down. I'm not sure what she did, but I do remember overhearing the question, "You don't want to go *back* to prison, do you?"

After exchanging insurance information and promising that I would never disrespect a man's Hog like that again, we were back on our way to the airport. As you might imagine, however, we were now *really* late and *very* emotionally agitated. I tell you this because when I climbed back into the SUV, Erin—trying to be helpful, I'm certain—said, "Make sure you look closely before pulling out this time."

I wish I could tell you that I thanked her for the thoughtful concern and assistance, but I'd be lying. Instead, we danced . . . Big Time!

But what if we had known how to deal with our dance? Here are five important choices Erin and I could have made differently and that you can make if you find yourself in a dance:

1. Create Space

Remember what the Incredible Hulk did to turn back into Bruce Banner? He would run off and go lay down somewhere. And then, after a few minutes of calming down, he would change back into Dr. Banner.

This is what we need to do. First and foremost, we need to create some space from each other. Another phrase for this is a "time out." This is when you get away, either internally or physically, so that you can calm down.

While sitting in the car next to Erin, instead of reacting to her, I could have said, "Erin, I love you and I want to talk about this issue; but right now my buttons are totally pushed and I need to take a break and deal with my buttons."

Perhaps you are thinking, *Oh, great. Greg, you just gave my fiancée permission to withdraw!* No, I did not! There is a huge difference between what we are suggesting and withdrawing. Withdrawal is when you shut down or move away, simply to stop the fight and avoid the pain. When you create space, on the other hand, you proactively get away so that you can get your heart back open. When you "Hulk up," the first thing that happens is that your heart closes to the other person—and this is what leads to many horrible reactions (affairs, drug or alcohol abuse, physical abuse, etc.).

The key is to verbalize in some way that (1) you care about each other, and (2) you will work this out later. You can't work it out at the moment, because you're the Hulk (or Hulkette), and so are not feeling "safe" in the conversation. But at a later time, you will become yourself again and then you can return to the issue and resolve it.

What would that sound like, in your own words? For your own relationship, talk about what phrase or "code word" you can use to explain that you are not withdrawing, but are creating space.

And how long should you maintain space? The key is to be away as long as you need to in order to get your heart back open. Some great research by Dr. John Gottman indicates that when your heart rate goes above one hundred beats per minute, you are in fight or flight mode (you've become the Hulk or the Hulkette). He discovered that it takes a minimum of twenty minutes for your heart rate to return to baseline (guys: seventy beats per minute; ladies: eighty beats per minute).[2] Therefore, we encourage you to take at least a twenty-minute break.

Now, here's the key: you cannot continue to entertain distressing thoughts during the space. You can't continue to grouse about the things your fiancée did or said, or dwell on how much your fiancé hurt you or how upset you feel. This will never get you to "de-Hulk." Instead, there are some helpful things we encourage you to do.

2. Identify Your Emotions

A great verse in James says, "Be quick to listen, slow to speak and slow to become angry" (1:19). Usually we hear this verse quoted in the context of our relationships with others. Usually we are encouraged to be quick to listen to the other person. But there's another valid application for this verse.

When your buttons get pushed and you've become the Hulk or the Hulkette, you must be quick to listen to *you* and not so much to the other person. If that sounds selfish, consider the reality. When you become the Hulk, you are no longer safe. There is no way you can effectively listen to the other person when you are all Hulked up. You can't listen because your heart is closed.

Have you ever tried to listen to your fiancé when your heart is closed? It's impossible. I don't care how relationally competent you are; when your buttons get pushed, you cannot listen effectively until you "de-Hulk."

The first part of de-Hulking is to identify your feelings, buttons, fears, hurts—your "stuff." Remember Matthew 7:5: "You hypocrite, *first take the plank out of your own eye, and then you will see clearly to remove the speck from your brother's eye.*" This is what we are saying: "Take the plank out of your eye *first.*" .

You do that by working to identify what the plank is. What button or buttons are being pushed right now?

When I hit the motorcycle, my "failure" and "making a mistake" buttons took a huge hit. I had cost my family money that we didn't have. In fact, the money it would cost to repair the motorcycle had to come from our vacation fund. *That's* failure. I also felt humiliated by the man's hysterical tirade and disrespect as he cussed me out. When I got back in our vehicle, my buttons were so activated that it took only a single comment from Erin to set me off again. When she "lovingly" encouraged me to pay closer attention when pulling out, I felt controlled and criticized.

It's critical at this stage to clearly identify your "stuff" (your emotions, buttons, fears, etc.). Ask yourself several key questions:

+ What's going on for me right now?
+ How am I feeling?
+ What specific buttons got pushed?
+ Where is this feeling coming from?
+ What is this saying about me, or what am I believing about myself right now?

Taking responsibility for your feelings means that you let your feelings and emotions (buttons) matter. You allow yourself to go to a place of compassion for yourself. You can always validate your emotions rather than ignoring them, detaching from them, or judging them. Be curious instead of judgmental about your feelings. Care and attend to your "stuff." Allow the feelings to have space to breathe. When you validate your own feelings, you're making it okay that you're feeling *whatever*. Learn to view your feelings simply as information, as the language of your heart. I'm adding a sidebar to say a little more about our emotions, because it's the key to breaking out of the dance.

EMOTIONAL INTELLIGENCE

We have been conditioned to believe that IQ is the best measure of human potential. In the past ten years, however, researchers have found that this isn't necessarily the case—that in actuality, your emotional intelligence quotient (EQ) might be a greater predictor of success, especially in marriage.

What is emotional intelligence? In the early 1990s, John Mayer, Maria DiPaolo, and Peter Salovey introduced the term "emotional intelligence" in the *Journal of Personality Assessment*. They used this term to describe a person's ability to understand his or her own emotions and the emotions of others and to act appropriately based on this understanding.[3] Then in 1995, psychologist Daniel Goleman popularized this term with his book *Emotional Intelligence: Why It Can Matter More Than IQ*.[4]

Why are emotions so important? For one thing, there are major health risks when we are unaware of what is going on for us emotionally. Look at some of the research:[5]

- Unaddressed emotions strain the mind and body.
- People who fail to use their emotional-intelligence skills are more likely to turn to other, less effective means of managing their moods. They are twice as likely to experience anxiety, depression, substance abuse, and even thoughts of suicide.
- Recent research studies have indicated an important link between emotional intelligence and susceptibility to disease. Stress, anxiety, and depression suppress the immune system, creating vulnerability to everything from the common cold to cancer.
- New medical research shows a definitive link between emotional distress and serious forms of illness, such as cancer.

These studies paint a pretty bleak picture for individuals who ignore their emotions. On the other hand, people who employ emotional intelligence tend to be more at ease with their surroundings and comfortable in their own skin. Why are emotions so vital to your well-being? Because they inform you about your needs and your deepest beliefs. When you feel a strong emotion—let's say dread, sadness, worry, or grief—your body is trying to tell you something important. Without your emotions, negotiating life would be like trying to drive a car with only one wheel.

God designed you to work best when your mind and your heart work together. You make the best decisions when you use your emotions to inform your brain. To get the best result, you need both your feelings and your intellect.

Yet it's here that problems often surface. What if you have been ignoring this major part of who God created you to be—your feelings? How do you learn to tap into your emotions? It's really a simple matter of listening to what they tell you. You're after *information*. Don't judge your emotions, but instead see them as great sources of information. Then ask yourself, "What are my emotions trying to tell me?" What could it mean, for example, if you are feeling stressed out, worried, sad, fearful, hurt, or frustrated?

Once you identify your feelings, at this stage don't try to figure out what to do with your emotions. Don't try to fix how you feel. Just work on learning how to become great at accurately identifying your feelings. You may want to ask yourself the following questions:

+ Do I pay a lot of attention to how I feel?
+ Do I notice my emotions as I experience them?
+ Can I accurately name my feelings?
+ When I experience emotions, do I know the reasons for them?
+ Do I pay attention to my thoughts, beliefs, and actions that could be causing how I feel?
+ Do I understand how my feelings influence my thoughts and actions?
+ Am I aware of how my emotions impact my fiancée?

It is so important to be able to identify your emotions. I had a hard time coming up with precise feeling words, even though I have a doctor-ate in clinical psychology and deal with emotions all the time. My struggle was that I just couldn't put a name to what I was feeling; I knew I was feeling *something*, but I just never really developed this *skill*. We are emphasizing the word *skill* because you can learn to accurately identify your feelings! To acquire this ability, you may want to use a feelings list that helped me convey more accurately how I felt. It's not a comprehensive list of emotions, but it is a start.

ANGER	JOY	SADNESS	HURT	FEAR
bothered	content	sad	lonely	uncertain
annoyed	peaceful	depressed	homesick	worried
bitter	relaxed	distraught	abandoned	anxious
angry	cheerful	despair	embarrassed	frightened
irritated	satisfied	melancholy	shame	scared
disgusted	joyous	grief	guilt	nervous
frustrated	excited	helpless	foolish	afraid
exasperated	ecstatic	hopeless	humiliated	terrified
furious	happy	miserable	hurt	overwhelmed

Remember, *God* is the creator of emotions—it was His design. Not only does God have deep feelings Himself, but He created us to experience emotions as well. Emotions exist to provide us with a valuable stream of information that we can use wisely in our relationships.

Another way to get the plank out of your eye is to clarify how you may have contributed to your buttons getting pushed. I can hear the objections: "Hey, I didn't do *anything*; my fiancée pushed my button!" But one of the most important lessons we've learned over the years is that it is *never* 100 percent the other person's fault when a button gets pushed. It's good to ask yourself several other questions:

✦ *Am I doing something to cause my buttons to be pushed?* Look at your stuff, your fear, your negative beliefs, etc. When Erin was a nurse and worked the late shift, every once in a while she came home late. If I looked up and noticed the clock read

1:30 a.m., and Erin wasn't home yet, I would automatically start imagining why. I would imagine that she had run out of gas, was attacked while walking to her car, or was lying in a ditch after being hit on the freeway. I would get so worked up! The point is, *I* was the one pushing my own buttons. Of course, Erin could have called to let me know she was going to be late; but I also did things that contributed to my stuff getting all stirred up.

✦ *What are my motivations and expectations?* One expectation I had that day at the gas station was that no one would speak to me in such a harsh and violent manner. Like I can control *that*.

✦ *What is my part versus the other's part?* I can always separate out my stuff from the other person's stuff. I certainly was responsible for knocking over the man's bike, but I don't have to take responsibility for his feelings and how he chose to react. That was *his* stuff.

Remember, you can't do anything to change the other person. Keep in mind your personal responsibility and the Serenity Prayer: "God grant me the serenity to accept the things I cannot change, courage to change the things I can, and the wisdom to know the difference." This is the part of "change the things I can." You can change *you*. You can take a look at the things *you're* doing to push your own buttons.

Many times a great place to start is to look at your expectations (chapter 4). We have so many expectations! Many times our buttons get pushed or the button that got pushed is exasperated by our expectations. But we can deal with our expectations—that's the good news.

3. Identify What You Want

Attend to your own feelings and wants—that is the opposite of controlling others. Some additional questions you can ask yourself include:

✦ *Is there anything I need emotionally in this moment that I can pro-vide?* I wanted to feel honored in that parking lot. I couldn't make that man treat me in honoring ways, but I could honor myself. I could have told myself that I made a mistake and that the man was saying untrue things about me. I could have thought about how God sees me and chosen to focus on that instead of what the man was saying.

✦ *What would I want to hear or receive from a friend in this moment?* Once I know that, I can figure out how I could provide that for myself. I can identify what I can do about my needs, in-stead of what the friend can do.

✦ *What would taking care of myself look like here?* I took care of myself by setting boundaries with the man. I told him that I was going to make it right, and that's why I didn't run off. But I wouldn't continue to talk to him if he was going to keep yelling and cussing at me. When he wouldn't stop, I walked back to my car, locked the doors, and called the police.

4. Take Your Feelings and Wants to the Lord

The secret to making all this work is to ask the Lord to help meet your needs and wants and to help care for your feelings and pain.

✦ Ask God if there is anything you are not seeing that He knows you need.

✦ Access the Lord in the provision of what you are wanting.

✦ Ask God to reveal His perspective and what the truth is about you and the situation you are in. Ask the Lord to lead you to a place of conviction if that's what you need. Ask with your heart and not with your brain:

　• What is the truth about me?

　• What do I need to take responsibility for?

- What do I need to seek forgiveness for?
- Who is the person I want to be in this moment (the person God created me to be)?

✦ Attend to your buttons.
- Depending on where you are and how much time you have, the goal is to "de-Hulk" and reprogram the automatic reactions (most people get caught in emotional ruts).
- The opposite is to neglect your buttons.
- Instead of judging, stuffing, or invalidating your feelings, you can be curious about them.
- Validate yourself (allow your feelings to matter).
- Ask yourself:
  - What hasn't worked in the past (in general and with this person)?
  - What have my reactions looked like?
  - What has worked before?
  - What are my options and choices?
  - What would a healthy response look like?

✦ Other tips: Take a few deep breaths, stand up and stretch, pray, read Scripture, listen to praise and worship music.

Why are you doing all these things? You do them to get your heart open and to fill it with God's love, so that you can respond (instead of react) to the other person.

5. Respond to Your Future Spouse

Our natural instinct is to react when our buttons get pushed, instead of responding. Reactions by definition are knee-jerk, like when someone hits our knee and our leg kicks out. Reaction mode doesn't involve conscious thought; we just react.

The goal here is to *respond* to your future spouse. Responding is thought out. When you respond, you do things that preserve your integrity. Responding is Christlike. When your heart is open and God's love is flowing through you, what comes out? Love.

And here is the cool part: "Love is patient, love is kind" (1 Corinthians 13:4). We don't have to figure out how to be patient, kind, and all the rest! Instead, the key is to become *love*. Then all these things come out of us. It's not what *we* do; it's what *God* does through us. Read these verses:

✦ What do you prefer? Shall I come to you with a whip, or *in love* and with a gentle spirit? (1 Corinthians 4:21)
✦ Do everything *in love.* (1 Corinthians 16:14)
✦ Instead, speaking the truth *in love* . . . (Ephesians 4:15)
✦ There is no fear *in love.* But perfect love drives out fear, because fear has to do with punishment. The one who fears is not made perfect *in love.* (1 John 4:18)

Do you see the common thread in all these verses? It's doing things in love. And that calls for a little reflection on what love really is.

What Is Love?

We often hear married couples say, "I don't feel in love with my mate anymore." Now, as marriage counselors, we just let that go, since it's not terribly important.

"How can you simply let that go?" you might ask. "Isn't not feeling in love with your spouse a *huge* problem?"

It's not that we ignore the statement; instead, we challenge the couple's beliefs about love and its origins. Let us ask you a question: Where does love come from? Have you ever thought about where love originates?

We normally blow by this issue of love in our work with couples because we know that love is not about chemistry (a fantasy). Couples tend to falsely think that love is magical or that they should have the ability to crank up the old love generator and create love. That's why, when we no longer feel love for our spouse, we put enormous pressure on ourselves, thinking that somehow we need to create love for him or her. As if that is something we can magically generate!

Worse yet, when we don't feel love for our mate, we conclude either that it is because we are incapable of generating love ("there must be something wrong with me!") or that there is something wrong with our mate ("she is unlovable!") or that there is something wrong with our marriage ("the love is gone, so we might as well just call it quits"). In reality, no love comes from us. We are not love's originators.

God is.

First John 4:7–8 insists that love comes from God and that God is love. Eleven verses later it declares that we love because God first loved us. The point? You do not generate a single drop of love. It *all* comes from God. By receiving God, you receive His love. You can then open your heart and share God's love with others.

Love feels good to all of us, but we are just passing it through from God to others. By making a conscious decision, you can pass love through to your future spouse.

When people tell us (usually, very gravely) that they no longer feel love for their spouses, we assume that, for some reason, they have closed the doors to their hearts. That is what prevents the flow of love. This is the common link in every couple who claim a loss of love; in reality, they have lost "heart." They have completely disconnected from their hearts, especially their emotions. They frequently use one of the following words to describe their dead hearts: detached, indifferent, numb, lifeless, heartless, alone, emotionally unavailable, or hard-hearted.

Do you feel that way? Do others accuse you of being this way?

It's like what the Tin Woodman said in *The Wizard of Oz*: "It was a terrible thing to undergo, but during the year I stood there, I had time to think that the greatest loss I had known was the loss of my heart. While

I was in love, I was the happiest man on earth; but no one can love who has not a heart, and so I am resolved to ask Oz to give me one."

This is why we have stopped making the issue about "how to love my spouse." Since we have no ability to create love, we make the focus the state of one's heart. So the real question becomes: "Is my heart open or closed?"

If your heart is closed, then love cannot flow from God, through you, to your future spouse. And so, quite naturally, you don't feel in love. If your heart is closed, then you have shut out God's love. This is what happens when people do not feel love for their spouses. They have simply closed their hearts to their mates (for good reasons, we're sure).

Your job is to do what Proverbs 4:23 says: "Above all else, guard your heart, for it is the wellspring of life." You *must* guard your heart! If you want to love as Peter talked about—"love one another deeply, from the heart" (1 Peter 1:22)—then you must discover why the door to your heart has closed; and then work to get your heart back open.

This realization has been extremely freeing for me. Instead of putting our efforts and energies into doing something we have zero ability to do (create love), Erin and I have learned to focus on the condition of our hearts. Are they open or closed? And we have total control over our hearts!

Get your heart open first, before you can truly love your future mate.

This is why we love 1 Corinthians 4:21. Read it again in light of what we just discussed:

What do you prefer? Shall I come to you with a whip, or in love and with a gentle spirit?

The only way you can come at your fiancée with a gentle spirit is through love. Furthermore, this is why Ephesians 4:15 becomes so powerful: "Instead, speaking the truth in love . . ." The only way you can speak the truth (which is from God) is by getting your heart open and allowing God's love to flow through you. And once your heart is open to your future mate, then you are in a position to respond to him or her.

What About Day-to-Day Stuff?

So you are responsible for yourself—but what about the day-to-day stuff? Who's going to finish the wedding plans, book the honeymoon, clean the bathroom, balance the checkbook, get the kids to the doctor, and pay the bills?

As an individual, you are responsible for your own well-being and becoming the person you were created to be. On the other hand, for your upcoming marriage to be great and everyone to feel thrilled, the division of labor has to be handled to everyone's satisfaction—but that is an issue of teamwork, not personal responsibility. We will address that topic thoroughly in chapter 9.

Still, in order to become a great team, players need to get themselves in order first. And taking personal responsibility is the essential first step.

COUPLE EXERCISES/HOMEWORK

1. List several examples of times you have tried to get your fiancée/fiancé to be responsible for how you have felt.

2. How does your fiancée/fiancé try to get you to be responsible for her/his feelings?

Go back to the Fear Dance Test on page 115. Review question 1 where we asked you to describe a recent conflict or negative situation with your fiancée/fiancé—something that really "pushed your buttons." With that recent disagreement in mind, answer the following questions:

1. On a scale of 0 to 10 (with 10 being completely closed), how closed was your heart toward your fiancée/fiancé at that time?

2. Looking back, what could you have done to create space? What could you have communicated to let your future spouse know that you needed space but would come back later to talk about the issue? What would that sound like, in your own words? For your own relationship, talk about what phrase or "code word" you can both use to explain that you are not withdrawing, but are creating space.

3. Identify your emotions. List the buttons that got pushed during that disagreement. Refer to the Your Fear Dance chart that you filled out at the bottom of page 125.

4. What did you do to push your own buttons (i.e., your fears, negative beliefs, expectations, etc.)? What was your part (your stuff) versus your fiancée's/fiancé's part (her/his stuff)?

5. List how you reacted to your fiancée/fiancé? Refer to the completed Your Fear Dance chart on page 125, (see Female's and Male's Reactions).

6. Looking back, what did you want from your fiancée/fiancé?

7. How could you have provided for yourself what you were trying to get from your fiancée/fiancé?

8. How could you have taken your wants, desires, needs to the Lord instead of to your fiancée/fiancé?

9. How could you have drawn in other "assistants" besides your fiancée/fiancé to help meet your needs (excluding opposite-sex friendships or other inappropriate relationships)?

10. What else could you have done to manage your buttons and keep from reacting (i.e., take deep breaths, stretch, pray, read scriptures, listen to music, exercise, walk, journal, etc.)?

11. Instead of reacting, how do you wish you would have "responded" to your fiancée/fiancé? What would "speaking the truth in love" have looked like?

Part Three

How Do *We* Stop Dancing?

7

Heart Talk

A woman has the last word in any argument.
Anything a man says after that is the beginning of a new argument.
—AUTHOR UNKNOWN

After living separate lives, a retired business executive and his wife discovered a painful reality. Sitting at home one evening, the couple called some friends to see what they were doing.

"Oh," said the other wife, "we're just talking and drinking tea." The executive's wife hung up the phone.

"Why don't we ever do that?" she demanded. "They're drinking tea and talking."

"So," said the executive, "make us some tea."

Soon they sat with their freshly brewed tea, staring at each other. And stirring. And staring. And stirring.

"Call them back," the executive barked, "and find out what they're talking about!"

Probably you have made the same discovery this couple did: a relationship will be only as good as its communication.

Become an Effective Communicator

After you take personal responsibility for your buttons and get your heart open, the next step in breaking the Fear Dance is to become an effective communicator. But understand that real communication takes more than understanding each other's words.

What?

Most of us have been taught that effective communication equals understanding words. As a matter of fact, countless techniques exist—speaker/listener, active listening, parroting, to name a few—that teach us how to accurately repeat what we hear the other person saying. Don't get us wrong! We do not disrespect these methods. They are extremely helpful to avoid misunderstanding. But we want you to enjoy the benefits of deep, emotional communication—a kind of talking that goes way beyond the actual words you use.

In reality, good communication takes place as each person understands the *feelings* that underlie the spoken words. People generally feel more understood, cared for, and connected when the communication first focuses on emotions and feelings rather than merely on words or thoughts.

Do you desire to feel deeply connected, understood, and cared for? If you answer yes, understand that it will involve many skills; but most important, it means learning how to listen to each other's hearts. We call this "emotional communication."

This type of listening takes time and work, and that's why so few practice it, much less master it. As a rule, your future spouse will desire communication with you to the same degree that he or she feels emotionally heard and understood. Who wants to talk with someone who never goes beyond mere words? The first step is to avoid some common pitfalls around communication.

"How Am I Doing?"

Let me introduce these common communication pitfalls by confessing one of the most bizarre conversations that Erin and I have ever had. It happened two weeks into our marriage.

"How am I doing as a wife?" she asked me.

I froze. I wasn't sure how to answer those seven seemingly innocent words, but since Erin and I had been married only two weeks, how hard could it be?

Silly boy!

"Fine," I said, avoiding eye contact.

Have you ever said something that you wish you could immediately retract or edit like a poor word choice on a computer screen? I felt like that at that moment. Erin's lack of words—actually, it was her lack of breathing—instantly caused me to wonder if "fine" was really the word she wanted to hear.

"*Fine?*" she demanded.

I had never realized, before that moment, that the word "fine," when said with so much passion, could actually sound like something negative.

"Uh . . . *what?*" I stammered.

Had I been a batter in a baseball game, you would have heard a gigantic whoosh, as I, for the second time in four seconds, hit nothing but air.

"You think I'm just *fine!*" Erin snapped again.

There it was again. The way she was able to verbalize my "fine" somehow sounded very different than how I had intended it. And then Erin asked something that still sends chills through my body.

"Zero to ten, with ten being the best," she instructed me, "rate how I'm doing as a wife."

I've heard the expression "the seconds seemed like days," but I'd never experienced the phenomenon until that moment. And suddenly I realized that everything I'd built as a husband over the past two weeks hung in the balance, based upon whatever I said in this next moment.

The key, I realized, was to stall!

"Did you say ten was the best?" I said in a shaky voice.

"You're stalling," Erin said, prodding.

She's good, I thought. And then I came to the sickening reality that I was going to actually have to answer her question. The horror!

"Well," I mumbled, starting to feel as if I were not just walking on eggshells but standing on the very heads of the actual chickens, "I would rate you as a . . ."

And then it hit me. I had the answer!

A confident smile pursed my lips as I said, "You're a 9.3."

I know what you're thinking: *Greg, you idiot. You blew it!* I know. But remember, you weren't there to slap me upside the head. You weren't there to say, "Greg, I'm not sure that's the answer your bride of two weeks is looking for." You weren't there to wave your arms frantically and scream, "NO!" like the guy on the deck of an aircraft carrier waving off a fighter jet about to crash into the side of the ship.

In my defense, I reasoned that since God is a perfect ten, and Erin isn't God and therefore has some room to improve, a 9.3 was pretty great.

I couldn't have been more wrong. It was as if I'd rated her a .0000439.

"What am I doing wrong?" came her immediate (let me emphasize the word *immediate*) response.

"What?"

Strike three!

"Why don't you think I'm doing a good job?" Erin asked, full of hurt.

"Honey," I begged, "a 9.3 is *awesome*. I meant that as a compliment."

"But I want to be perfect for you," Erin sobbed.

And once more, I could have said something very different from what I had in mind. But oh, no!

"Erin, only God is perfect. So the best you could do is a 9.9, and I thought I'd leave you a little room for improvement."

You're thinking it again, aren't you? *Greg, you idiot!*

Erin and I lay in bed that night, arguing about her score. We argued for a good forty-five minutes before we both rolled over and closed our eyes, deeply hurt. And I won't even tell you what I was thinking as I drifted off to a very unrestful sleep. (I don't need to hear, one more time, *Greg, you idiot!*)

Over the years, we have identified several ways most of us communicate in order to break the dance that, in reality, are a complete waste of time. Do you use any of the following to try to break free of the dance?

1. Focus on who's right and who's wrong.

Any time you try to convince your fiancée that you are right and she's wrong, you are wasting your time. When you do this, you are sending a very hurtful message: "My ideas, thoughts, or feelings are valid, and yours are worthless." This is a total waste of time.

Of course you think you're right; if you thought you were wrong, then you would change your thought to something you believed was right, wouldn't you? No one consciously thinks, *Hey, since I believe Idea X is totally wrong, I'm going to believe it!* That just doesn't happen. I normally think I'm right, and Erin normally thinks she's right. You normally think you're right, and your future spouse normally thinks he or she is right. That's completely normal. So how do you determine who is actually right?

You don't!

But we promise, you *will* do the dance to try to figure it out!

Remember when Erin asked me to rate her as a young wife? When she reacted as she did, I immediately began arguing about whether she was actually a 9.3.

"It's my decision!" I kept telling her.

"There is no *way* I'm below a 9.5," she shot back.

So, who was right? *What difference does it make?* Suppose I somehow could have "proven" that Erin really was a 9.3. Do you think that suddenly she would have felt utterly satisfied and said, "Oh, my darling genius, *now* I see how right you are. My bad!"? Hardly! Nor would I have felt better if Erin had been able to empirically demonstrate that she really deserved a 9.5. Being right or wrong simply wasn't the issue.

But so long as we made it the issue, we danced.

2. *Focus on what really happened.*

We err when we focus on the "facts" and details. We dance whenever we try to correct what we perceive as faulty information or lies the other person is telling about what actually happened. We do this when we say things like:

+ "It wasn't *yesterday*, it was *three days* ago!"
+ "I didn't say it like *that!*"
+ "I *did* do it; you just didn't notice."
+ "It was in the *car*, not in the *house*."
+ "Oh, 'I never do that'? Well, what about last week?"
+ "I *always* do that? Well, did I do it *yesterday*?"
+ "It wasn't like that . . . it happened like this . . ."
+ "I never said that!"
+ "You're exaggerating!"
+ "You're minimizing how you said it."

This particular error is very hard for me to stop. If I feel Erin has an inaccurate perception, then it's almost as if the voice of God is telling me to correct her sinful take on the situation. (I think it's more like the devil's voice!)

This strategy is a waste of time because people have very different perspectives on what actually happened. What happens when an investigator interviews eye witnesses to the same crime? He often gets completely different stories. Why? Because people perceive things very differently.

Erin can see things very differently than I do. I see things very differently than she does. So how do we determine whose perception is more accurate?

We don't!

At least, not without more dancing.

3. Focus on who's to blame or whose fault it is.

This occurs when you try to determine who is more at fault for the argument. You may say things like:

+ "We wouldn't be in this mess if *you* hadn't . . ."
+ "*My* fault? *You* were the one that . . ."
+ "Everything would be fine if you would stop ____ (or start ____)."
+ "You *always* do . . ."

"This is all *your* fault!" Erin said that night. "What kind of husband rates his wife a 9.3, just two weeks into their marriage!" (Notice that this wasn't a question.)

"*My* fault?" I shot back. "What kind of wife asks her husband to rate her, just two weeks into their marriage!" (Again, not a question.)

And then my wife came back at me with one of my all-time favorite slams: "Well, at least I'm not a 4.9 like *you* are!"

If that hadn't completely pushed my buttons, I would have appreciated the banter much more—like I do now!

4. Make the current issue (money, work, etc.) the real issue and topic of focus.

If you focus your communication on whatever the topic or issue happens to be—whether money, communication, future in-laws, affection, leisure time, household tasks, work, whatever—you are missing the real issue.

And what *is* the real issue? We hope that, by now, you get that the real issue is *always* that your emotional fear buttons get pushed.

Erin and I spent a whole hour arguing the validity and reliability of my rating of her. Sadly, we never once talked about our buttons. I felt like a failure and that Erin was trying to control me. Erin felt invalidated and worried that she wasn't measuring up as a wife.

5. Focus on the other person's reactions.

If you focus on how your fiancée is reacting to you, then you are completely wasting your time. Why? When someone points out that she doesn't appreciate what you are doing, how are you likely to react? That's right. You are likely to react with even more intensity, or withdraw.

One of our favorite verses encourages us to guard against wasting our time in this way: "Do not pay attention to every word people say" (Ecclesiastes 7:21). Isn't that great advice? No wonder King Solomon is considered one of the wisest people ever to walk the earth!

That night, Erin and I continued to try to get the *other* person to notice his or her poor reaction.

"Do you *hear* how you're talking to me?" I kept saying to her.

"Why do you have to keep defending your *obvious* mistake?" Erin demanded. "Just apologize and we can go to bed!"

6. Mind reading.

Do you ever try this one? You mind read when you tell someone how he really feels, what he is *really* thinking, or what he *really* meant. You say things like, "I know what you *really* think or how you feel!" It never works real swell.

What happens when someone tells *you* how you really feel and what you're really thinking? You probably tell the person to take a long walk off a short pier. Others will get right to the point and say, "Drop dead!" Either way, we all get defensive and argue how we really feel. Again, a total waste of time!

7. Focus on solutions or how to fix the problem.

Most guys love to fix things and solve problems (whether they can actually do so or not is a different discussion). It seems so productive. But this, too, is a total waste of time in the beginning stages of the dance, because people usually want to feel heard, understood, validated, and cared for before they're ready to think about solutions.

It's also a waste of time because by jumping so quickly into fix-it mode, you may miss the real issue. It would be like going to the doctor, reporting that your knee hurts, and getting a prescription shoved in your face as the doctor shows you to the door and says, "Have a good day." You might well have a deeper problem that requires an MRI for an accurate diagnosis.

In a similar way, the particular issue is never *the* issue. If you don't take time to explore the buttons that got pushed, you won't have all the necessary information.

These seven things are total wastes of time because they focus merely on surface or trivial issues. They concentrate on the mind and completely neglect the heart. They keep you distracted from the real issues (what's going on in your heart).

Furthermore, each of these is debatable, so agreement is almost impossible to achieve. Each person may see the facts and details of what happened differently. Truth really is in the mind of the beholder, especially in interpersonal relationships. These things ultimately keep you stuck and spinning around in the Fear Dance.

Two Great Uses of Time

If, in the beginning, you instead focus on the following, you are using your time wisely:

+ Share and care about your feelings (your fear buttons, feelings, emotions, hurts, etc.).
+ Ask and care about your fiancé's feelings (his fear buttons, feelings, emotions, hurts, etc.).

These two activities waste no time because they are matters of the heart. They keep you focused on the real issues, the core, and not on trivial things.

Furthermore, these activities are not debatable. In other words, feelings and emotions are not right or wrong; they are just information.

Heart Talk

Heart Talk begins with understanding an important component that goes missing from many relationships: caring.

Deep caring and love are important components for any great marriage. Caring about another person is always optional, and it is also risky. The moment you choose to care, you set yourself up to be hurt, rejected, and/or disappointed. Loving someone who does not return love can be a very sad, lonely, and painful experience. But the only alternative is to choose not to care, or to limit your caring.

Unfortunately, that doesn't work.

Not caring may protect you from rejection or disappointment, but this strategy achieves a hollow victory at great cost, since your ability to experience meaningful intimacy is a function of your capacity to love and care. A portion of your love hunger will not be satisfied and will grumble for attention, should you choose not to care.

People find all sorts of ways to address unmet longings. Sadly, many of these reactions are unhealthy or destructive and often take the form of illicit sexual affairs, drugs or alcohol, overeating, shopping, emotional distance, and numerous other escapes. All of them will leave you unfulfilled.

The essence of genuine love and caring has to do with feelings and emotions. For a relationship to progress to the next level, emotions become central. At the basic level, people need to feel that their overall well-being and feelings are protected. This is why Erin and I talk so much about safety.

Furthermore, to feel loved and cared for, people need to know that others care about their feelings and consider those feelings extremely important. When you care about and accept how your fiancée feels, this does not mean you necessarily agree with the feeling or that you have the same feeling. You can let your fiancée know you care how she feels even when you see and feel very differently. This is really more about communicating: "I care about how you feel because I love you. You matter to me; therefore, your feelings matter to me."

For people to feel emotionally cared for, their feelings need to be accepted without judgment. They need to be recognized as important and valuable. To judge, ignore, or try to change your partner's feelings, indicates either that you believe his or her feelings are wrong, or that you don't care. Because people generally don't consciously choose their feelings, telling them that their feelings shouldn't exist or that they should be different puts them on the defensive. They instantly feel they are wrong for being who they are. Defensiveness is strong evidence of not feeling safe (you don't *defend* if you're not feeling *attacked*).

When your feelings are being judged, or when you are in a relationship with someone who doesn't care how you feel, it will be difficult for you to feel safe. Additionally, when one partner sends the message, "I don't care how you feel," that message will *never* feel like love.

On the other hand, when you communicate that you care about how your fiancée feels, she will usually translate your message into, "I care about you." That is a message of love and contributes to creating an emotionally safe environment.

It might seem that when you choose to care, you take a big risk, and the one you care about is the one who benefits. But when you choose to care, you create an opportunity to experience for yourself the love, warmth, and affection that accompanies caring.

While choosing not to care may feel safer to you, not caring tends to create an empty, cold, and lifeless aftereffect. Choosing to care feels vital and alive. When experienced within the safety you create in your relationship, caring allows love to flow freely—and that benefits everyone involved. Caring and love is a clear indicator of a good relationship and creates the potential for a *great* marriage.

"My Other Daddy"

When we first moved to Siloam Springs, something upset Erin. We were lying in bed one night and she said, "I forgot to tell you what *your* son has been telling people."

I love it when *our* children become "my" children. The declaration is usually followed by something they did that was wrong, bad, or evil. Unfortunately, it had been a long day at work, and I just wanted to fall asleep.

"What happened?" I responded, only half awake.

"This woman that I've been getting to know over the past few weeks came over for lunch today. The entire time we ate, I felt like there was something that she really wanted to know but was afraid to ask."

"Uh huh," I mumbled, almost completely unconscious.

"Are you listening?" Erin asked as she poked me with her elbow.

"Ouch!"

"Good! You're awake."

"Toward the end of our lunch," Erin explained, "she asked me how long you and I had been married. And the strangest part was when I told her almost fourteen years, she seemed surprised by my answer. So I asked her how long she thought we'd been married."

She got even more animated and then said, "*Listen* to what she said!"

How could I sleep now?

"She thought we'd been married only a few years," Erin declared. "Can you believe it? She even knows that Taylor is in middle school. I was shocked!"

"Why did she think we'd been married only a short time?" I asked, now curious.

"I'll tell you why," Erin leaned up, staring at me. "Your son—"

"Garrison?"

"Unless you haven't told me about another son you have, yes—Garrison!"

"What did he say?" I asked cautiously.

"Well," Erin explained, "it seems that your son told this woman that his *old* daddy is in jail because he hurt him and me. And now he has a new daddy named Greg who he really likes."

By now she was shouting.

"I was humiliated! She even asked me if I was scared that my first husband would find us!"

I could think of only one thing to say, and it probably was not something Erin wanted to hear at that particular moment: "I can't believe you've hidden this from me all this time! You think you know someone, only to find out they've been married before!"

It got so quiet that I could actually hear crickets chirping—and nothing else.

I quickly changed tactics and asked, "You're not taking this *seriously*, are you? Erin, it's no big deal. It's actually kind of funny, if you think about it."

And that night, for good ol' times sake, we took a few spins around our Fear Dance.

It always amazes me how quickly I can get drafted into a conversation and end up in trouble. The point of this story, of course, is not to set the record straight about Erin's first husband. Actually, Garrison made up that story; I am Erin's first and only husband. The point is this: sometimes I do things with Erin's heart that don't get us to where we want to be.

It also amazes me that I have found it so difficult to really care for Erin's heart and emotions. I've always struggled when Erin gets emotional. Although I grew up in a great home and have a wonderful dad, I never learned how to deal effectively with emotions.

When Erin and I got married, her emotionality surprised me. It freaked me out whenever she got emotional. I would instantly feel overwhelmed by the intensity of her feelings. Since I wasn't sure what to do, I did what came natural: I tried to fix her feelings or solve them for her.

And she just *loved* that.

I spent a number of years trying to save Erin from her own emotions. I felt convinced that without my logical and analytical mind, Erin would go off the deep end.

Can you relate in any way? Think about the different ways many of us communicate that suggest we don't really care how someone feels:

+ "You shouldn't feel that way!"
+ "Why do you get so emotional?"
+ "Your emotions are out of control."
+ "That *can't* be how you really feel!"

I have used all these statements (and many more, I'm sure) throughout our marriage—and every time, Erin has ended up not feeling cared for.

I'll never forget the day she'd had enough of me trying to manage her emotions. As I told her logically how she could resolve a prickly situation with a friend, she screamed, "Do you think I'm a complete idiot?"

Since it seemed to me that, just maybe, she didn't really want me to answer her question, I kept my mouth shut. Wisely, I just listened.

"Greg," she said, her voice full of exasperation, "I know that you are actually trying to help me by offering a solution. But do you have any idea what message that sends me, every time you try to *solve* my feelings and emotions? It makes me feel like you think I'm incompetent, like I can't resolve my own issues unless *you* figure out a solution. It's as though you think I'm ready to go off into an emotional abyss."

For the first time in our marriage, I realized that I *did* think she would go off the emotional deep end. Moreover, I understood how responsible I felt to help her manage her emotions and feelings.

"But you get so worked up when you talk about your emotions," I said. "Sometimes, it actually scares me. I'm just trying to help you calm down so you can think about things from a more logical standpoint. Did I mention that I love you?"

And then we had one of the best talks in our entire marriage up to that point. For the first time, I really understood how my discomfort around her feelings affected Erin. I ended our conversation by telling her that I didn't want to be responsible for managing her emotions. I wanted her and the Lord to do that job. And I told her that I was releasing myself from that job.

"My job from now on is just to listen and care about how you feel," I said. "Not to fix or solve your emotions."

I wish I could tell you that I felt this huge weight lift off my chest. To be honest, I felt like throwing up. I was so convinced that without my help she would not be able to manage her feelings—that soon she would be an emotional wreck.

But you know the truth, don't you? Over the next few months, I watched my wife do an amazing job with her feelings. Although she would still get very, very, *very* emotional at times, she also worked through her feelings and would always get to a good place. And you know the best part?

I no longer got into trouble, like I did whenever I tried to "fix" her.

In the same way, many people remain stuck in the Fear Dance at precisely this point. They stay with their brains when their partners want to express their hearts. The problem is the mismatch: brain to heart.

If you ever feel as though you are not connecting with your future spouse and he or she seems to be getting frustrated, ask yourself if your loved one is trying to share his or her heart, while you are listening with your brain. If your fiancée wants to talk about her feelings or deepest concerns, the best thing you can do is to go heart-to-heart with her.

Couples remain stuck until they finally learn to look for the deeper emotions present in whatever the particular issue happens to be at the moment. They find freedom only when they discover how to go beyond the words and get to the deeper feelings and emotions. When you both *care* about each other's fear buttons, it's amazing how hurt and frustrations melt away and how the dance just ends.

Make Caring Your Goal

As a guy, I always need a goal. So I made caring one of my top relational goals. It's irrelevant if your fiancée's feelings are illogical, true, accurate, rational, truly reflect how you feel, or make sense. *None of that matters.*

This was a difficult lesson for me to master. Nevertheless, I really tried to make my goal to care about Erin's feelings and emotions—her heart. When you are trying to care about someone's heart, the goal is not to get *you* to feel understood; it's to have your *fiancée* feel deeply understood. In order to accomplish this, I had to understand something very important about caring—what it is and what it is not. Caring for your fiancée's heart does not equal:

+ resolving or "fixing" the issue
+ agreeing with what she says or how she feels
+ being responsible for her feelings
+ making changes
+ admitting guilt/fault or apologizing

In order to be free to care, I had to remind myself of these realities. I still do. Every day.

But oh how much better life has become!

Put It into Action!

Heart Talk is listening and speaking with your heart. Your fiancée will feel emotionally cared for when you listen to her deepest feelings. It's so easy to get trapped into listening to someone only with your *head*—that is, using your brain to focus on content and words without paying attention to the underlying emotion. You understand, of course, that there's still an issue that must be resolved—wedding plans, where to live, how much to spend on a wedding dress, finances. And that takes brainpower. Still, you can't neglect the heart.

We promise that we will teach you a wonderful method of resolving your issues in a way that makes you *both* feel great about the solution. It's at this point that you will want to use your brain in addition to your heart. But the order here is critically important; we want to be very intentional about that. *Before* you talk about solutions, you have the incredible opportunity to care for one another's hearts. Don't miss this amazing opportunity that is before you! You have the opportunity to get heart-to-heart with each other.

That is why we say, "Don't use merely your brain to listen." When we use our brains, we tend to focus on the facts, details, words— information. The problem is that the conversation then usually stays in the cognitive realm. This explains why, when someone simply parrots or repeats back your words, it tends to feel robotic and disingenuous. Trust us! There is no better way to reconnect after the dance than to listen, understand, validate, and care for *both* hearts that were wounded as buttons got pushed and reactions flew. Don't miss this golden opportunity!

In order to put emotional communication into action, follow seven simple steps:

Make Safety Your First Priority

We can show you the latest research, we can coach you to use the finest skills and tools, you can have the strongest purpose—but you will still fail if your fiancée or fiancé feels unsafe. All the tools, knowledge, skill, insight, and desire are meaningless if two people don't feel safe with each other.

When the relationship feels emotionally safe, it makes Heart Talk easier; and in turn, Heart Talk creates more safety. Isn't that *great*! They literally work off each other to improve your relationship, because when people feel safe, they don't worry about being attacked, rejected, shamed, or punished for sharing their feelings, thoughts, and ideas. As a result, people are more inclined to open up and share their deepest thinking and emotions.

Replace Judgment with Curiosity

Judging your fiancée results in defensiveness and closes down your relationship, while curiosity results in openness and safety, giving life to your relationship. When your fiancée refuses to judge your motives and instead tries to understand why you acted in foolish or hurtful ways, her compassion encourages your heart to open up—and deep connection ensues. The walls come down, and the conflict ceases.

Listen to the Words the Other Is Saying

You don't have to agree with anything your future mate is saying, or fear that you might have to change your behavior because of what he or she is saying. You are just listening to gain a greater understanding of who this person is and how he or she feels about your discussion. The more safety that exists in your relationship, the more openness, real intimacy, and connection will occur. Again, when a person feels safe, he or she is more inclined to become a willing participant in the relationship.

Listen with Your Heart

If you listen with your heart (and not just your brain) to the point that the other person feels deeply understood and cared for, then you increase the person's sense of safety. This is exactly what the Bible says to do: "love one another deeply, from the heart" (1 Peter 1:22). When you listen with your heart, you say to your fiancée, "I care how you feel. Your feelings matter to me." And when your fiancée gets this message, she feels deeply cared for. That's when she feels loved. But if you don't relay this message—even if you understand the words she has spoken—she still will not feel loved, and real communication will grind to a halt.

Reflect Back What You Heard

Don't react to any particular word, but start trying to ferret out the emotions underneath the words. Repeat the words back to the speaker by using words of your own, and then say, "Is that what you said?" After the speaker confirms that you heard the words right, ask about his or her feelings. Ask questions like, "What were you feeling when that happened to you?" or "How does that make you feel?" or "When that happens to me, I sometimes feel like this or that—is that how you feel?"

Sometimes you need to prime the person's emotional pump. Suggest several feelings and let him or her pick the one that seems closest.

Allow Her Emotions to Touch You

When you allow your fiancée's feelings to touch your heart and you allow yourself to really feel her fear, hurt, or frustration, you are giving her the gift of empathy. Empathy is the ability to recognize, perceive, and directly feel your fiancé's emotion—to put yourself in his shoes. Your ability to empathize with your future spouse requires that you recognize and accurately identify his or her feelings. Like any skill, you can improve your empathy by doing the following:

- Allow yourself to feel your loved one's joy and pain.
- Tune in to the feelings of your future spouse.
- Identify the specific feelings of your future mate.
- Expand your emotional vocabulary.
- Notice your fiancée's pain, even if she doesn't talk about it.
- Attempt to understand why your fiancé feels the way he does by being curious.
- Place yourself into the inner life of your fiancée and imagine how you would feel if you were in her place.

Empathy goes beyond *understanding* feelings and allows those feelings to touch your heart—to sample the emotions of your future mate. This is one of the best ways to help your fiancée feel cared for and loved.

Don't Take Responsibility for What He Does with Your Caring

Remember, you cannot change or control others. If you try to do so, you will only end up frustrated. For the same reason, you have no control over what the other person does with your caring. You can focus on creating a safe environment, replace your judgment with genuine curiosity, listen with your heart, accurately reflect back his or her feelings, and allow your heart to be impacted by those feelings—but in the end, it may still not achieve the desired results.

When someone's heart is closed or she feels really unsafe, she will not respond in a positive way to caring actions. We know that is painful! Allow your heart to grieve the pain and disappointment. If your buttons get pushed, manage your emotions and work to get your heart back open. It is always possible that you are attempting to care in ways that do not communicate caring. You may want to ask for specific things that you can do to show you care. In the end, you can control only the choice to be a caring person. Whether your future spouse responds is up to him or her.

Adjust Your Expectations

If you go into Heart Talk expecting things to flow easily and without a lot of effort, then you're just kidding yourself. We recommend that you adjust several key expectations.

Expect Your Buttons to Get Pushed

A couple drove down a country road for several miles, not saying a word. An earlier discussion had led to an argument, and neither of them wanted to yield. As they passed a barnyard of mules, goats, and pigs, the husband asked sarcastically, "Relatives of yours?"

"Yep," the wife replied, "in-laws."

This is the place where most people get tripped up. They say with hope, "Now that we've broken out of the Fear Dance and are focusing on each other's hearts, everything should flow smoothly."

Don't spend one moment in this la-la land! Since you're dealing with matters of the heart and sharing deep feelings—both positive and negative—you will *certainly* get your buttons pushed as you listen to each other. Remember, you can't keep people from pushing your buttons! It is going to happen.

Knowing that, make your attitude, "So what! No big deal." Get great at noticing when your buttons get pushed (you know, when you become the Hulk), and then take the time to deal with your "stuff" (de-Hulk, as described in chapter 6).

Expect to Misunderstand Each Other

We all make mistakes communicating; that's what humans do. Even those charged with producing the Sunday bulletin for church commit some real whoppers. Our favorite is this one: "Thursday at 5:00 p.m. there will be a meeting of the Little Mothers Club. All wishing to become little mothers, please see the minister in his study."

Communication is tough! When communication fails, both people are to blame. Many times Erin and I don't understand our own feelings. This makes communicating very difficult when we feel confused or are unaware of what is going on at a deep emotional level. We also fail miserably at times to understand each other.

Count on it—you *will* feel misunderstood. But if you *expect* that you will probably misunderstand each other from time to time, then when it happens, your buttons are less likely to get pushed. And when they do get pushed, work yourself through the previously described five steps (see "How Do *I* Stop Dancing?" pages 138–148).

Expect to Need a Lot of Patience

If you want your communication to feel relaxed and be more effective, keep repeating the phrase, "Heart Talk takes time." You may not connect or understand each other even after several botched attempts. Don't get impatient, because this shuts down genuine understanding. Instead, try to be patient with one another as you express your hearts. The Amplified Bible says, "Living as becomes you with complete lowliness of mind (humility) and meekness (unselfishness, gentleness, mildness), with patience, bearing with one another and making allowances because you love one another" (Ephesians 4:2).

Remember, look beyond the words your fiancée uses and *slowly* discover the emotions behind what is being said.

The Heart of Intimacy

One afternoon a lawyer was riding in his limousine when he saw two men along the roadside, eating grass. Greatly disturbed, he ordered his driver to stop so he could get out to investigate.

"Why are you eating grass?" he asked the first man.

"We don't have any money for food," the poor fellow replied. "We have to eat grass."

"Well, then, you can come with me to my house and I'll feed you," the lawyer said.

"But sir, I have a wife and two children with me. They are over there, under that tree."

"Bring them along," the lawyer replied.

Turning to the other poor man the attorney said, "You also come with us."

In a pitiful voice, the second man replied, "But sir, I also have a wife—and *six* children with me!"

"Bring them all," the lawyer declared.

They all gladly hopped into the car, which was no easy task, even for a vehicle as large as the limousine. Once under way, one of the poor fellows turned to the lawyer and said, "Sir, you are too kind. Thank you for taking all of us with you!"

"Glad to do it," the lawyer replied. "You'll really love my place! The grass is almost a foot high."

Ah yes, communication. A tricky thing! And yet communication lies at the heart of intimacy. If your heart's desire is for the other person to feel truly loved and cared for, then master the art of Heart Talk. Good communication happens when you choose to make your primary goal understanding rather than being understood.

Use the following summary to guide you through the Heart Talk process:

HEART TALK

SPEAKER	LISTENER
1. Focus is on myself. • Who am I focused on? Me. • I feel . . . • If you say, "I feel like/that you . . . ," it's not a feeling.	1. Repeat back what the other says. • Who am I focused on? The other. • No judgment—just curiosity.
2. Talk about my heart—feelings, emotions, buttons, fears, hurts, or wants/desires. • What am I talking about? My feelings. • Speak in bite-size pieces so the listener can repeat back what I say.	2. Focus on the other's heart—buttons, feelings, emotions, wants, etc. • What am I repeating back? The other's feelings (heart). • Allow the words to impact me—let the other's feelings touch my heart.

COUPLE EXERCISES/HOMEWORK

Again, go back to the Fear Dance Test on page 115. Review question 1, in which we asked you to describe a recent conflict or negative situation—something that really "pushed your buttons." With that recent disagreement in mind, answer the following questions:

1. To break out of the Fear Dance, which of the things that are a waste of time did you use (e.g., focusing on who's right and who's wrong instead of on what really happened, on who's to blame or at fault, on whatever issue got you into the argument, on your fiancée/fiancé's reactions, on mind reading, on fix-it or problem-solving mode)?

2. Since those things never get you out of the Fear Dance, take 10 to 20 minutes to practice Heart Talk from this chapter. Here are some hints to help you be successful:

   a. Remember that your goal in Heart Talk is to "care" about how your fiancée/fiancé feels. You don't have to agree with her/his feelings, fix the issue, be responsible for her/his feelings, make changes, admit fault, or apologize. Instead, without any hint of judgment, you want to communicate: "I care about how you feel because I love you. You matter to me; therefore, your feelings matter to me."

   b. If your buttons get pushed while caring for your fiancée/fiancé's feelings, simply go back and repeat the steps of what to do when your buttons get pushed, on pages 138 to 148.

   c. Use the following summary to guide you through the Heart Talk process:

HEART TALK

SPEAKER	LISTENER
1. Focus is on myself. • Who am I focused on? Me. • I feel . . . • If you say, "I feel like/that you . . . ," it's not a feeling.	1. Repeat back what the other says. • Who am I focused on? The other. • No judgment—just curiosity.
2. Talk about my heart—feelings, emotions, buttons, fears, hurts, or wants/desires. • What am I talking about? My feelings. • Speak in bite-size pieces so the listener can repeat back what I say.	2. Focus on the other's heart—buttons, feelings, emotions, wants, etc. • What am I repeating back? The other's feelings (heart). • Allow the words to impact me—let the other's feelings touch my heart.

8

Will You Forgive Me?

I can remember the excitement I felt as I boarded my flight to Denver," Erin recalls. "I was going to visit Greg, whom I hadn't seen in months. I was anticipating a *great* reunion with my fiancé! At the time, Greg was living in Denver while I stayed in Phoenix to continue working and planning our wedding.

"I worked a strange schedule at the hospital—ten days on, then six days off. This worked out great, because it gave Greg and me almost a week together every several months to dream about being married.

"On this particular trip, I had high expectations of Greg, of how he would greet me, what we would do while I was there, where we would eat, and finally how he would send me off, back to Phoenix. Instead of going into the details of what I expected, however, I'll simply tell you that *nothing* I wanted came to pass—so I was left feeling very deflated.

"The trip began with Greg picking me up at Stapleton Airport in Denver. He met me at the curb outside of baggage claim, not as I had imagined—at the gate with a pathway of rose petals leading me down the Jetway. We then drove immediately to Denver Seminary, where I had the privilege of sitting in on his Old Testament theology class—again, call me crazy, but not my idea of excitement. After class, instead of a romantic candlelight dinner at our favorite restaurant, we returned to

Greg's studio apartment and ate leftover chicken spaghetti that, quite honestly, had almost no taste.

"The next day, when we were to meet at my hotel, Greg picked me up late. I was absolutely furious, because once again I felt like more of a nuisance to him than a priority. *He doesn't even have the decency to show up on time!* When my hotel phone finally rang, Greg let me know he was in the lobby. I stormed down to him and immediately started criticizing him for being late. He stood there, stunned, with that 'deer in the headlights' look. He piped back at me with some comment about his class running late and my being overly critical. We began our dance right there in the hotel lobby, having no idea that 'dance' is what we'd call it more than ten years later.

"The rest of our 'romantic getaway' continued down the same ugly path. It culminated with his dropping me off at the curb of the airport terminal with a quick kiss and a 'see you soon' as he sped away. I stood on the curb that day, deeply hurt and confused. *Does this man truly desire to marry me?*

"After boarding the plane, the tears began to fall, and I realized my hopes had vanished into the great, blue sky. In the 'catastrophizing' thought processes I can so easily get hooked into, I had determined that our engagement was over and that we were moving on without each other.

"Later that evening, I called Greg and told him how I felt. My experience made him feel sad, and through our conversation, he realized he had been distant during my entire visit. He confessed that not only was he preoccupied with school, but that he was also having some doubts about our impending marriage; he felt as though he couldn't do anything right the whole time I was there. He then asked me to forgive him for how he had treated me and wondered aloud if I would be willing to come back in two weeks so he could make it up to me.

"As I sat on the other end of the phone, I realized I had a choice to make—to forgive or not. I felt deeply hurt and wasn't sure if I *could* forgive him for how he had treated me. Once I told him I did forgive him, however, I truly began to realize how negative beliefs had taken over from the minute I stepped off the airplane and failed to get those rose petals. My high expectations of the trip had set him up for failure, long before he hurriedly met me at the curb.

"I then asked him to forgive me for viewing everything he did in a negative light. Today, of course, it is clear to me that my 'unimportant' and 'invisible' buttons were clearly being pushed. Back then, however, I didn't have the language to explain it, or the self-insight to understand what was going on for me.

"Still, the bottom line was that forgiveness needed to take place—and it did, that very day on the phone. We were able to reach a very deep level of understanding and intimacy once we realized that we did love each other profoundly and that we both were committed to our relationship and to our future marriage."

Starting Off Right!

Ephesians 4:32 says, "Be kind and compassionate to one another, forgiving each other, just as in Christ God forgave you."

While you certainly want to start your new marriage off right by offering whatever forgiveness may be needed for past hurts, forgiveness in your marriage, as you can imagine, will be a minute-by-minute, moment-by-moment exercise. When one or both of you feels that trust has been broken, you may need to get help from a mentor couple or counselor to assist you in the healing process. At times, you might not agree with your future mate's feelings or take on what happened (we'll discuss this in a moment). If you truly want to be free from the torture of your own personal prison, you really must choose either to seek or to offer forgiveness. Jesus has a word for you here: *forgive your future mate.* He offers you no other key.

Forgiveness and Marital Satisfaction

Some time ago, Erin and I began wondering just how much forgiveness really impacts the state of a marriage. We were not surprised to find out that the level of forgiveness in a marriage has a direct impact on the level of marital satisfaction.

Although we had experienced forgiveness entering into our marriage, we wish now that we would have known just how important this was to our new marital relationship. Again, forgiveness is not just *our* idea, it is *God's* idea. It is spoken about in the Scriptures repeatedly, and our prayer for you as a couple is that you begin to place high priority on continually practicing forgiveness in your marriage.

What Forgiveness Is Not

Many of the couples we have worked with have feared offering forgiveness to each other because they believed it was "letting the spouse off the hook" or meant that "the sin was forgotten." It is very important to understand that forgiveness is not either of these things. Basically, when you forgive your mate, you are saying, "I'm pardoning you from what you have done." Again, forgiveness empowers us to move beyond what has happened to us, and ultimately this will help us continue to mature and grow into His image. Our other option is to reflect bitterness, anger, and hurt.

William Meninger once wrote:

> *Forgiveness, then, is not forgetting. It is not condoning or absolving. Neither is it pretending nor something done for the sake of the offender. It is not a thing we just do by a brutal act of the will. It does not entail a loss of identity, of specialness, or of face. It does not release the offenders from obligations they may or may not recognize. An understanding of these things will go a long way towards helping people enter into the forgiveness process.*[1]

In your marriage, this does not mean that the trust is immediately re-built, or the painful memories are magically gone. This all takes time and God's hand in the process. However, at the forefront we must remember that He died on the cross to forgive us!

Will You Forgive Me?

All couples, no matter how healthy their relationships are, will have the op-portunity to seek forgiveness and to offer forgiveness. You may be thinking, *But we don't fight.* Remember, again, that whether you withdraw or brawl, both are equally damaging to a relationship. Our goal is to encourage you to make your relationship the safest place on earth, and part of this is continu-ally forgiving each other. Here are some helpful hints in seeking forgiveness:

Reflect Tenderness

When you realize someone's heart is closed, the first step in opening it is to express a softness or tenderness. To reflect tenderness, do your best to . . .

+ lower your voice
+ become gentle in heart
+ get down on bended knee
+ speak slowly
+ relax your facial expressions
+ become pleasant in your demeanor

All of these reflect honor and humility, and, as the Bible suggests, "A gentle answer turns away wrath" (Proverbs 15:1). When you become tender, you communicate four important things. You're saying:

+ Your future spouse is valuable and important. You express this in nonverbal ways: You're slow to move toward her. Your head may be bowed, and you're obviously grieved that you have hurt her.

+ You don't want to see his heart closed. You care about him.
+ You know something's wrong. You acknowledge by your softness that an offense has taken place, and you're going to slow down long enough to correct whatever has happened.
+ You're open to listening. It's safe for her to say how she feels about what has happened, and you're not going to get angry or hurt her again.

"When I called Greg to tell him how hurt I was over my experience in Denver," Erin says, "Greg did a phenomenal job of reflecting tenderness. Although I couldn't see his nonverbal communication over the phone, he definitely communicated to me through his words that he cared and valued me. His voice was caring and gentle. This set the conversation up to succeed, because my heart began to melt—and best of all, it came open."

Once you become soft, the next step is to better understand the other's pain.

Increase Your Own Understanding

It's important to genuinely understand the pain your future spouse feels and how he or she has interpreted your offensive behavior. Ask for his or her perspective on what occurred, so you can validate those feelings or needs. Taking the time to see your loved one as unique and very valuable is true friendship. Resist the urge to defend yourself, lecture, or question why he or she did or didn't do something.

Empathy means identifying with and understanding the other person's situation, feelings, and motives. Empathy is easy to give. You start by taking a guess at what your fiancée or fiancé may be feeling.

Listening and empathizing communicates that you believe your fiancée has something valuable to say; consequently, she feels valuable. Listening shows that you respect your fiancé as a person; empathy communicates that you understand him. Listen to understand rather than to react. Desire to understand more than to defend yourself. In other words, listen with your heart—hear her pain, feel his needs.

When you really listen, you don't need to tell anybody that's what you're doing—it's evident. You can bet your fiancée knows whether you're truly listening or faking it! You show you're listening by your body language, by nonverbal responses like facial expressions and eye contact, and by the follow-up questions you ask. Furthermore, you give cues that demonstrate you're paying attention. A good listener:

+ is attentive, not distracted; does not look around or do something else at the same time;
+ does not rush the speaker;
+ is focused on the person speaking;
+ does not interrupt;
+ maintains good eye contact;
+ does not grunt responses.

When you're really listening and empathizing, you focus your attention squarely on the other person—who will, therefore, feel like the most important person in your world at that moment. Listening does *not* require attempts at problem solving. Your fiancée merely wants to know that you understand her point of view. She wants to sense from you that it's okay to be upset and to show emotion.

Good listening takes time and work, which is why so few people practice it, much less master it. But know this: if your fiancée doesn't feel she's being heard, it's unlikely that your relationship will improve. As a rule, to the same degree that she feels listened to, she will grant future opportunities for communication. After all, who wants to talk with someone who doesn't listen? For that matter, who wants to be in a relationship with someone who doesn't listen?

"That night on the phone so long ago," Erin says, "Greg could have corrected my experience and told me how wrong I had it. Instead, he listened and empathized with my pain. Still, this became one of our biggest challenges in our first year of marriage."

Early in our marriage, when Erin would share her deepest feelings, I would often jump in to "fix it," "stop it," or "shut it down." I usually feared that if I didn't take control, Erin wouldn't be able to stop the feelings, tears, etc., on her own. I admit that I felt totally overwhelmed with Erin's emotions and just wasn't sure what to do—so in reaction mode, I tried to get them to stop.

Now that you're becoming soft and tender and are listening and empathizing to understand your beloved's pain, the third step in opening a closed heart is to admit your mistakes.

Admit the Offense

When someone hurts you and does not take responsibility for the hurtful actions, it can be discouraging. Perhaps your fiancée feels like one of the monkeys at an unusual zoo. "That's incredible, having a monkey and a lion together in the same cage," said a zoo visitor. "How do they get along?"

"Pretty well, for the most part," answered the zookeeper. "But once in a while they have a disagreement, and then we have to get a new monkey."

Your fiancée may feel much like that monkey. Each time the two of you get into a disagreement, you come down on her like a roaring lion. Instead of tending to her wounds by admitting your wrongdoing, you simply reject her feelings as invalid.

It can be hard to say, "I was wrong," but it can work wonders.

Admitting you're wrong (when you obviously are) is like tending to your fiancée's wounds. Or, to change the analogy, it's like drilling a hole in her "anger bucket" and allowing that unhealthy emotion to drain away. Once she senses that you understand your mistake and she hears you admit it, the anger—the hurt, frustration, and fear—has a way of flowing out of her life.

Sometimes you may not be wrong about the facts or specifics of a disputed matter, but your attitude might be dead wrong. Or perhaps the way you've done something is offensive. If your attitude is harsh and angry when telling your fiancée about legitimate problems, you're still wrong. The Bible affirms this: "The anger of man does not achieve the righteousness of God" (James 1:20 NASB). Stopping short of admitting you're wrong can leave a dangerous gap between you and your fiancée that may not mend quickly—or at all.

When you don't admit your mistakes, you can delay the reopening of your fiancée's heart. On the other hand, people feel valuable when they hear you admit your mistakes and see that you understand how they feel. Sometimes that's all it takes to open a closed heart.

On the phone with Erin that night, I not only took responsibility for what I had done, but I offered some helpful background information as to what was going on for me. I wasn't defending or explaining it away but really tried to share my heart with her.

"Nothing is more precious," Erin says, "than having someone—especially the man you love—take responsibility for hurting you."

The last step in opening a closed heart is one of the most honoring things you can do. It's like giving a large bottle of cold water to someone dying of thirst in the desert.

Seek Forgiveness

If you do everything else and then neglect to seek forgiveness, the one you love will be left feeling violated and angry, just like the man who discovered a gigantic dent in the back of his new car one morning. By the look of things, the damage would cost him thousands of dollars to repair. He felt relieved, however, to find a note under the windshield wiper from the guilty party—until he actually read the note: "As I am writing this, your neighbors are watching me. They think I am giving you my name, address, license number, and insurance company. I'm not!"

It's important to give your fiancée the opportunity to respond to your confession—to ask if she can find it in her heart to forgive you. This is a wonderful opportunity to model seeking forgiveness. Your fiancée or fiancé may need to see the importance of asking someone for forgiveness, when one has made a mistake.

Erin and I had an ongoing discussion early in our marriage. Erin often thought all that was needed was for me to apologize. Inevitably I would say, "it isn't fair for me to apologize—*you* have to do it, too!" As you can imagine, this tactic didn't get us far, other than launch us into yet another power struggle.

"Our phone call went very differently," Erin says, "because he was soft and tender, empathized, and then apologized."

Forgiveness Takes Time

One of the most powerful experiences that has taught me (Erin) about forgiveness, actually has nothing to do with my marriage, but often comes to mind when I need to forgive Greg. I have a hard time remembering people's birthdays. However, several months ago I actually remembered to call a dear friend to wish her a "Happy thirtieth birthday!" What my friend didn't know was that I was calling her to throw her off—because there was a massive surprise party planned for her later that evening, and I was planning on being there.

However, in the midst of being excited for her party, I realized that there was also a battle going on within me. On the one hand, I was so excited to celebrate my friend's special day, but on the other hand, I knew it meant facing another friend, one who was not happy with me. This gal had quit speaking to me over two years ago, and our paths had not physically crossed since then. It was one of the most painful experiences I had ever had in my life. To call someone "friend" one day and have her blast you with cruel words the next day was a new experience for me. Unfortunately, she didn't keep these unpleasant words just between us but chose to build allies with other women in town and to share her dislike of me with them.

Although we had moved to another state over sixteen months ago, I had been in shock with how much time and energy she was taking in my daily thought life. I began to realize that I might as well have packed her on the moving truck with the rest of my belongings. It was as if she sat on my shoulder reminding me what a horrible friend I had been to her and that she didn't really know me after being friends for over two years. The guilt, anguish, and helplessness I felt seemed to never end. I continuously sought the Lord and pleaded with Him to release me from this bondage, and I also prayed for conviction over what I truly needed to seek forgiveness for from this friend. Time and time again, I asked "Sarah" to forgive me for whatever I may have done to lead her to this place of anger and dislike of me. She refused to grant me forgiveness and typically never returned my attempts to make contact with her.

Over the months of tears and confusion, I finally realized that I could only be responsible for me and my actions, and I felt I had attempted to carry myself with integrity. I was well aware that I was not the perfect friend, but I couldn't understand her unwillingness to extend grace to someone who was truly broken. But it wasn't me doing this, and I soon landed on the fact that I had to release her to the Lord and let Him deal with her heart. I knew that I was called to love her—but how in the world could I possibly do that?

As the day of the party came closer, I returned to my very familiar position of kneeling and begging the Lord to help me—as I had done numerous times before. I got my Bible out and asked Him to speak to me that very day as to whether or not I should be putting myself into the same room with this woman. So I opened my Bible and was led to Matthew 9:1–8.

> *Jesus stepped into a boat, crossed over and came to his own town. Some men brought to him a paralytic, lying on a mat. When Jesus saw their faith, he said to the paralytic, "Take heart, son, your sins are forgiven."*
>
> *At this some of the teachers of the law said to themselves, "This fellow is blaspheming!"*

Knowing their thoughts, Jesus said, "Why do you entertain evil thoughts in your hearts? Which is easier: to say, 'Your sins are forgiven,' or to say, 'Get up and walk'? But so that you may know that the Son of Man has authority on earth to forgive sins . . ." Then he said to the paralytic, "Get up, take your mat and go home." And the man got up and went home. When the crowd saw this, they were filled with awe, and they praised God, who had given such authority to men.

At first I began to think . . . *what does this have to do with me? I am not a paralytic . . . physically.* However, I soon began to realize that I sure was one emotionally. That was it . . . I realized I had been emotionally paralyzed with fear over what "Sarah" thought of me, what she said about me, and what she did to me. And He was now telling me to "Get up and walk!" While it was easy to read these words, it was much more difficult to reverse my case of "paralysis." Jesus backed up His words with action . . . and I knew that was what He was calling me to. Talk is cheap, but our words lack meaning if our actions do not back them up. We can say we love God or others, but if we are not taking practical steps to demonstrate that love, our words are empty and meaningless. Truly, I reflected on, *How well do my actions back up what I was saying?*

The real truth is that the Lord had told me over and over again that I was called to "love" my enemies. I couldn't understand how I could truly do this . . . as my friend truly had broken my heart.

I guess I had never really allowed myself to accept two things . . . that people will let you down and that they will break your heart. But I also realized there are good days and bad days—that's just what life is about—and that time can bring our faith and love back around. However, this is only possible through the loving and gentle care of our heavenly Father. He cares that we are heartbroken and holds us close if we ask Him to. The greatest truth that I was reminded about was that He *can* heal my broken heart and that I will be restored to the place of offering His love out to my friends again—even those who had broken my heart.

After my day of "internal processing," I packed my kids in the car and headed toward the party. Soon I was walking into the thirtieth birthday party and was awaiting the arrival of the birthday girl. However, I was soon aware of Sarah's presence—she was glaring at me from across the room. The words, "Stand up and walk" rang in my mind. So I did. I stood up and walked over to Sarah and gave her the biggest hug and asked how she'd been. Now, you have to understand, this wasn't an easy walk. I felt much like I'm assuming the paralytic man felt—full of fear and anxiety over what was going to happen. I'm sure the paralytic wondered, *Will I be able to walk if I stand?* In my emotional paralysis, I knew that by truly walking in faith I would be set free from this burden and season. It seemed like the longest walk of my life . . . and I was met with a shallow hug from my former friend's lackluster arms. And that was it— we didn't speak the rest of the night.

I spent the rest of the night visiting with old friends. I left the party and picked up my kids—heading to another friend's house to have a fun sleepover. The most exciting thing was awakening the next morning with the deepest breath I had been able to take in a long time. Truly, I felt the burden gone, and the Lord gently spoke to my spirit, *In faith you walked, and you have been set free!* Thinking of the freedom, I couldn't wait to document my experience with the Lord so I could always return to the moment of "being set free" as I am sure the paralytic did day after day. The Lord truly backed up His words with His actions in my life on the night of the thirtieth birthday party!

We pray for you that you, too, can "stand up and walk" in freedom by offering forgiveness in your marital relationship. There will be opportunities for daily forgiveness in your relationship; however, there might be the times when you feel like your heart has been truly broken as a result of something your spouse has done. We pray that you can trust the Lord to speak to you and guide you through the process of forgiveness, much like He did for me on the day of the thirtieth birthday party!

What If He/She Refuses to Forgive?

If you follow the prior four steps and your fiancé still refuses to forgive you, then there are several possible reasons:

+ The offense was deeper than you realized.
+ He wants to see your behavior change first.
+ She may have been offended by someone else as well.
+ He may need more time to think through what happened.
+ She has a general resentment toward everyone around her.
+ Simply asking forgiveness doesn't erase everything that has happened.
+ You can't possibly understand how deeply he has been hurt.

Be Patient

Whatever the reason, the best thing to do is be patient. Don't feel that just because you have started doing some things differently and have sought forgiveness, you will be forgiven right away.

Picture your offended fiancée as someone who has been out in cold weather for too long. After her skin becomes numb, she can no longer feel the painful wind. In the same way, some individuals seem indifferent or callous toward others because the relationship has gone on so long without the warmth of forgiveness. Once you seek forgiveness, however, it's like soaking that numb skin in warm water. Although the warm bath (forgiveness) is healthy, it doesn't bring instant relief. Instead, it initially causes a painful, tingling sensation. It first makes the skin feel worse before it begins to feel better. Likewise, it might take your hurting fiancée some time to warm up to your forgiveness.

No matter what reaction you get, never drop the issue altogether simply because the person isn't ready to forgive. Let the situation "warm up" for a while on its own; then come back and repeat the four steps.

Or perhaps your act of tenderness was not what your fiancée needed. You may need to choose another way to demonstrate softness.

Yet again, maybe your fiancée did not feel that you listened to her pain. We can't emphasize enough the importance of listening! Ask yourself, *Did I really listen to her? Was I trying to defend my actions or justify why I behaved the way I did?* If you're not sure, then go back and listen carefully to her pain and frustration.

It may also be that your fiancé did not feel you were sincere in taking ownership of your part of whatever conflict closed his heart. Perhaps you came close to taking responsibility but didn't clearly acknowledge your fault. If that's the case, it will be difficult for your fiancé to forgive you. It's like trying to build something on sand; the foundation will always remain shaky. But taking ownership of your mistakes is like laying four feet of reinforced concrete as the foundation of your relationship.

Honor His or Her Walls

Another powerful way to honor your fiancée if she doesn't want to forgive you is to honor her "walls."

Some people make their relationships feel unsafe by misunderstanding and dishonoring walls. We know, of course, that emotional walls stand in the way of achieving intimacy and connection with those we care about. Therefore, it seems only natural and reasonable that we try to break down the walls that stand between us.

But as logical as this may sound, it has the unfortunate effect of making your journey toward forgiveness far more difficult.

People erect walls when they feel unsafe or threatened. They actively maintain those walls in response to a perceived threat. When anyone, themselves included, attempts to tear down those walls, scale them, attack them, or dishonor them in any way, the result is to *increase* the feeling of threat. The person behind the wall feels less safe, not more. And the more threatened the person feels, the more he or she works to maintain the wall—thus making intimacy more difficult.

The alternative is to honor the walls and care about the feelings involved. When you recognize that your future spouse erects walls only when he or she feels unsafe, then anytime you encounter a wall in your relationship with your fiancée, you know that the person behind the wall feels unsafe. That gives you the opportunity to choose to care more about that person and those feelings than about getting what you want. But what if the perceived threat is only imagined? That's irrelevant. Just the fact that the person *feels* unsafe is what matters.

If you are committed to not doing anything to cause your loved one to feel more unsafe, and instead you choose to find ways to care about and protect the frightened individual behind the wall, then that person will generally take down the wall . . . in time. After all, it takes a lot of energy to maintain walls and fortresses, and most people would rather use that energy to live and love and have a good, satisfying, intimate, and *safe* relationship.

So before you take a sledgehammer to some wall, think about why that wall got erected in the first place. Walls always get built by people who feel threatened. Behind every wall quivers a person who feels unsafe. That person doesn't want to stay closed and defended, but because the environment feels unsafe, he or she builds the wall for protection and self-preservation. If you are about to marry someone like this, you must take the time to understand why the walls are up—and over time, your fiancée will start trusting you again, *so long as you work to create a safe place for her.*

When you see a wall separating you from your loved one, it's natural to think, *I have to get rid of that wall.* But as soon as you take out the jackhammers or call out the bulldozers, you confirm yourself as a dangerous threat, forgetting that the reason the wall went up in the first place is that the person didn't feel safe with you.

So does the wall help build the relationship? Not really. At some point, if your relationship is to flourish, it has to come down. What, then, can you do to encourage your future spouse to take down the wall, brick by brick?

First, he or she needs to know that you understand the wall is there for a reason and that you accept its presence. The person needs to know that his or her well-being is the most important thing to you; therefore, the wall can stay up as long as it is needed.

Second, let your fiancé know that you're not going to require him to be open with you or break down the walls until he feels safe. Your job is to give your fiancé every reason in the world to feel safe, while still honoring his right and responsibility to take care of himself.

You can even try imagining yourself as a sentry. Let your loved one know, "I understand that the wall is there because you feel unsafe. And I want you to know that I am going to stand outside this wall as a guard and work on *me* so that you can eventually feel safe. I'll try to keep my mouth shut and start discovering what I've done to create such an unsafe place for you. I won't rest until you finally feel relaxed enough to open up and be yourself around me. I'll even try to protect you from others who create this feeling of apprehension."

Respect the wall! The other person has built it for a reason. And when you create a safe environment in your relationship—when the other person no longer needs to protect himself or herself from you—then that wall will eventually come down and forgiveness will take place.

If you have tried all these steps and still your fiancée refuses to forgive you, then you may need to try some additional things. Don't adopt the attitude, "Well, if she won't forgive me, that's *her* problem. I did my part!" If you take that mind-set, the problem may never be resolved.

But this also means not assuming all the responsibility. Just as you are in charge of forgiving your fiancée for hurtful words and actions, so your fiancée is responsible for forgiving you, as well. You can be faithful to seeking forgiveness and owning your part of the problem. But you cannot take an inferior or guilt-ridden position if your fiancée consistently refuses to forgive you.

You may want to have someone hold you accountable for how you handle the situation—for correcting your mistake and seeking forgiveness, yet not taking more than your share of the blame. It's possible to try too hard and to get locked into feeling guilty and shameful. God does not want you to get stuck in shame if one of His children refuses to forgive. Do your part, but then allow God to work in your loved one's life.

It's All About Opening Closed Hearts

Remember, opening your fiancée's or fiancé's closed heart involves reflecting tenderness, increasing your own understanding, admitting the offense, and seeking forgiveness. If this process doesn't work, repeat the steps—but make changes from the way you tried them the first time. If you keep doing things the same way, you're likely to keep getting the same results.

There's no set number of times to repeat these steps if he or she won't forgive you. Remember Jesus's famous exhortation: "Peter came to Jesus and asked, 'Lord, how many times shall I forgive my brother when he sins against me? Up to seven times?' Jesus answered, 'I tell you, not seven times, but seventy-seven times'" (Matthew 18:21–22). Each situation is different, and so is each person. Turn the process over to God, find an accountability partner, and continue to love and forgive your future spouse.

COUPLE EXERCISES/HOMEWORK

Again, go back to the Fear Dance Test on page 115. Review question 1 where we asked you to describe a recent conflict or negative situation—something that really "pushed your buttons." With that recent disagreement in mind, answer the following questions:

1. What choices, behaviors, words, or actions in that situation do you need to take responsibility for and to seek forgiveness for? In addition to your own ideas on this, it is always important to ask what are your fiancée/fiancé's ideas because you might not be aware of everything about your hurtful actions.

2. Here are some hints to help you be successful in the forgiveness process:
   a. Reflect tenderness (lower your voice, become gentle, speak slowly and softly, relax your facial expression).
   b. Increase your own understanding of the pain you caused. Ask: What was that like for you when I did . . . ? How did you feel? What buttons got pushed?
   c. Admit your specific behaviors or words that caused fear, hurt, or frustration.
   d. Seek forgiveness. Say the words, "Will you forgive me for . . . ?" And then allow time for a response. This may

be immediate or it may take time depending on the offense. Remember, honor your fiancée/fiancé's emotional walls. If your betrothed doesn't want to forgive you, give her/him the space and time to work through the hurt. You focus on being a safe person.

9

Teamwork

During my doctoral studies, I had to take a statistics class. My trouble began when, during the first class meeting, our professor recited a list of formulas that we should all know. My stomach sickened when nothing he said sounded even remotely familiar. I rushed home and informed Erin that I was dropping the class.

Unfortunately, Erin didn't agree, and a major argument erupted.

"You are *not* dropping the class," Erin exclaimed. "You won't be able to finish on time, and it will cost us money."

It seemed to me that she was saying I needed to "cowboy up" and work through this tough situation like a man. Okay, maybe that is what I heard and not what she said—but she was *thinking* it!

"Give me a break," I reacted. "It won't cost us anything, and I can take it next semester and still finish on time. Besides, I have a really tough schedule and this class is going to push me over the edge."

"Can't you get into a study group or something?" Erin probed. "I just think you need to stay in it."

"Trust me," I asserted, "It will be fine. You'll see that I'm right."

Our dance might have lasted longer, except our then-two-year-old daughter, Taylor, interceded.

"That's enough, guys!" she yelled, and then smacked me on the backside with a huge wooden spoon. The shock of being reprimanded by a two-year-old broke our dance and caused us to double over with laughter.

By the way, I remained in the class and got an A. But that's not the point! The point is that we were destroying our relationship by getting into power struggles like this one, again and again. Our basic problem boiled down to this: Each time we danced, we became adversaries. It became me against Erin. We stopped being married teammates and instead squared off as opponents.

Has that ever happened to you?

Beware of Power Struggles

All couples have to make decisions during their engagement and married lives. Some issues allow for easy decisions, like the color of the bridesmaids' dresses, the style of reception music, the flavor of wedding cake, who handles the remote control, or where to eat dinner. Others require more careful consideration, because they involve weighty issues like career choices, where to live, which church to attend, when to have children, major investments, who pays the bills, whether to buy or rent, and how much debt to take on.

As you both face significant choices, it's important to have a method of decision making that allows you to remain in harmony. Even more important, however, you need a system that will allow you to work effectively together as teammates.

One of the greatest forces for positive change in my marriage came when Erin and I finally understood that we were constantly allowing ourselves to get into power struggles. A power struggle erupts when you face off against your fiancée and both of you take up opposing positions. This relational tug-of-war can occur over differing opinions, concerns, or expectations.

As Jesus explained, power struggles are destructive because, "Any kingdom divided against itself will be ruined, and a house divided against itself will fall" (Luke 11:17). Any time Erin and I square off against each other, the outcome is already assured. We become divided; unity melts away.

When this consistently happens over time, the relationship begins to feel very unsafe. How safe can a marriage be if you feel like you're living with an adversary? And when you feel unsafe, your heart will close and you will disconnect from each other. Eventually, people stop trying to work through issues and nothing gets resolved. When you stop trying to resolve your differences, you start making adjustments on your own— and not too far down that road, loneliness sets in. Once people start to feel lonely in a marriage, divorce becomes a very real possibility.

Win-Win versus Compromise

To combat disunity in your relationship, we urge you to learn how to find win-win solutions. Quite possibly you've already used this strategy to make decisions regarding your wedding. And then again, no doubt there have been times when you haven't.

Think about some of your disagreements as you've had to make choices about a wedding date, how many people to invite, how much to spend on the wedding, how many bridesmaids and groomsmen to have, where to go on your honeymoon, where to register for gifts, the type of stationery to send out—you know what we're talking about.

Have you ever compromised a few times along the way? In other words, although you wanted to find the perfect win-win solution, have you ever had to settle for an occasional win-lose?

The latter occurs when you make a decision that produces one winner and one loser. This is exactly what happened to Erin and me over my graduate class. Erin wanted me to stay, while I wanted to drop the class. I ended up staying, just to please her. We're not saying it's bad to put someone's desires before your own! Philippians 2:3 says, "Do nothing out of selfish ambition or vain conceit, but in humility consider others better than yourselves." Furthermore, Romans 12:10 says, "Be devoted to one another in brotherly love. Honor one another above yourselves."

Acting as a servant can be a great thing—unless, of course, you feel as if you've lost and your mate has won. That is exactly what happened to me in grad school. Although I went along with Erin's solution (I stayed in the class), I felt as if I had lost. In effect, we had created a win-lose situation.

For many years in our marriage, we often accepted a win-lose decision. When I "won," I would justify my actions by rationalizing that Erin simply needed to submit to my authority as the leader of our family (that worked *real* well, by the way). When Erin "won," she would validate her decision by thinking that I would warm up to the idea once I realized how right she was.

Do you know the real problem with a win-lose situation? You actually end up with *two* losers. You get, not a win-lose, but a lose-lose.

In marriage there is no such thing as a win-lose, because you are both on the same team. As a team, you either win together or you lose together. There is no other option.

This truth changed our marriage. Although Erin and I believed we were on the same team, we often didn't act like it. So many times when attempting to make a decision, we abandoned our team and became adversaries. And make no mistake:

Any time one team member loses, every member of that team loses.

A No-Losers Policy

Our good friend and former colleague Dr. Robert Paul taught us an amazing concept called a No-Losers Policy. Basically, this is a mind-set that says, *members of a team win together or they lose together; therefore, in a premarital relationship, I can't win unless my future spouse also wins.* As we learned and practiced this concept, we made it unacceptable for either of us to walk away from any interaction feeling as if one of us had lost. Erin and

I agreed that we both need to feel good about whatever solution we dream up.

Let's revisit Philippians 2:3 for a moment. Paul wrote, "Do nothing out of selfish ambition or vain conceit, but in humility consider others better than yourselves." Consider well the very next verse: "Each of you should look not only to your own interests, but also to the interests of others."

There it is! Paul describes a win-win, in plain and simple language. In this verse, the apostle encourages you to look not only to your own interests (win) but also to the interests of your fiancée (win). That means that to make the idea work in your relationship, you must come up with a different definition of winning. If winning is about getting your own way, then you'll never be a successful team. The key is to redefine winning as *finding a solution that both of you feel good about.*

Erin and I had a choice to make that day when wondering what to do about my graduate class. We could have decided that the only acceptable solution was one that we both felt great about. Sadly, that's not what we did. Instead, we chose an adversarial path that resulted in our whole team losing.

To be honest, we finally just got tired of losing all the time. We knew we needed to make a change—and that change came in the form of a No-Losers Policy.

But Does It Work in the Real World?

Although a No-Losers Policy makes complete sense to most people, some doubters hesitate to implement the strategy in their own relationships. Why? Most of the time their greatest concern sounds something like this: "It looks great on paper, but in the *real* world, there is no way this will work. It just takes too much time."

We have a simple answer to their objection. We just return to Matthew 12:25, where Jesus insists, "Every kingdom divided against itself will be ruined, and every city or household divided against itself will not stand." That's pretty clear! *A house divided will fall*—and in the long run, nothing takes longer than failure.

Your future household will be divided if you feel you have to defend your territory. As this happens, you tend to dig in your heels for a tiring tug-of-war. The battle continues until one or the other person just wears out—and that can take a long, long time. We've counseled many couples who have had the same argument *for more than twenty years!*

What, that's *saving* time?

Don't avoid implementing a No-Losers Policy in your future marriage for fear that it will take too much time! While it may take a little time and effort to get used to—especially if you have tended to become adversaries during a conflict—in the end, it can save you decades of time. Quite literally.

7 Steps to Creating Win-Win Solutions

But how do you implement this strategy in your relationship? We're happy to report that it's actually very easy! All you need to do is follow some simple steps. And they'll work regardless of the conflict, as the following story illustrates.

Although we began at opposite ends of the spectrum, Erin and I finally reached a decision. It wasn't easy, and it took us a long time to arrive at our answer—but yes, the Smalley family would adopt a Ragdoll kitten.

This was no ordinary kitten like one you might get for free in the Wal-Mart parking lot! We wanted a real mellow and relational cat, and everyone kept telling us that we needed to get a Ragdoll. *What in the world is a Ragdoll?* we wondered. *It sounds like a cloth baby our mothers used to play with.*

After researching the benefits of this type of cat, Erin finally agreed to having one in our home. According to the experts, the male Ragdoll was the best.

And so the day finally arrived that I was to drive with Taylor and

Maddy to Eureka Springs, Arkansas, to pick up our kitten from its breeder at a store called Kitty, Kitty, Kitty. (Yes, this was an actual location and, as you might guess, a store designed to meet every need any cat might ever have.) The name itself should have tipped me off that something bad was going to happen.

The girls and I headed out early in the morning with high anticipation of meeting our first pet. Well, I should preface that statement by saying, "the first pet that might stay around longer than two weeks." A few years earlier, I had "surprised" everyone with a puppy. I thought it was a brilliant idea. "Every kid needs a dog," I insisted. The rest of the family came home from a trip to meet Holly in the living room. She immediately jumped up and scratched the kids' legs. They began to cry.

Need I say more?

Holly then proceeded to potty on the living room floor and chew on the corner of the couch. Normal puppy behavior, right? Well, it would be, if you actually *desired* to be the proud owner of a puppy. I went out of town right after Holly arrived, and during my absence, Erin conveniently found a single friend of ours to take in Holly.

So, as you can imagine, this little bit of family history put an increased fear in Erin's mind over assuming responsibility for *any* animal, even a cat.

As we drove to Eureka Springs, my girls and I talked about names for our new kitten. Since it was Christmas time, the girls arrived at Bumble. Do you remember the abominable snowman in the classic cartoon *Rudolph the Red-Nosed Reindeer*? Perfect name for a male cat!

Several hours later, we slowly pulled into the parking lot of Kitty, Kitty, Kitty and looked for Laverne, the cat breeder. We saw a woman leaning up against an older automobile, wearing a dark trench coat with large sunglasses. Strangely, she had no kitten in hand.

Well, that's different . . . maybe the cat is in the car, I thought as I approached the woman. I pulled alongside her and rolled down my window.

"You have the money?" Laverne whispered.

A bit shaken, I took out several large bills and handed them over. And almost as quickly, the cat lady pulled her trench coat open and shoved a small kitten into my arms. And then—she was gone.

I quickly scanned the area and wondered what illegal activity I had just been part of. Instead of a drug deal, it appeared to be a cat deal.

As my daughters and I drove away, we joked about Bumble's crazy arrival into our lives. The girls lovingly cared for him all the way to Siloam Springs.

When we got home, it was clear Erin still felt a little hesitant about our new family member. *Will this cat be a good mix for our family?* she wondered. But when she saw how beautiful he was and how sweet and mellow he seemed to be, she immediately laid those fears to rest.

Bumble fit right in to our family. Several months later, however, his behavior became very odd. Erin told me, "If I weren't certain this cat is a male, I'd say it's in heat!" We laughed out loud at the absurd notion.

But Bumble's strange antics continued to the point that Erin could take it no longer. She couldn't stand the loud squeals at all hours of the night. She decided we needed to take our deranged cat to the veterinarian to see what medication for schizophrenia she could give us.

Erin signed in Bumble as a male—and then felt abruptly shamed by the vet's technician when she loudly asked, "Who signed this female cat in as a *male?*"

So, as I am sure you have guessed by now, Bumble was, in fact, a girl. She needed to be "fixed" immediately. We're happy to say that Bumble is still a valued member of our family.

What we really want you to get from this story is not the happy ending but the happy way we made the decision in the first place. Instead of dancing around the decision, compromising or losing together, we worked hard to find a solution that we both felt thrilled about. The great news is that you can do the same thing in your own relationship. May we show you how?

Reaffirm Your No-Losers Policy

The most powerful place to start is by reminding each other that you are on the same team. This creates a positive environment that improves how you treat each other. As a matter of fact, if this is all you do when making a decision, you will see an enormous improvement in your relationship.

Couples relax when they actively search for a solution that both people feel great about. Why? The worry simply dissipates and is replaced by feelings of safety, because neither of you has to worry about protecting your own agenda. You no longer feel anxious that your feelings won't be considered.

Discover the Win Nugget for Each Person

In the last chapter we encouraged you to listen for each other's hearts. The difference here is that you focus, not on your feelings and emotions, but instead on trying to understand the win for each person.

"Why do you prefer this particular solution or want to go in that specific direction?" You're really looking for the golden nugget of why your fiancé's idea or solution seems so important to him. Usually you will find one or two reasons why his position is so important—but usually you have to dig for it. The key is to keep asking questions and being curious: "What will it help you to accomplish? What is it that you really want? Why is your solution so important?" The bottom line is to be curious about his ideas.

Never argue or debate her solutions. Don't try to manipulate your fiancée toward your solution!

One newlywed couple saw the negative effects of manipulation when they were buying life insurance. Despite a great sales pitch, a salesman could not convince the young couple to purchase his policy.

"I absolutely don't want to pressure you into a decision," he proclaimed while walking toward the door. "Please sleep on it tonight, and when you wake up in the morning, let me know what you've decided."

Think of the process like a funnel. You want to sift through a lot of material to funnel down to the absolute nugget, which is, "what is it that I really want, down deep?" To discover the deepest wants and desires, you simply listen to your fiancé and repeat back what you hear him saying. Again, don't attempt to convince him why his ideas are wrong, stupid, illogical, or won't work. Just listen.

Choose one person to go first. In our adventure with Bumble, Erin and I decided that Erin would start our win-win process.

"Why don't you want a cat?" I asked Erin.

"It's not that I don't want a cat," she replied. "I actually like cats. It's just that the last time we got a pet, you surprised me with it. If you remember, we *kind of* talked about it, but we never made a firm decision. Instead, you decided to make the final decision on your own. I felt left out."

"I hear you saying that you felt left out of the decision to get a dog."

"Yes," Erin continued. "And since I will be the one most likely who will take care of a cat, I really want to be included in the decision. I want a voice, and I want my voice to matter to you."

"I hear you saying that you want me to value your opinions, and you want to be included in the decision."

"Absolutely," Erin affirmed. "That is the real win for me."

"That's easy," I teased, "You actually want to be a valuable part of making the decision this time. By the way," I said with total humility, "I'm so sorry that I bought the dog without talking to you first. That was wrong!"

"Thank you!"

"Although," I teased, "you *did* give our dog away all on your own!"

"Now we're even!" Erin joked. "No, I'm kidding. That was equally as wrong, and I'm sorry, too." She paused, then said, "Greg, help me to understand why you want a cat so badly."

"I don't know," I said. "I always had cats, growing up. I loved having a cat sleep on my bed, and I would like our kids to experience that."

"So I hear you saying that you'd like our kids to experience having a pet, just like you did while growing up."

"Yes. But, I'm not sure that is *really* what's going on for me. I think what I really want is for you to understand and value my feelings about having a pet. When I've brought this up before, I usually end up feeling minimized when you jump in so quickly with all of the reasons why owning a pet would be a bad idea. Beyond actually getting a pet, I just want you to care about why it's important to me."

"Wow," Erin said, stunned. "I had no idea you felt that way. I can totally see why you would feel that way. I do jump really fast to why it's a horrible idea because I'm so afraid that you're going to go right out and buy another animal. I'm so sorry for doing that! Your feelings do matter to me."

"Thank you."

"So I hear you saying that your win is for me to really understand and care about how you feel about having a pet."

"Yes," I responded. "I want you to value my opinion."

"You got it!" Erin said, smiling.

Erin and I continued to talk about why I wanted a pet so badly. Finally I was able to express some things to her that we never discussed in the past. Regardless of whether we actually bought a pet, it felt really good for her to care about me. In the end, by using curiosity, we were able to identify the following golden nuggets:

+ Erin: *to be included in the decision*
+ Greg: *to have my reasons valued*

Once you find these nuggets, both must be factored into your solution. That's how you get to a win-win solution. If you take what is most important to you and what is most important to your future spouse, and you put both into the mix, you always end up with a win-win solution.

Seek the Lord's Opinion

This third step adds yet another layer of safety. When you pray together, you seek out the Lord to see whether He has an opinion. But make sure you lay aside your ideas first! This only makes sense, for if the Lord actually does have a direction He would like you to go, wouldn't His solution be the best?

You'll be amazed at how many arguments get resolved once you ask the Lord whether He has an opinion on what you ought to do. In addition to praying about the situation, make sure you talk about what the Bible says about the issue. Obviously, the Bible will not speak to every issue; but a direction will not be Christ centered if it violates biblical truth.

The best part about praying together is that when a man and woman get down on their knees as a team to seek out the Lord's will, this very act instantly restores unity. We love the scripture verse that reads, "Be completely humble and gentle; be patient, bearing with one another in love. Make every effort to keep the *unity* of the Spirit through the bond of peace" (Ephesians 4:2–3). Another verse has a very similar message: "My purpose is that they may be encouraged in heart and *united in love*, so that they may have the full riches of complete understanding, in order that they may know the mystery of God, namely Christ" (Colossians 2:2). The message in both texts is pretty clear: Christ desires that we maintain unity. And prayer together is an outstanding way to reestablish unity.

Erin and I prayed together about the decision to get a cat. Although we didn't walk away feeling a peace that God was leading us one way or another, we definitely agreed that He wasn't discouraging us, either.

(I did bring up the fact that Noah had at least two cats aboard the Ark. Therefore, I insisted, owning a cat would not violate the Scriptures.)

Brainstorm Possible Solutions

This is the fun step. Here is where you generate all possible solutions. The best advice here is to get creative and refrain from judging or critiquing the ideas generated. Allow both people the opportunity to share their suggestions and ideas. The only rule is that any solution mentioned must consider both people's nuggets.

Remember our two nuggets? Erin wanted to be included in the decision; I wanted to have my opinions valued. We then started throwing out possible solutions that contained both of our wins.

Pick a Solution

At this step you evaluate and critique the possible solutions and pick something that you both feel great about. You want to consider the ideas generated at the last step, highlighting the ones that seem to offer the most in solving your dilemma. If you feel you need more input, do some research on the Internet or at the library (that's the big building with all the books!). Sometimes you may need to consult with an expert or talk to friends. The goal is to pick what you both see as the best possible solution.

We settled on the solution of sitting down *together* to talk about getting a cat. Part of the conversation would give me plenty of time to share why having a cat felt so important to me.

Do you see how that ended up being a win-win for us?

Just Do It

After you discover a solution that excites both of you, try it out. Take it for a test drive. See if it feels as good as you thought it would. But go into it with the same spirit that helped you to identify this option—making sure that both of you still consider it a win-win.

After Erin and I had a great discussion about getting a cat and why that was so important for me, we both decided to "go for it." Hence, this is how Bumble the boy/girl cat (we really should have named it Pat) came to live at the Smalleys.

In the end, it doesn't matter who came up with the idea; the only important thing is that both of you consider it a win. There will be plenty of times you end up doing exactly what the other person wanted to do; but by the time you get there, you will feel great about it (win-win). At other times, you will do exactly what you suggested in the beginning; but by the time you get there, the other person will feel great about it (win-win). And there will be times you'll come up with a completely different solution that neither of you proposed beforehand.

In our case, instead of getting a cat, we might have decided upon an iguana (hey, it could happen). In any event, the goal is always to find a solution that makes you both feel great.

Reexamine the Solution

Many times, after trying out a win-win solution, you will discover that your solution doesn't feel quite like you thought it would. In the past, I would say something like, "No, Erin! We're *not* changing now. You had your chance to give your input and feedback. We went through all of that work, and we're going to live with this solution!" I would never say that now, because the moment a solution feels like a loss to Erin, what happens to my team? We lose!

And I hate losing.

If this happens to you, don't worry about it. Just repeat the seven steps and rework your solution. Remember, your goal is to make sure that your team stays on the successful side of things and that both people feel great about the solution.

But What If We Can't Agree?

At this point, someone always asks, "But what if we try to find a win-win and we can't find one? Who makes the decision then?"

You want to know the honest truth? In all the years that Erin and I have been using a No-Losers Policy, we have *never* run into a situation that frustrated our attempts to find a solution we both felt great about. And we've had to make some gigantic decisions, like moving, having children, changing careers, graduate school, investments, and so on.

You know why this is true, don't you? It's because we recognize that the problem is rarely *the* problem.

The real problem *always* has to do with our buttons getting pushed and our deep wants and desires going unfulfilled. If you follow the above seven steps, we are convinced that you will find some kind of happy agreement.

"But what if we don't?" you plead. Then let us tell you something else we've discovered.

Most urgent decisions—things that drive us to hurry up, that tell us we're almost out of time, that insist we're about to miss the opportunity of a lifetime—almost always end up being less than urgent. The opportunity either was not as good as it looked, or an even better opportunity had not yet presented itself. We often look back to realize that if we had moved on the first decision, we would have missed out on the second.

That is why, in general, we prefer to hold off on such decisions until we can arrive at a place of unity. But if the decision really does need to be made, we try to determine who appears to be the most qualified to make it—based on experience or training or something else—and then let that person decide. Too often guys say things like, "Listen, I'm the man—so therefore you need to submit" (the dreaded *s* word)!

(A quick word here for the husband trying to follow biblical truth: Ephesians 5:21 says, "Submit *to one another* out of reverence for Christ." We are *both* to submit to each other; one does not rule over the other. In fact, Jesus says that if you want to be the leader, then you must become the servant of all (see Matthew 20:25–28). Paul says the husband must actually follow Christ's example and "give up his life" (Ephesians 5:25 NLT) for his wife, as Christ did for us on the cross.

Remember, the only other possibility is for your team to lose. Don't make the issue about submitting! Make it about finding a win-win. That is honor. That makes the marriage feel safe.

These days, if I feel compelled to make a decision that Erin opposes, I'll do so only with great caution. I'll say, "I feel led to make this decision, but I have to tell you that because you and I are not together on this, I'm open to the possibility that I might be wrong. Therefore, I will make the decision; but I want you to know that I will also take the heat if I'm wrong. And I will be the one to answer to God. You are off the hook." This is very different from saying, "I'm the man, so back off and submit, because *I* make the decisions around here!"

Who Does the Work?

A friend read me an email he received the other day. It went like this:

> Who's working, anyway?
>
> The population of this country is 300 million. 160 million are retired; that leaves 140 million to do the work.
>
> There are 85 million in school, which leaves 55 million to do the work.
>
> Of this, there are 35 million employed by the federal government, leaving 15 million to do the work.
>
> 2.8 million are in the armed forces, preoccupied with killing Osama bin Laden, which leaves 12.2 million to do the work.
>
> Take from that total the 10.8 million people who work for state and city governments, and that leaves 1.4 million to do the work.

At any given time, there are 188,000 people in hospitals, leaving 1,212,000 to do the work.

Now, there are 1,211,998 people in prisons. That leaves just two people to do the work.

You and me.

And there you are, at your computer, reading jokes!

Dang! Do I have to do *everything*?

The truth is, if you want your marriage to really work, both of you have to be on the same team. Both of you have to be working together, as teammates, figuring out how to win as a unit.

In a marriage there is no such thing as a win-lose solution. There is either win-win, or lose-lose. No other options exist!

Remember that, act on it, and then enjoy the benefits of discovering solutions that you both feel great about!

COUPLES EXERCISE/HOMEWORK

1. As a couple, review pages 207 to 220 so you can create your own No-Losers Policy. Here are some hints to help you be successful:

   a. Make it unacceptable for either person to walk away feeling as if he/she lost.

   b. Redefine winning as finding a solution that both feel good about.

   c. Agree that ALL conflicts and major decision making will be handled using your No-Losers Policy.

2. Go back to the Fear Dance Test on page 115. Review question 1 where we asked you to describe a recent conflict or negative situation—something that really "pushed your buttons." With that recent disagreement in mind, work through the seven steps to creating win-win solutions:

   1. Reaffirm your No-Losers Policy.

   2. Discover the "win" nugget for each person. Remember, this is not about understanding how each other feels. If you still feel like your fiancée or fiancé doesn't understand your feelings, go back to the Heart Talk exercise on page 181. Instead, this step is about unearthing why your loved one's idea or solution is so important to him/her. You usually have to be extremely curious (no judgment) and dig for the one or two nuggets by asking questions like these: What will it help you to accomplish? What is it that you really want? Why is your solution so important to you?

List your fiancée/fiancé's nugget(s):

List your nugget(s):

3. Seek the Lord's opinion by putting aside your individual nuggets and praying together for His direction.
4. Brainstorm possible solutions.
5. Pick a solution that you *both* feel good about.
6. Just do it—put it into action.
7. Reexamine the solution and rework if necessary.

10

Putting It All Together

I n this chapter you'll take the new skills you've just learned and apply them to real issues. Some of them you'll face as you and your fiancée plan your wedding; others you'll encounter as you navigate through your first year of marriage.

What follows is exactly the process Erin and I use to deal with our issues. To see how it works out in real life, let's use a conflict we had regarding our wedding plans.

A Song of Conflict

One of my greatest regrets is that I did not get more involved in the planning of our wedding. Erin did a wonderful job, and we had a beautiful wedding, but when I didn't get more involved, I sent a message to Erin that I didn't truly value our wedding.

The only aspect I really did get involved with took place about one week before the ceremony. Erin sent me the order of the ceremony "run sheet" and told me to look it over. I remember looking at all the songs for our wedding and noticed that the one song I had asked for didn't seem to be listed.

I'll fix that, I remember thinking as I dialed Erin's number.

"I like the ceremony order," I said in my sly (read "manipulative") way, "especially the songs!"

"Great," Erin responded, "I'm so relieved, because I've worked so hard to get every song we wanted in the ceremony, and we've filled every possible time slot."

"We've?" I said sarcastically.

"What do you mean?" Erin replied, a little confused. "I'm not following you."

"I noticed that the *one* song I asked for is missing," I answered, "so when you say *we* have filled every possible time slot, you really mean *you*."

I wish that sometimes the little voice in my head—the one that says, "shut up, fool!"—were louder!

"Are you being *serious*?" Erin yelled, clearly in reaction mode. "You never mentioned that you wanted a song! What song are you talking about?"

"'When I Fall in Love.' I've only mentioned it like twenty times."

"You've *never* mentioned that song!"

You can imagine the rest of the conversation. The only thing we eventually agreed on was that we both had very different perceptions of this issue. So, here's the question: how could we have handled this issue differently back in the late spring of 1992?

Step 1: Create some space. Remember, it takes two to tango. All it ever takes to stop the Fear Dance is for one person to decide to quit dancing. Either of us could have said, "My buttons have been pushed. I need to take some time to figure out what's going on with me. Let's take a break and get back together in a little while."

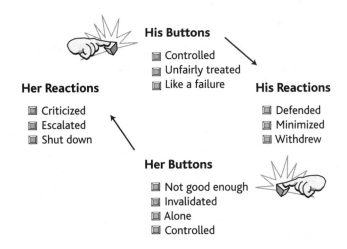

His Buttons

☐ Controlled
☐ Unfairly treated
☐ Like a failure

Her Reactions

☐ Criticized
☐ Escalated
☐ Shut down

His Reactions

☐ Defended
☐ Minimized
☐ Withdrew

Her Buttons

☐ Not good enough
☐ Invalidated
☐ Alone
☐ Controlled

***Step 2: Identify what buttons got pushed for each person and how you re-
acted to each other.*** Several of my buttons got pushed that day. I felt controlled (Erin was making all the decisions), unfairly treated (it wasn't fair
that my one song wasn't included), and like a failure (when I realized I
had made a mistake and actually *hadn't* told Erin about my song). Several
of Erin's buttons also got pushed. She felt not good enough (she had
worked endlessly on all our wedding plans and it *still* wasn't good
enough for me), invalidated (I didn't seem to care or acknowledge how
difficult it was for Erin to make all the plans on her own), alone (she did
all the planning without any help from her future husband), and controlled (we had one week until the wedding, and *now* I wanted her to
change things?).

I reacted by defending myself ("This is the first time I've seen the
ceremony order. How was I supposed to know my song wasn't there? If
you had let me see this a few weeks ago, I could have changed it then!"),
minimizing Erin's feelings ("I don't know why you're making such a big
deal about this. It's one song. How hard can it be to change it? You get
so emotional over the smallest things!"), and then I withdrew
("Fine . . . forget it . . . it doesn't matter . . . I don't want to talk about
it").

Erin reacted by becoming critical ("You always do this . . . you wait until the last minute to tell me what you want"), escalated ("I'm so tired of making all these plans on my own . . . it's *our* wedding and not just mine!"), and then she shut down ("Whatever . . . I'll figure it out later . . . good-bye!").

Step 3: Take your buttons to the Lord. After we had created some space (remember, that space is not the same as withdrawing, because you are intentionally dealing with your buttons in order to get your heart back open), we could have each individually taken our "stuff" to the Lord.

"Lord, I'm not even exactly sure what is going on with me right now. I'm so mad at my fiancée and I feel hurt. I'm not sure what buttons have gotten pushed for me. Help me understand what's going on in my heart right now, Lord; search my heart. I'm feeling controlled, that things are unfair, and like a failure. Lord, reveal to me Your truth about this situation. I know that I'm fully capable of misunderstanding my fiancée and misperceiving what happened. Lord, I don't want to react to her. She is too precious. You have made her in Your image, and I don't want to dishonor You or her. Lord, give me the strength to respond to her. Lord, help me reopen my heart to You and to my fiancée. Thank you!"

Step 4: Care for each other's hearts. After you spend enough time in your space (about twenty minutes) dealing with your buttons and getting your heart back open, now you have the opportunity to care for each other. Remember, in this step you are not trying to solve anything ("Do we put Greg's song in the wedding or not?"). Instead, you are just trying to care about how each person felt—care about what buttons got pushed.

It's irrelevant whether your fiancée's feelings are logical, illogical, true, accurate, rational, truly reflect how you feel, or make sense. Right now, the goal is to care about his or her feelings, emotions, and heart. Caring for someone's heart does not equal resolving or "fixing" the issue, agreeing with what he says or how she feels, being responsible for his or her feelings, making changes, admitting guilt or fault, or apologizing. Instead, caring means that you feel each other's pain and allow your heart to be "touched" by the other's emotions.

All those years ago, if we had dealt with our own stuff and got our hearts back open, we could have cared about each other.

"I'm sure I pushed your buttons," I could have said. "I care about how you feel, Erin. What was going on for you when I called?"

"I just have felt so alone in this process," Erin might have replied. "I know that you've been trying to finish up your first year of seminary. I know you've been gone—but I just feel so alone."

"I hear you saying that you've felt alone. I'm so sorry! My mind has been so preoccupied with school that I can't imagine what it's been like for you to plan everything by yourself."

"That's exactly right. Thanks! When you talked about adding your song, I felt instantly overwhelmed, realizing that I've filled every conceivable time slot. So I was afraid that you would be upset and disappointed in me."

"I can totally see how you would feel that way. You are feeling completely overwhelmed anyway. Then, you must have felt helpless trying to figure out how to please me and include my song. I'm so sorry you felt that way! That's no fun to feel alone and helpless."

"That's exactly how I've been feeling. Thank you for listening. I'm not sure what was going on for you."

"I think my failure button got pushed as I realized I may not have told you about my song. I felt stupid and didn't want to admit my mistake."

"I know how difficult that is for you when you feel like you've made a mistake or have failed in some way. I know that is a painful feeling for you."

"Thanks. And, whether this is true or not, I felt controlled that you had the final say-so on whether my song could be in the wedding. It didn't feel fair to me. It's funny, because on the one hand, I haven't helped you with the details; and yet, on the other hand, I wanted to feel like I'm included in the decisions. I know that might not make sense, but I know that's what was going on for me."

"That makes perfect sense. I hear you saying that you want to feel that I include your input when decisions have to be made."

"Yes . . . that's exactly right."

"The bottom line is that it sounds very important for you to have that song in our wedding. And because it's important to you, it's important to me."

Step 5: Seek forgiveness for the damaged caused by the dance. This step involves taking responsibility for your hurtful reactions. Although we are not responsible for our fiancée/fiancé's buttons and feelings, we *are* responsible for our actions.

"Erin," I might have said, "I want to apologize for defending myself, for blaming you for not including my song, and for being sarcastic. I didn't honor you at all. I'm so sorry for that."

"You were already forgiven!" she could have replied. "Likewise, I want to seek forgiveness for criticizing you and getting angry. I don't ever want to treat you that way. You are just too valuable to me. I'm sorry."

Step 6: Find a solution that you both feel great about. In this step you discover a win-win solution by using the No-Losers Policy. Remember, you are not finding a compromise, but something that both people feel great about. By the way, what follows is the exact conversation we ultimately had all those years ago. Here's the solution we found together:

"In terms of the song," I said, "let's find a solution that we both like."

"That sounds great," Erin replied. "Greg, tell me what it is that you really want."

"That song just means a *lot* to me. I've always wanted it in my wedding, from the first day I heard it."

"So you just want the song, and it doesn't matter when or where it is played?"

"Yes, that's correct. I just want the song to be somewhere in our wedding. What is it that you really want? What would be a win to you, Erin?"

"The win for me is to be able to keep the order we already have. I've worked so hard organizing the flow of the ceremony! If I change any one thing, then I risk having the domino effect take place. In other words, if we make one change to the order, then we probably have to redo the entire thing."

"So the win for you is not to change the order."

"Yes!"

"Is there any place that could have a song that doesn't already have one?"

"The only place I can think of is when the groomsmen and the bridesmaids are walking down the aisle. We don't have a song there, and we actually could have one if we wanted."

"That sounds great to me. I will be already up there, anyway. So I would get to hear it. I love it!"

"You love it? That's *great*, because then I don't have to change anything! And I really wanted the secretary at my hospital, Teresa, to do something in the wedding, and she has a great voice. Could she sing the song?"

"I really don't care who sings it. If you think Teresa would do a great job, then that works for me."

Time for Practice

Now it's your turn. Look over the common wedding-planning issues below and pick two that either you've had some conflict around, or something that you're dealing with right now.

"Okay," you might be saying, "but with so many deeper issues that we need to deal with, why do you want us to practice with such simple issues?"

Great question! We have a very simple answer. First, how you handle the little things will dictate how well you'll handle the major decisions from this day forward. It's the principle emphasized by Jesus: "Whoever can be trusted with very little can also be trusted with much" (Luke 16:10).

Second, we want you to be successful, and the best place to start as you develop your new skills is with less emotionally charged issues. Of course, we are not suggesting that the following wedding-planning issues won't bring up intense emotions! These issues may well push your buttons and stir up some powerful stuff that you will need to work through.

Third, these are the issues staring you right in the face. Why not use some of the things that are ripe for the picking—the low-hanging fruit?

Here are the top wedding-planning issues:

+ Who will do our premarital counseling?
+ Picking a wedding date and time.
+ Type of wedding—size, formality, and setting.
+ Budgeting—determining how much to spend, who will pay for what, and how expenses will be shared.
+ Bridesmaids and groomsmen—how many groomsmen and bridesmaids will we have? Which friends and family will serve as wedding attendants?
+ Wedding guest list—whom to invite, and how many can we have at the reception?
+ Reception and catering plans—type of entertainment, reception location, catering, musician or disc jockey, favors, wedding and groom's cake, color schemes, and seating arrangements.
+ Professional photographer and videographer.
+ Florist
+ Wedding rings
+ Wedding dress and headpiece
+ Men's wedding attire

+ Bridesmaids' dresses and accessories
+ Honeymoon and location
+ Marriage license
+ Gift registry and your gift choices
+ Invitations and related stationery needs
+ Wedding-day transportation
+ Ceremony—where we will get married, who will marry us, readings for ceremony, music selections for ceremony, and each parent's role in the ceremony
+ The rehearsal dinner
+ Attendants' parties (bachelor party and bridal shower)
+ Accommodations for out-of-town attendants and guests
+ Wedding-ceremony rehearsal—instructing your wedding party on what they will be doing on the day of the wedding

Wow! Our heads swim just thinking about the massive number of decisions you are about to make. It's no wonder that engaged couples who have been spared a lot of conflict suddenly can't seem to make a decision without arguing. If you haven't gotten into any disagreements around these issues, either you have a fiancé who doesn't have an opinion and who wants you to make all the decisions because you've been dreaming about this day for your entire life (and have six folders full of magazine clippings), or he just doesn't want to get involved. If it is the latter, then probably you are harboring some level of resentment. You will need to work through that.

At any rate, when you need to make so many decisions, it's absolutely normal to have arguments, differences of opinion, fights, and conflict. If you ever build a house, you'll go through the whole thing again. Just ask any couple who have built a home, and we guarantee you 95 percent of those couples will roll their eyes and gasp, "Don't *ever* build a house if you want to stay married!" Why not? Like getting married, building a house requires that you make eight million decisions in a very short period of time. The resulting stress—feelings of being overwhelmed and trying to blend two individual sets of ideas into one decision—creates a breeding ground for conflict. Accept it! It is what it is.

The point is, control what you have control over. Put your time and energy into what matters most—your relationship. Every time you encounter a decision that results in an argument and hurt feelings, you have an opportunity to grow deeper in your relationship as you manage the issue in an honoring way.

So, have you picked your two issues? Great! Then walk through the following steps together.

Step 1: Create some space.

Step 2: Identify what buttons got pushed for each person and how you reacted to each other.

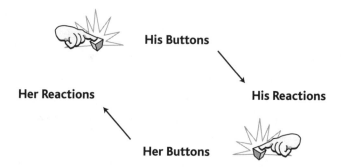

Step 3: Take your buttons to the Lord.

Step 4: Care for each other's hearts.

Step 5: Seek forgiveness for the damage caused by the dance.

Step 6: Find a solution that both of you feel great about.

Your First Year of Marriage

You will never forget your first year together. All the planning and dreaming of a life together can't compare to the reality of the "until death do us part" piece. The newness and excitement of starting your life together, the newness of each situation—there is an amazing feeling of freshness in the air. Think about it, the excitement of being with someone you love *on a full-time basis.*

At one of our marriage seminars, we asked couples to remember their first year and describe what they considered the best part. Here are a few of their responses:

+ Being able to sleep together (finally!) and hold one another—there was a slumber party every night.
+ Our first tiny apartment, we were both working and coming home to "our place."
+ Knowing we were now our own family, just the two of us.
+ Freedom! Being responsible for ourselves and making our own decisions about life—it was the first time I felt like an adult.
+ Having a best friend with me all the time.
+ Waking up next to my spouse.
+ Making new traditions and simply knowing that we were a team tackling problems, situations, and ideas together.
+ Feeling a sense of adventure.
+ Sharing our life goals, future plans, and dreams.
+ A complete sense of calm, permanence, and stability.

But the first year can also be a source of pain for many couples. As newlywed couples begin their lives together, they face situations that cause stress and conflict. If the couple lacks the tools and skills to successfully manage their issues, the resulting stress will have a negative impact on their marriages.

The newlywed years are often most difficult because couples have a hard time transitioning from being single individuals to being a couple. They also struggle going from their family of origin to being a new family. The common denominator is potential conflict.

Even if you are both fairly passive and "flight" is your normal reaction, it is vital to learn to manage your differences. In the midst of daily life, many undesirable traits of your future spouse will be revealed.

But so what? The key is how you will work through these irritations when you encounter them.

What are some of these issues? We asked more than four hundred adults at one of our marriage conferences to name the most difficult part of their first year of marriage. Read through their answers, not because we want to scare you, but because we want you to have a realistic picture of the challenges many couples face.

#1 Answer: Adjusting to the Marriage

+ Realizing that dating and marriage are very different
+ Adjusting to each other's living styles and to unfamiliar habits
+ Getting used to someone always being there
+ Understanding how to live together once the newness has worn off
+ Getting over the honeymoon phase to have a realistic view of married life
+ Learning to share my life with someone else who does things very differently

#2 Answer: *Managing Differences*

✦ Learning the differences in each other and how to make them blend

✦ Blending personalities—not trying to make my spouse conform to my ways of thinking and behaving

✦ Discovering our differences and the conflicts they produced; it seemed like we had so much in common before marriage

✦ Having very different ideas of how we plan or make decisions or even just run a household

✦ Understanding and accepting/resolving our cultural differences

✦ Learning about some characteristics I had not known about before

✦ Adjusting to his temperaments and little quirks. (We also had a child in our first year, so it was difficult to transition from the roles of husband and wife to those of mom and dad.)

#3 Answer: *Dealing with Expectations*

✦ Unmet or unfulfilled expectations

✦ Too many unrealistic expectations

✦ We both had very different expectations—many of which were never verbalized, but we "found" them during those first few years.

#4 Answer: *Dealing with Conflict*

✦ Sharing feelings and working through conflicts

✦ Getting through all the arguments

✦ Lots of stress and arguments

✦ Fighting over stupid stuff

✦ We had conflicts and didn't know how to resolve them.

Do you notice a common theme? These top four issues all boil down to managing or working through differences—whether those differences have to do with adjusting to marriage, personality quirks, or expectations.

We want to make this as simple as possible. If you are to focus on any one task to transition from a successful engagement to a successful marriage, we encourage you to focus on developing awesome conflict-management skills to deal with the "differences" that you *will* bump into. By this point, we have taught you how to break out of the dance, both as individuals and as a couple. You've practiced managing your wedding-planning issues. Now we want you to practice your new skills on real issues that impact most (if not all) newlywed couples during their first several years of marriage.

The Two Biggest Issues

Our research and that of other marriage experts suggests that the top two issues most couples will face during their first two years of marriage are *money* and *sex*.

Finances

Married couples fight over finances more than any other topic. Why? So many issues are wrapped up in money. It is impossible to narrow finances down to one issue that trips up couples.

First, most new husbands and wives have drastically different financial philosophies. They simply don't think about money in the same way. Some are savers, while others are spenders.

Think about your own attitudes and beliefs about spending, saving, debt, budgeting, credit cards, retirement, vacations, buying gifts for others, tithing, who will pay the bills and manage the checkbooks, who will be the primary breadwinner, making major purchases, and the list goes on. See what we mean? To further understand the differences in money philosophies, think about these scenarios:

◆ Does money make you feel powerful because you can buy the things you want, or because you can hold it as an asset?

◆ When you talk to your friends about money, are you more likely to mention a great bargain you purchased, or the great undervalued stock you bought?

◆ If you fall short of money at the end of the month, is your attitude, "that's what credit cards are for," or is it, "I won't buy anything"?

◆ If you don't have enough cash, will you hit the corner ATM or will you put off the purchase because you hate paying ATM surcharges?

◆ When you're out shopping, do you think most about the stuff you're buying, or the money you're spending?

◆ When you make an impulse purchase, do you feel a rush, or are you thinking right now, *What's an impulse purchase?*

◆ When you put money into savings, do you feel you've done your duty, or do you feel excited?

◆ At the current rate you're saving, do you have any idea how much you'll be worth when you retire?

Money problems in a marriage also can lead to an inability to develop a specific plan for spending and saving. If you can't agree on how you view money, then how in the world can you decide how you're going to spend it?

A final issue is that, probably, you both have been earning income separately and have had separate accounts at financial institutions. You have been making most of the decisions separately for many years, and the two of you may have very different ways of handling finances. We hope you heard the word "separately" that we've used over and over. The issue that trips up many newlyweds is that you go from managing your money *separately* to merging your finances *together*.

Erin and I took several major stumbles over this issue in the first four years of our marriage. It all came out in a big way when one day I brought home an "extra" thousand dollars from some conference work I had done. We hadn't budgeted for this money, and we didn't have to earmark it for bills. So I thought we could just split it and each of us use our $500 for whatever we wanted.

Erin didn't see it quite that way. To her, the whole thousand bucks was *ours* and so she should have a say in how I spent *my* half, just as I would have a say in how she spent *her* half. I didn't know this, of course, at the time. So when I spent a good chunk of my half on an antique football helmet, she took immediate exception to what she considered my wasteful ways. We argued loudly and soon started dancing in a very hurtful way.

So, was money our real problem? Or was it something else? We hope you understand by now that financial arguments are not really over money. The real issue always lies beneath the surface, connected to our buttons. Finances provide the veneer for much deeper issues, often involving power, control, trust, and feeling secure in the marriage. That was exactly the case for us.

When Erin questioned why I had bought the helmet, I felt controlled. So I reacted by trying to take back control. "Listen," I said, "this isn't an area that we even need to discuss. If I want to buy the helmet, I will. We already talked about this." Of course, as you can imagine, Erin felt completely invalidated and invisible. She reacted by criticizing me— and our whole dreary dance began to pick up steam until Erin finally shut down and withdrew.

It didn't have to happen that way, of course. We could have moved through the same process we've shown to you.

Step 1: Create some space. We always have the option to create some emotional space instead of reacting to each other. That way, we can identify and understand what is going on emotionally for each of us.

Step 2: Identify what buttons got pushed for each person and how you reacted to each other.

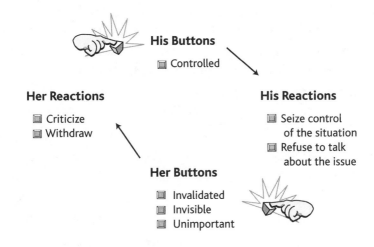

His Buttons

☐ Controlled

Her Reactions

☐ Criticize
☐ Withdraw

His Reactions

☐ Seize control
  of the situation
☐ Refuse to talk
  about the issue

Her Buttons

☐ Invalidated
☐ Invisible
☐ Unimportant

Step 3: Take your buttons to the Lord. The moment we got into the dance, our hearts closed down to each other. Therefore, our main goal must be to go to the Lord and get our hearts open to each other. Remember, hearts open to each other when we feel safe. The safest relationship in our lives is with the Lord: "The LORD is my light and my salvation— whom shall I fear? The LORD is the stronghold of my life—of whom shall I be afraid? . . . For in the day of trouble *he will keep me safe in his dwelling;* he will hide me in the shelter of his tabernacle and set me high upon a rock" (Psalm 27:1, 5). Any time we want to feel safe, all we need to do is close our eyes and imagine being hidden in the shelter of the Lord's tabernacle. And once we are safe in His dwelling, we can tell Him exactly how we feel. He will never judge our feelings or tell us that's a stupid way to feel. With His help, we can do the same things with our hearts. We can validate our pain and care about how we feel. We can acknowledge our buttons: "Lord, I'm feeling controlled right now. But I want You to have control over my life. I don't want to control me. I don't want someone else to control me. I want You. My life is Yours." As we seek the Lord's comfort, our hearts naturally begin to open. Now we are safer to care about how our spouses feel. Remember, we want to be imitators of Christ. Let's emulate Him by caring for our spouses' hearts like He does ours.

Step 4: Care for each other's hearts. Once our hearts were open, Erin and I had the option to listen, understand, and validate each other's feelings. I had the opportunity to care that Erin felt invalidated because she didn't think her feelings and opinions mattered to me. Now, I could have said, "Erin, that's not at all how I felt. Your feelings *do* matter to me." But that is the worst thing I could have done. The moment I start reacting and defending myself, my heart is going to close, as is Erin's. This step is all about caring. So here's a better way for me to show how her feelings of invalidation matter to me. "Wow . . . I can totally see why you would feel that way. That must have really hurt you to feel I didn't care about talking to you first. I'm sure you felt totally invisible and that your opinion didn't matter to me." Remember, I'm not responsible for Erin's feelings, neither do I need to change based on how she feels. I just want to *care*.

Erin also has the opportunity to care about my feelings. "I can totally see why you felt controlled. That's not fun when someone tries to tell you what to do. I'm sure you felt very confused and helpless, based on the fact that we had talked about each of us having the freedom to spend our money as we wanted." It would have felt so good to see her caring about my feelings.

Step 5: Seek forgiveness for the damage caused by the dance. Because we want to feel safe with each other and want our hearts to be fully open, we can seek forgiveness for our choices in how we treat each other. I tried to control Erin and end the discussion. But I could have said, "Erin, I am so sorry for reacting to you and trying to control whether we talk about something or not. That's not who I want to be. That's not how Christ would respond to you. Will you forgive me?"

Erin could also have used this opportunity to help me feel safe. "Greg, I'm so sorry for demanding that you talk about your intended purchase. I don't want you to ever feel controlled into talking to me. I want you to feel safe—I want you to experience me as a safe person so you'll want to talk. I'm sorry for criticizing you and for withdrawing. Will you forgive me?"

Doesn't that feel safe? When two people are aware of their "junk" and own it, hearts are so much more likely to open . . . and stay open.

Step 6: Find a solution that both of you feel great about. In this situation, a win-win solution could have taken many forms. Erin and I agree that one possible win-win would have worked perfectly. Erin's win was the desire to discuss things; she never actually wanted to make the decision for me. She simply wanted to talk about it. Simple enough!

My win was to have an agreed-upon amount that I could spend and then to have the freedom to buy what I wanted within that limit. A win-win could have been to agree on a spending limit. We also could have agreed to talk about whatever we wanted to buy. The purpose would have been to connect and share opinions, not to vote on a purchase. That would have felt good to both of us—a win-win!

Sex

Three couples went in to see the minister to see how to become members of his church. The minister said they would have to go without sex for two weeks and then come back and tell him how it went.

The first couple was retired, the second couple was middle-aged, and the final couple was newlywed.

Two weeks went by, and the couples returned to the minister. The retired couple said it was no problem at all. The middle-aged couple said it was tough for the first week, but after that, it was no problem. The newlyweds said it was fine until she dropped the can of paint.

"Can of paint?" exclaimed the minister.

"Yeah," said the newlywed man. "She dropped the can, and when she leaned over to pick it up, I just couldn't restrain myself." The minister just shook his head and said they were not welcome in his church.

"That's okay," said the man. "We're not welcome at Home Depot, either."

Sex can get you into trouble at home when you have a radical difference in expectations regarding the frequency and quality of your sexual contacts. You might go from making love three times a day on your honeymoon and then get back to real life—to work and school and doing the dishes and having responsibilities. The issue can manifest itself in several ways:

+ differing levels of interest in sex between husband and wife
+ dissatisfaction with the amount of affection received from one's partner
+ sexual disinterest between partners
+ difficulty talking about sexual issues
+ an inability to keep the sexual relationship interesting and enjoyable

If the issue is a difference in the level of interest in sex or feeling dissatisfied with the amount of affection received from one's spouse, the initiator may end up feeling rejected, unwanted, not desired, or disconnected. The spouse who isn't as interested in sex, or is not as affectionate, may end up feeling guilty, not good enough, like a failure, and invalidated. Since couples have difficulty talking about sexual issues anyway, there is little likelihood that they are talking about what buttons get pushed.

Let's say that the wife initiates sex and the husband has had a difficult day at work and doesn't respond to her playfulness. Her rejection button gets pushed (she already felt disconnected because he was withdrawn as a result of what had happened at work), and she criticizes him by saying, "What's your problem? I was just trying to be nice. You said you had a tough day at work, so I was just trying to make you feel better. Don't take it out on *me!*" Her criticism then pushes his failure button (which had already been pushed at work), and he reacts by withdrawing further from her. The husband simply rolls over in bed, as far away from her as he can get. Although he says nothing to her, she can feel the disconnection, which pushes her *rejected* and *unwanted* buttons even more. With a powerful tug on the covers, she rolls over onto her side and says sarcastically, "What's wrong with you? You can bet it will be a cold day in hell before I initiate anything with you again!" And then it's over. What took a matter of a few seconds resulted in two people feeling hurt and disconnected from each other.

What could they do to avoid this?

Step 1: Create some space. Both people always have the option to create some emotional space instead of reacting to each other, so that they can identify and understand what is going on emotionally for themselves.

Step 2: Identify what buttons got pushed for each person and how you reacted to each other.

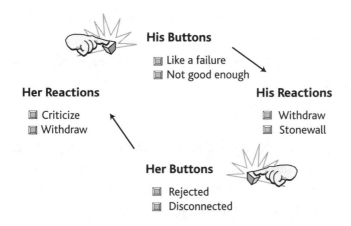

His Buttons
- [ ] Like a failure
- [ ] Not good enough

Her Reactions
- [ ] Criticize
- [ ] Withdraw

His Reactions
- [ ] Withdraw
- [ ] Stonewall

Her Buttons
- [ ] Rejected
- [ ] Disconnected

Step 3: Take your buttons to the Lord. Since both hearts have closed to each other, their first priority is to go to the Lord and get their hearts open. Prayer and focusing on the Lord gets our hearts open. The other part of getting our hearts open is by understanding and validating how we feel. Each person, with the Lord's help, can validate his or her own pain and emotions. The result usually is a heart that begins to open. This then makes the individual feel safer.

Step 4: Care for each other's hearts. Once hearts open to each other, this couple has the option to turn around and care about how each other feels. This doesn't have to happen the same night. We don't need to resolve anything before we go to bed. Sometimes, the best thing we can do is give each other space. But before I go to bed, I want to spend some time with the Lord, getting my heart open.

Then, the next day, this couple could talk about what was really going on for each person and then care for each other. He could make his goal to care about how she feels—really allow her pain to touch his heart. As a result of their caring, hearts would continue to open to each other. This is the beauty of caring for each other's hearts and allowing our feelings to matter.

Step 5: Seek forgiveness for the damage caused by the dance. Once both people felt heard, understood, and validated by the other, they also have the option to seek forgiveness. He could seek forgiveness for shutting down and withdrawing after work; she could seek forgiveness for personalizing his withdrawal.

Step 6: Find a solution that both feel great about. What did the wife want? Probably she wanted to feel connected—that was the win for her. On the other hand, what did her husband want? This is more difficult. Perhaps he wanted space to deal with his difficult workday.

So what could have been a win-win solution? They could have agreed that the next time he feels stressed out at work, he will let his wife know about it, and that he needs some time alone. The win for her is that he connects with her by telling her what's going on with him; the win for him is that he gets his space and has the opportunity to recharge.

Use All Your Safety Tools

While in high school, my friend Keith Blue and I were sitting in my parents' Jacuzzi, talking about deep issues, when a wild-eyed fowl jumped on the side of the Jacuzzi and scared us to death. We thought it was a vulture coming to eat us. We ran as fast as we could back into the house and came back out with my BB gun.

We both felt completely humiliated once we realized the ferocious attack bird was merely a chicken. We vowed never to tell anyone.

Of course, I just broke that vow. I hope he'll forgive me! The point is that Keith became my best friend as the result of countless hours we spent doing things together and developing knowledge about the other by talking about deep issues.

The tools you've just learned and practiced are designed to help you develop deep, heart-level knowledge about your future spouse. Use them well and wisely, and you'll create a home that feels like the safest place on earth. And no chicken will ever be able to come between you two.

COUPLE EXERCISES/HOMEWORK

Individually write down your expectations for your wedding night, and then discuss them (this includes expectations for before and after sex).

Other issues that you will need to talk about:
+ where to live
+ jobs/career decisions
+ religious matters
+ affection
+ how much time with friends
+ hopes, dreams, vision, and purpose in life
+ amount of time spent together and separate
+ setting up a household
+ leisure time interests

Part Four

Oneness

11

Leaving

I will never forget standing up in front of the church at my wedding and listening to the preacher quote from the Old Testament: "In Genesis chapter two . . . ," he began.

Genesis two! I thought as my eyes rolled. *There are sixty-six books, including the New Testament—and the best he can do is start with the second chapter of Genesis? At least he could start with something interesting, like the Song of Solomon or Proverbs 31!*

My mind continued to wander as he drove home his points. *Better yet,* I thought, *he could refer to a more recent Old Testament book like Habakkuk or Haggai. No one reads a good verse from Habakkuk at weddings anymore.*

"Then the LORD God said, 'It is not good for the man to be alone,' " intoned the preacher. "I will make a helper who is right for him."

I snapped out of my mental drifting and thought, *Now he's talking.* I felt like yelling out, "Preach it, brother!"

The minister continued reading: "So the LORD God caused the man to sleep very deeply, and while he was asleep, God removed one of the man's ribs. Then God closed up the man's skin at the place where he took the rib. The LORD God used the rib from the man to make a woman, and then he brought the woman to the man. And the man said, 'Now, this is someone whose bones came from my bones, whose body comes from my body. I will call her "woman," because she was taken out of man.'"

By now, the preacher definitely had my full attention. Looking back, however, I wish I had more fully understood what he was *about* to read. This next verse is one of the most important passages a couple can apply in their relationship. If Erin and I had grasped this verse better, we would have saved ourselves years of relational pain and suffering. Although we didn't know it at the time, there is no better place to begin a wedding and a new marriage than in Genesis chapter two, verse twenty-four:

> *For this reason a man will leave his father and mother and cleave to his wife, and they will become one flesh. (Genesis 2:24 KJV)*

This verse hits the reader out of nowhere. In the span of seven verses, you read about how Adam named every animal, wild and tame, plus all the birds in the sky. No small task! You can't tell me that the entire process didn't slow down when he got to the duck-billed platypus. Anyway, at the end of all that, God puts Adam to sleep and rips out one of his ribs to create Eve. And it is at that point that what may be the most fundamental marital verse in all of Scripture gets thrown at us.

Unfortunately, a lot of us miss its significance—perhaps because it tends to get overshadowed by the next verse, which talks about two naked people. As if there is any guy in the world who could concentrate on the previous verse after hearing about naked people!

Nonetheless, verse twenty-four is where it's at.

Building the Proper Foundation

Understanding the significance of "leaving and cleaving" is one of the most important things you can do to prepare for your marriage. If the proper relational foundation is not put in place before you attempt to construct your marriage, then problems can—and almost certainly will—wreak havoc in your relationship.

So what does it mean to "leave and cleave"?

Few things are more important to your future marital relationship than understanding and acting upon these two words. In this chapter we will look at the first word, "leave," and give you some very practical advice about how to implement that divine instruction in your marriage. But first, I want to confess to you what a difficult time I had leaving my own family and cleaving to my wife.

After our honeymoon in Hawaii, Erin and I returned to Denver, Colorado. I was on summer break from graduate school and Erin had not yet started her job as a labor-and-delivery nurse, so we had some extra time to play around. We decided to drive up to Montana and Wyoming to visit Yellowstone National Park (the one with the Old Faithful geyser). We had a wonderful time getting to know each other as husband and wife.

The only problem was that our trip lasted only a week. Why only a week? Because I had committed us to joining my family on a trip to Europe. Although we felt a little hesitant at first about vacationing with my family so soon after our wedding, the lure of Europe proved too strong. So we figured, "Hey, it's only a few weeks. What could be wrong with that?"

Plenty, as it turned out.

Erin and I didn't realize that we had not yet "cleaved" as a married couple. So spending time with my family so soon immediately pulled me out of my role as husband and put me back into my role as a son.

The moment we arrived in England, Erin began to notice changes in me. "Why are you so quiet?" She'd ask. "Why don't you stand up for yourself?"

Of course, I got defensive and turned on her because it felt easier to argue with her than with my family. One time in particular, we stayed at a bed-and-breakfast in Bath, England. Late one night my sister and I had an altercation, and in Erin's opinion I failed to stand up for myself or us. We ended up arguing well into the night. We yelled and screamed, slinging awful words at each other.

But it got worse when we soon discovered our room had paper-thin walls. Even more disturbing, my sister and her new husband had a room to one side of us, while my parents had a room on the other. They all had clearly heard every negative word of our nasty argument.

At breakfast, my parents even asked if everything was okay. Erin and I both felt mortified.

I wish I could tell you that things quickly got better after that for Erin and me, and that we learned how to be a married couple around my family in Europe that summer. But we didn't. We continued to butt heads over issues directly related to leaving and cleaving. I made a number of poor choices during the trip that caused Erin to seriously question my loyalty as her husband. In fact, she says, "I wondered if I had made a mistake in marrying Greg. I just wanted to go home to my mommy. I had hives all over my body. I just wanted to get on the plane and get out of there." And being the spiritually mature giant I was, I thought, *What a momma's girl. I mean, come on! We have one little fight, and now you want to go home and scrap the whole thing?*

As a result of that disastrous three-week trip, we did serious damage to the foundation of our new marriage—damage that took years to undo.

Our European experience is one big reason why we're so passionate about leaving-and-cleaving issues. If you do not think through these concerns before you marry, you may innocently walk into some situations that could cause permanent harm to your union.

We have heard of couples who filed for divorce after only a few weeks of marriage, all because of difficulties with leaving and cleaving. Although Erin and I never got close to divorce, we did endure a great deal of relational pain—all unnecessary—because I failed to really leave my family and cleave to my wife.

If you think this all sounds crazy, then listen carefully to the following couple's story, told by a distraught woman named Krista.

My husband and I have been married barely two years, but already we have discussed divorce, due to his mother's actions. She mutated after our wedding, changing from a sweet and sincere woman to a manipulative, controlling, whining nag. My husband had been a bachelor until he was forty, permitting his mother to do everything for him. The problem was that she did not want anything to change after he became married. She still imposed her taste on our home decorations, even permanently hanging some tacky art on the walls.

Once, when I had stopped wallpapering the dining room to run an errand, she ripped several sheets of very expensive paper from the walls, telling me, "You wanted those sheets taken down. They were coming off at the corners, and I know you wanted me to take them down." That imposition cost me $200.

These are just a few of the things that have happened in our relationship. The biggest problem, however, is that my husband refuses to do anything about his mother. No matter how severely this woman runs over me emotionally, he minimizes the impact. His typical response is, "She's just being Mom. Cut her some slack—she's old and won't be around forever." What he doesn't understand is that if he continues to favor her over me, I won't be around forever.

You can't tell me that leaving and cleaving doesn't matter! It sure does to Krista, and it sure did to Erin early on in our relationship.

Calling All Men

If you're a man, listen up. Although leaving-and-cleaving issues are important to both the man and the woman, it's *especially* vital for the man. How tied a husband remains to his parents can make or break a new marriage, according to a new study on marital adjustment among newlywed couples.

Researchers discovered that a husband's lack of independence from both his parents was the biggest predictor for both spouses not adjusting well to the new marriage. Both spouses reported higher levels of adjustment and satisfaction in their marriages when the husbands were free from excessive guilt, anxiety, mistrust, responsibility, inhibition, resentment, and anger in relation to their mothers. The couples also were better adjusted in their new marriages when the husbands possessed a greater ability to manage and direct practical affairs without the help of their fathers.

Furthermore, wives' adjustment to marriage seemed to depend on how well the husbands separated from their parents, whereas husbands' adjustment to marriage depended on how well *both* spouses separated from their parents' influence.[1]

Additional research shows that men who divorced late (after twenty to fifty years of marriage) were premaritally more emotionally close to their mothers than those who remained married.[2] Likewise, men who divorced were likely as young adults to have depended strongly on their mothers.[3]

What It Means to "Leave"

Let's take a closer look at two specific aspects of "leaving" before we deal with the who and what we are to leave.

Separation

Webster's New World Dictionary defines leaving as "to go away from, to abandon, or to depart." Leaving first and foremost means to separate from someone or something.

What areas of your life will be difficult for you to detach and separate from? In a general sense, separation means that you forsake everything and everyone for the sake of your future spouse. In terms of your parents and family of origin, separation means that you leave the dependence, comfort, and security of your parents' authority. You are literally breaking apart the old parent-child relationship—"mommy" and "daddy" no longer exist for you as they once did. You are also separating from your siblings and extended family.

It's not that you are cutting ties with these dear people; instead, you are forging a new relationship with them, based on the fact that you are married and your highest-priority relationship has now become your spouse and you. You will also need to shift the priority of your friendships, separate from past romantic and opposite-sex relationships, and leave behind your single lifestyle.

Leave also means "to terminate association with." We love this part of the definition. Leaving literally means that you disengage from anything that could potentially interfere with your "cleaving" to your new spouse.

As we talk about disconnecting from family, friends, and past experiences, we are not talking about severing those relationships. Severing means that you totally cut off those relationships and allow them to die, in the same way you would amputate a diseased, dysfunctional limb. We don't advocate *that!* Instead, we encourage you to lessen the emphasis you formerly placed on previous core relationships.

Leave of Absence

Another way to look at this leaving is to think of it in the same way the military grants a leave of absence to its personnel. This is a time to be "absent from duty" or "the period for which this is granted." Interestingly, the Bible itself makes exactly this provision for newlyweds:

> *If a man has recently married, he must not be sent to war or have any other duty laid on him. For one year he is to be free to stay at home and bring happiness to the wife he has married. (Deuteronomy 24:5)*

As a couple forms a new marital relationship, the two need to be given permission to be absent from the duty of being someone's son, daughter, sibling, or friend. A new couple needs to be granted a period of time to formulate their new relationship without the pressure of maintaining other kinds of relationships. They literally need a "leave of absence" in which others do not expect the new couple to be proactively working on outside relationships.

A logical question might be, "how long should the leave of absence last?" After all, most workplaces give new parents six weeks leave of absence. Since couples differ, there is no standard amount of time. Instead, we encourage you to think about what specific things need to take place in order to cement your new relationship. Once those things occur, then you could end the leave of absence.

Remember the movie *Dances with Wolves?* In that film, a woman has to mourn for her dead husband for a specific amount of time, determined by her father, who had to sense when she had grieved long enough. Your time of absence will be up when you both feel you have bonded and cleaved to each other as man and wife.

One word of caution here: feeling a special closeness and bond as friends, boyfriend and girlfriend, and betrotheds is much different than cleaving as husband and wife. If you've had a long dating history or engagement, or if you've known each other many years, you still need extended time to become one as a married couple.

Erin and I had been good friends for three years and had been dating and engaged for almost two years, yet we still fell into the trap of going on an extended trip (in a twelve-seat van!) with my family right after we returned from our honeymoon. Big mistake! We should have used those months to cleave to one another, instead of hanging around my family for the summer.

Who or What Do You Leave?

We believe that the act of leaving involves withdrawal on several levels:

+ physically, mentally, emotionally, and spiritually breaking away from parents, siblings, and extended family
+ shifting the priority of your friendships
+ separation from past romantic and opposite-sex relationships

✦ leaving behind your single lifestyle

✦ resolving past emotional baggage

Leaving Parents and Family of Origin

A young couple got married and left on their honeymoon. Back at home for a few days, the bride called her mother.

"Well, how was the honeymoon?" asked the mother.

"Oh, Mama," she replied, "the honeymoon was wonderful! So romantic . . ." Suddenly she burst out crying. "But Mama, as soon as we returned, Sam started using the most horrible language. He's been saying things I've never heard before! All these awful, four-letter words! You've got to come get me and take me home! Please, Mama!"

"Emily, Emily," her mother said, "calm down! Tell me, what could be so awful? What four-letter words has he been using?"

"Please don't make me tell you, Mama," wept the daughter, "I'm so embarrassed! They're just too awful! You've got to come get me and take me home! Please, Mama!"

"Darling, baby, you *must* tell me what has you so upset. Tell your mother these horrible four-letter words!"

Still sobbing, the bride replied, "Oh, Mama . . . words like dust, wash, iron, and cook."

Unlike the young bride who wanted to run back to her mother, leaving your family means that you understand the change about to take place in your family constellation. You and your spouse will constitute a new family, greater in importance to you than your family of origin. This is where you go from being defined primarily as a son or daughter, to being a husband or wife. Although you will always be a son or daughter, the Bible insists that your primary identification will be as a husband or wife.

Your *immediate* family will be your wife or husband and your children. Your *extended* family will be both sets of parents, siblings and their families, and the horde of other relatives—grandparents, uncles and aunts, cousins, and the like.

Understand that we are not being picky or trying to split hairs. We want you to grasp the very real difference coming to your family constellation: the major difference between immediate family and extended family. Your primary allegiance is always to your immediate family. That is where your main loyalties and devotion are to reside. Your primary obligation and connection will be to your spouse, and then to any children that you may have, and no longer to your parents, siblings, grandparents, uncles and aunts, or cousins.

Leaving Friendships

It's extremely important to alter your priorities by making your extended family and friends secondary to your spouse. This intentional reorganization of your priorities will not need to be so rigid after you establish a new family system with your mate; after the appropriate foundation is in place, then you can begin to reintroduce extended family and friends into your marital relationship. But do not misunderstand! It is *imperative* to allow the leaving and cleaving process to take place.

And don't imagine that we discount friendships as a valuable and important part of married life. Erin feels so strongly about this issue that she recently coauthored an entire book on the importance of friendships in women's lives.[4] She says, "In the midst of coauthoring that book, I was amazed to discover the health benefits of women having close female friendships. Women who have healthy, intimate female friendships tend to live longer, have less incidence of cancer, get fewer respiratory infections, and typically have more energy to give their families. I cannot speak strongly enough to husbands to encourage their wives to form healthy friendships with other women. It will benefit not only their wives, but also the marriage. God created women to draw near other women in times of stress. This speaks to me profoundly, that God actually created women to be deeply ministered to through female friendships."

The Scriptures offer us a look at some precious female friendships, females who deeply ministered to one another. Think about how Ruth followed Naomi to a foreign country, leaving her family and giving up all she ever knew. Ruth clung to her mother-in-law after Naomi had told her to leave not just once—but four times! Elizabeth and Mary are another great example of the amazing support you get from your girlfriends. Right after finding out she was carrying Christ, Mary went to Elizabeth's home and stayed with her for about three months (Luke 1:39–56). I can only imagine how much wisdom, faith, joy, and reassurance Elizabeth offered Mary when she found herself in an unexpected situation. Two female researchers from UCLA found that during high-stress times, women *congregated* together, while men seemed to *isolate* from others.[5]

We are huge advocates of friendships! What changes after marriage is the *priority* of those friendships. Although this shift in priorities might be more difficult for couples who remain in their hometowns, it is necessary to say, "My priority is my spouse, and that means my friendships need to take a backseat now." Friendships will always be important, but your marital relationship must always come first. That's the way to create a home that feels like the safest place on earth.

Leaving Past Romantic and Opposite-Sex Relationships

Many engaged couples ask us, "are opposite-sex friends okay when you're married?" The answer is this: while many people who get married have long-term, opposite-sex friendships, those friendships, great when they were single, may not be appropriate in marriage.

The best advice here comes from King Solomon: "My son, preserve sound judgment and discernment, do not let them out of your sight; they will be life for you, an ornament to grace your neck. Then you will go on your way in safety, and your foot will not stumble" (Proverbs 3:21–23). Distancing yourself from previous romantic relationships is a wise move and helps to put safety into your relationship both during your engagement and after your marriage.

Erin dated Jack in high school and off and on through college, and when they broke up for the last time, they became great friends. They continued talking frequently on the phone until we got engaged; then the calls subsided.

After our wedding, however, we discovered that Jack was living on the same island where we had our honeymoon. He harmlessly invited us to visit him. I remember saying, "It's nice that he invited us over and all, but it is a little strange to be going to visit your former boyfriend on our honeymoon." Erin respected my feelings and didn't push the issue.

Ironically, the next day on the beach, we ran smack into one of *my* former girlfriends. She was also honeymooning in Hawaii! What are the chances?

Several years later, Erin received a phone call from Jack. She hadn't heard from him in several years, but he called to let her know he was in California (where we were in school) and wanted to stop by that weekend to say hello. She really did want to see him—not romantically, but because he truly was a special friend in her life. That weekend, however, I was traveling out of town. Erin considered meeting Jack somewhere, but deep inside she knew she needed to protect our marriage, and so she declined the meeting. She was keenly aware of the importance of keeping distance, both emotionally and physically, from previous romantic relationships.

Do you continue to have interactions with a previous romantic interest? Have you allowed your fiancé to influence how you continue this friendship? We cannot stress enough the importance of guarding your relationship from outside romantic influences. *No* old friendship is worth running the risk of injuring your relationship.

Although it's possible for a married couple to have healthy opposite-sex friendships, we tend to err on the side of extreme caution. We made a decision early in our marriage that it was not okay for us to have opposite-sex friends. It's not that we ignore people; instead, we do not nurture those friendships apart from each other.

If you are wondering whether some close friendship with a person of the opposite sex might pose a threat to your future marriage, Dr. Todd Linaman has developed a list of questions for you to answer. He asks:

+ Is your future mate unaware of your opposite-sex friendship?
+ Would you ever behave differently around your friend if your future spouse were present?
+ Would you feel uncomfortable if your fiancé had the same quality of friendship with someone of the opposite sex?
+ Do you prefer to spend time alone with your opposite-sex friend, rather than in a group setting?
+ Are you physically and/or emotionally attracted to your friend?
+ Is your friend someone you would consider dating if you were single?
+ Have you ever entertained romantic fantasies about your friend?
+ Do you ever compare your future spouse to your friend?
+ Do you think about sharing important news with your friend before you speak about it to your fiancée?
+ Do you and your friend ever exchange highly personal details about your lives or complain about your relationships to each other?
+ Do you often reference or talk about your friend with others?
+ Has your future spouse ever expressed concern about your friendship?
+ Is your relationship with your friend ever a source of tension or conflict between you and your future spouse?
+ Have you ever ignored or minimized your fiancé's requests to end or modify the relationship with your friend?
+ Have you ever deceived or misled your future spouse about matters concerning your friendship?

+ Has anyone other than your future spouse ever cautioned you about your opposite-sex friendship?
+ Do you do things with your friend that your fiancée is unwilling or uninterested in doing?
+ Does your friend fulfill needs that you wish your future spouse would meet?

If you answered yes to one or more of these questions, then your opposite-sex friendship poses a real threat to the quality of your upcoming marriage. It may be in the best interest of your relationship either to significantly limit or actually end your close friendship. Be completely honest with yourself and your future spouse, and pray that God will give you the wisdom, discernment, and courage to do what is best.[6]

If you choose to have these kinds of friendships, you need to create strong boundaries around them, especially if you ever dated the person. For example, it wouldn't be okay if I innocently met a female friend for coffee on a regular basis to shoot the breeze. We apply this boundary even to opposite-sex work colleagues. I would never take a female colleague out to lunch alone or travel alone with a female. When faced with this dilemma, I have taken separate flights or taken another male along. If this isn't possible because of your boss's decision, talk about what the boundaries need to be so both of you feel comfortable. Here's the bottom line: make sure you're committed to guarding your relationship from even the *tiniest* virus. While it is possible for married people to have healthy opposite-sex friendships, we highly encourage you to maintain some clear boundaries:

+ Nurture a best-friend relationship with your future spouse.
+ Develop and consistently nurture close relationships with same-sex friends.
+ Make sure your future spouse knows your friend and is completely comfortable with the type and level of interaction you have with him or her.

+ Honor your fiancé's wishes concerning your friendship—even if it means ending that relationship.

+ Avoid establishing close friendships with opposite-sex singles.

+ Avoid developing a close friendship with someone to whom you are physically and/or emotionally attracted.

+ Avoid close opposite-sex friendships if you are struggling in your premarital relationship.

+ Don't share with others what you haven't shared with your fiancée.

+ Regularly discuss the nature of your friendships with your future spouse.

+ Although it can be healthy to get an opposite-sex perspective, you should not regularly share intimate issues with someone who is not your spouse-to-be.

Do you know our real concern? Even a totally innocent relationship could end up causing unnecessary harm to your future spouse and marriage, if you don't keep it closely in check. If you want a home that feels like the safest place on earth, then you must pay careful attention here.

Leaving Your Single Lifestyle

As you get married, you must leave something behind: your single lifestyle. Realize that many of the life patterns you have established may be difficult to change just because you say "I do." Perhaps you'll have to stop hanging out with friends after work. Or maybe you must change your habit of leaving your laundry piled up until you have nothing left to wear. Or again, it may be changing your pattern of neglecting grocery shopping until you have nothing left but a gallon of milk in the fridge.

It's difficult to pinpoint every area of challenge, because going from single to married means something different for each of us. How you and your future spouse join your two worlds and how well your prior single lifestyles overlap will determine how much the impending change of your marital status will impact you. The number of years you have been single may also impact your adjustment. Those who marry at an older age may have more difficulty breaking away from some things related to their single lives.

One of our dear friends got married later in life. He married a younger woman, and they often talked about their different tendencies. Sam would often be ready for bed by 8:30 p.m., when Michelle was just getting going; she often invited people over about this time. Michelle also quickly learned that Sam used only white towels for showering; therefore, she returned all the vibrant-colored towels she received as wedding gifts. Although neither minded finding win-win solutions to their differences, they quickly learned how different many of their habits really were.

Before we got married, Erin had become quite accustomed to working out around 10:00 a.m. every day, because she worked the 3:00–11:00 p.m. shift. She would work out, meet her friends at the mall food court for a fun lunch, then go home, shower, and go to work. She would return home around 12:30–1:00 a.m., and her roommates and she would stay up until 2:00–3:00 a.m., talking and catching up on the day.

Once we got married, all of that changed.

She had no idea that I didn't share her love of the very late hours of the night. One of our first nights in our new apartment, I jumped in bed at 9:30 p.m. Erin felt stunned, then fought an internal battle over whether she should also climb in bed. She soon learned that I had *never* pulled an all-nighter all the way through college. That was second nature for Erin; she thought that when you have a bunch to do, you just stay up until it is done. I would much rather go to bed early and then get up early the next morning to complete a task.

And eating at the food court every day was out of the question. I thought it cost too much money and was unhealthy, and anyway I preferred to watch TV while I ate my tuna or turkey sandwich.

So as a thoughtful new husband, I went out and purchased Erin a new stationary bicycle so she could work out at home with me. She quickly realized, however, that part of why she liked working out at a gym was to be with a large group of people while she listened to the music and activity going on around her. I couldn't understand why she still wanted a membership to a gym.

As you can see, neither of us tried to tell the other that his or her ideas were right or wrong, better or worse. They were just different! And that's our point. Married life will bring different ways of doing things, and ultimately this may lead you to grieve the loss of your single lifestyle.

Leaving Past Emotional Baggage

Although we all carry emotional baggage into marriage, the goal here is to make sure your baggage amounts to small carry-on pieces instead of steamer trunks full of traumatic issues. Perhaps you're dealing with the effects of your parents' divorce or your own failed previous marriage; with overcoming thoughts of former romantic relationships; the issue of premarital sex; a pregnancy or abortion; past abuse; dysfunctional families; controlling relationships; and so on.

The key is to understand that you will need to work through the issues that you did not have to work entirely through before because you could just walk away from them. If you know of some issue that you fear will negatively impact your upcoming marriage, we cannot encourage you enough to seek a counselor's help.

Although we cannot deal with every conceivable past issue here, Erin and I do want to focus on one important question that repeatedly comes up in our counseling sessions: how do we regain our virginity before getting married? Even if you are a virgin, don't skip this section. We will provide valuable information that can help you maintain your virginity, as well.

Two brooms hanging in the closet got to know each other so well that after some time they decided to get married. (Of course, one broom was the bride broom and the other the groom broom.)

Come the wedding day, the bride broom stunned everyone in her white dress, while the groom broom looked handsome and suave in his tuxedo. They had a lovely ceremony, and at the reception dinner the bride broom leaned over and said to the groom broom, "I think I am going to have a little whisk broom!"

"Impossible!" replied the groom broom. "We haven't even swept together!"

We wish the problem were as slight as our bad joke. Unfortunately, untold numbers of couples today are "sweeping" together before marriage. Premarital sex is a reality for millions of engaged couples. Even thousands of Christian couples are falling sexually.

In 1997, we surveyed our seminar attendees—mostly Christian couples who reported having a good relationship with each other—about their sexual history. It shocked us to learn that 79 percent reported they had engaged in premarital sex. Furthermore, 67 percent reported they had engaged in premarital sex with their current spouse.

Like many other Christian young people, when I was in college, I also fell to sexual temptation. As a result, one of the most painful experiences of my engagement was telling Erin that I hadn't "waited" for her. Nothing is worse than trying to explain to someone you love why you did not wait. The pain is almost beyond description.

To this day, I wish I could have glimpsed that future sorrowful conversation back when I was making choices about my virginity. Perhaps through that peek into my future, I would have seen Erin's face as she tearfully accepted my confession and grieved her own premarital mistakes. Maybe I would have seen how Erin had to suffer through thoughts of inadequacy and comparison. I would not wish that day or conversation on anyone!

To some, the thought of regaining a lost virginity may seem ludicrous. We do not intend to mislead anyone here. The physical act of sexual intercourse cannot be undone. And the consequences—some of them lifelong—that go along with violating God's principles cannot be dismissed, either.

But the good news is that a person's body is only part of his or her being. When we speak of regaining one's virginity, we are talking about the emotional, mental, and spiritual aspects as well. The following four steps will help you to regain and maintain your virginity.

Turn to Christ through confession and repentance. Making God your first love again begins with confession and repentance. The word *confession* simply means to "admit it" when you know your actions grieve God. It's agreeing with God that your behavior is not His best for you. It's naming your behavior for what it is: sin.

In addition to confession, repentance is necessary. *Repentance* means to "turn around and go in the opposite direction." This means to stop your sinful behavior and go the other way. It's doing a 180-degree turn. The Bible says to run from anything that takes us away from God's best (see 2 Timothy 2:22).

As we turn back toward God, He promises *that all things become new to those who are in Christ Jesus* (see 2 Corinthians 5:17). The Almighty God can restore anyone who has fallen—no matter how far. This is a major theme throughout the Bible. We can point to many individuals who once lived lifestyles of disobedience to God, but when they confessed their sin and repented of it, He restored them completely. The same can be true of you.

Forgive yourself by treasure hunting the pain of the sexual experience. I lived for years with the guilt "stain" of my premarital sexual experience, but I could have lived with the restored sense of joy and freedom that God clearly gives to the repentant, regardless of the past sin.

God loves to bring "beauty" out of "ashes,"[7] and it's our job to locate these precious gifts by "treasure hunting." We treasure hunt by looking for any shred of positive residue left behind by some difficult trial. A trial such as premarital sex might produce things like increased sensitivity, empathy, humility, or a renewed desire for a relationship with Christ. Find whatever gifts are buried under the pain or hurt of losing your virginity. By discovering these treasures, you can greatly increase the value of your painful experiences.

Become aware of your choices, and build a buffer zone away from sexual temptation. I believe it was Edwin Hubbel Chapin who once said, "Every action of our lives touches on some chord that will vibrate in eternity." Do you realize that every action you take has a lasting impact on yourself and others? Even the smallest movement can have a major impact. Like throwing a tiny pebble into the lake, you never know how far the ripples with reach.

One thing that can lead to making a poor choice is rationalization. We rationalize when we use statements such as, "It's no big deal," "It's all right—everyone's doing it," "I'm not hurting anyone," "It's only wrong if you get caught," or "Trust me!" These statements can start a tragic pattern. Each time you cross a line, no matter how small the step, you risk stepping out of bounds.

Stepping out of bounds is a major factor in the battle for your virginity. As you develop purity, it's crucial to learn where to draw new lines. Personal lines consist of things such as: how far you will go on a date; what type of clothes you wear; how much time you spend alone together; how much kissing you do; and whether to watch R-rated movies. Everyone is different, so every couple needs to draw its own lines. But we *all* need to draw many lines, or we risk tragedy.

During a football game, have you ever noticed which part of the field gets most damaged? It's usually the middle. This is true because the closer a player gets to the sideline, the more likely he is to run out of bounds. So he typically tries to stay away from them. Satan, like an opposing football team, tries to get us to step out of bounds. The closer we get to the sideline, the closer Satan gets to influencing our lives.

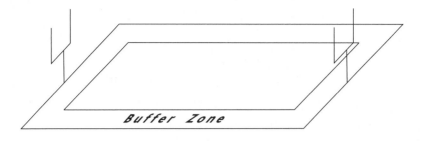

As Dr. Gary Oliver notes in the book *Seven Promises of a Promise Keeper,* the key is creating a new sideline—ten yards away from the original line.[8] In other words, leave room for error. If you have had sex, then you need to develop a new purity line. For some, the new line won't permit going beyond kissing or holding hands, or may prescribe a no-contact period. If the former line allowed kissing, then stepping ten yards back might be not kissing while lying down or no passionate kissing. Since everyone makes mistakes, having room before you step out of bounds may mean the difference between losing a few yards and losing the game.

In addition to forming new lines, you need to stop asking what's *wrong* with certain choices. Instead, you need to ask what's *right* with them. A great question to ask is, "How will this decision lead to the enrichment of myself and others?" If we can decide based on whether our actions are moving us closer to or further away from purity, then we will have won a major battle. If we desire virginity, then we must carefully watch our choices to ensure that they bring us closer to, and not further away from, Christ.

Seek out accountability. One of the most important ways to help maintain or regain your virginity is to become accountable to someone, whether to a family member, friend, coach, counselor, or pastor. Or it might be to a group of people who have made a similar commitment to purity. Accountability greatly improves your ability to say no to sex before marriage.

Accountability is simply being responsible to another person or persons for goals and commitments you have made. When you become accountable to someone, the important ingredient is giving that person the right to ask the difficult questions: "Did you compromise your standards on your date last night?" or "Have you given in to sexual temptation this week?" Such questions force you to carefully and prayerfully consider your choices, because you know that someone will be checking.

And what a great source of strength when you face difficult times! If you desire to be pure, we encourage you to ask a mature friend, youth minister, teacher, or coach for accountability. And then begin praying for the right person to come around. As this person begins to work in your life, you will understand why Ecclesiastes 4:9–12 says,

> *Two are better than one,*
> > *because they have a good return for their work:*
>
> *If one falls down,*
> > *his friend can help him up.*
> > *But pity the man who falls*
> > *and has no one to help him up!*
>
> *Also, if two lie down together, they will keep warm.*
> > *But how can one keep warm alone?*
>
> *Though one may be overpowered,*
> > *two can defend themselves.*
> > *A cord of three strands is not quickly broken.*

Next Stop on the
Marital-Oneness Train

To begin your exciting journey on the train toward marital oneness, two things are required, according to Genesis chapter two: Leaving father and mother, leaving the past, leaving your old way of doing and thinking—and cleaving to one another. Let's take a look at cleaving next.

COUPLE EXERCISES/HOMEWORK

1. What could potentially interfere with you "cleaving" to your future spouse?

2. What areas of your life will be difficult for you to detach and separate from when you get married (e.g., parents, siblings, extended family, friends, habits, past experiences, past romantic relationships, certain opposite-sex friendships, past emotional baggage, etc.)?

3. What things or relationships need to be shifted in terms of priorities so that your highest priority is your spouse?

4. What will it look like for you to leave your single lifestyle behind? Are there specific things from your single lifestyle that you are worried about giving up or that will change now that you are getting married?

5. As a married person, describe what a new relationship will look like with the following people:
    + your mom
    + your dad
    + your sibling(s)
    + your extended family (grandparents, aunts, uncles, cousins, etc.)
    + your best friends
    + your opposite-sex friends or coworkers.

6. Talk about how you will communicate to both sets of parents, siblings, extended family, friends, colleagues, church members, and pastors that you are taking a "leave of absence" to strengthen your new marriage.

7. Talk about how you will communicate (both in words and actions) to your new spouse that your loyalties, devotions, and allegiance are to him/her.

8. What boundaries will you need around opposite-sex friendships and work colleagues?

9. How will you and your future spouse join your two worlds (single lifestyles)? What concerns do you have about joining your two lifestyles? Talk about things like breakfast preferences, exercise routines, TV habits, cleaning preferences, hanging out with friends, laundry preferences, making the bed, which side of the bed to sleep on, meal times, eating out, who will grocery shop, cook, do dishes, take out the trash, mow the lawn, etc.

10. We strongly encourage you to spend at least six sessions with a counselor to talk about the emotional baggage you both are bringing into the marriage (i.e., dysfunctional family, effects of your parents' divorce, effects from a former romantic relationship, premarital sex, a pregnancy or abortion, past abuse, controlling relationships, etc.).

12

Cleaving

When Bill and Mary got married, they couldn't afford a honeymoon, so they went back to Bill's parents' home for their first night together. In the morning, Bill's little brother, Johnny, got up and had his breakfast. As he was going out the door to school, he asked his mom if Bill and Mary had gotten up yet.

"No," she replied.

"Do you know what I think?" Johnny asked.

"I don't want to hear what you think!" his mom shouted. "Just go to school."

Johnny came home for lunch and asked his mom, "Are Bill and Mary up yet?"

"No," she replied.

"Do you know what I think?" he asked again.

"Never mind what you think!" his mom replied once more. "Eat your lunch and go back to school."

After school, Johnny came home and asked for a third time, "Are Bill and Mary up yet?"

"No," said his mother, this time a little concern in her voice.

"Do you know what I think?" Johnny asked again.

"Okay, now tell me what you think."

"Last night," Johnny said, "Bill came to my room for the Vaseline . . . and I think I gave him my airplane glue."

How's that for cleaving?

Great marriages involve two people committed to their own personal journeys and eager to help each other along the way. Although we are not responsible for each other's individual journey, we do have the opportunity to love, honor, encourage, and assist each other in those journeys. The Lord said this clearly in Genesis 2:18 when He declared, "It is not good for the man to be alone. I will make a *helper* suitable for him."

You are to be a "helpmate" or an "assistant" to your future spouse in his or her journey. This is what Erin and I believe cleaving means—coming together as one to assist each other to become more like Christ. Remember, God created marriage for male-female companionship, so that each mate could assist the other on this journey toward become increasingly like Jesus.

And yet, God also said something else—admittedly, something a little unexpected. Despite everything we just pointed out, He also said, "It is not good for the man to be alone."

It Is Not Good for Man to Be Alone

God's purpose for marriage is that you become Christlike. But He also created marriage for male-female companionship, to provide mutual assistance on this journey to become increasingly like Christ.

From God's perspective, everything in the garden was good except for Adam's being alone. Adam's loneliness was more than not having others around. His aloneness resulted from having no one around *suitable* for him. He had no one to complement him, and by that we mean everything from biological to complex psychological and spiritual complementation. He was the solo piece of a puzzle, designed for another piece where none yet existed.

After seeing Eve, his future mate, Adam understood this profound truth. He realized God had made male and female for each other, and so he cried out, "together she and I are one bone, one flesh"—in essence, one being.

Do you begin to see now why pursuing God's design for marriage is essential if you want to help fulfill God's purposes for mankind?

God's design (not purpose) for marriage is for a man and a woman, in all their masculine and feminine differences, to come together and become "one." Married individuals are not carbon copies of each other, but two people who are both being transformed into the image of Christ. The more each individual in a couple is transformed into the image of Christ, the more both can move toward oneness. God's design is that by moving toward oneness with your future spouse, you will learn to love, you will mature, and you will develop as a human in a way impossible in any other relationship. Put simply, marriage makes us more like God wants us to be.

When God created man and woman, His goal was that "the two shall become one flesh." God's design for marriage is that two people with completely different orientations to life—one male, the other female— might yet experience oneness.

Genesis tells us when two people marry, they begin the process of becoming one. What does this mean exactly? Oneness in marriage is about reflecting the oneness that we have with Christ. Jesus talked about oneness in John 17:23, "I in them and you in me. May they be brought to complete unity . . ." This happens as two hearts become united together in marriage.

So Who's Responsible?

Every marriage begins with two individuals, each on a journey to become the fullest expression of who God created each one to be—conformed to the image of the Lord. Each journey is unique, and each individual has his or her own needs, desires, challenges, and obstacles.

The responsibility for each person's individual journey lies with the individual. That means you are 100 percent responsible for your journey, and your future spouse is 100 percent responsible for his or her journey. The future husband is completely responsible for becoming the man God created and called him to be, while the future wife is totally responsible for becoming the woman God created and called her to be.

When you stand before the Lord some day to give an account of your journey toward Christlikeness, what didn't work for Adam will most certainly not work for you: "The man said, 'The woman you put here with me—she gave me some fruit from the tree, and I ate it' " (Genesis 3:12). Blaming your future spouse will not fly any better for you than it did for Adam. You and you alone are utterly responsible for becoming conformed to the image of Christ.

When viewed correctly, marriage can be a great adventure. An incorrect view of it, however, will leave you feeling lost and confused, like dazed out-of-towners. But this journey becomes the essence of what God wants to do with you. In the journey lies the destination.

Remember, the most important opportunity we have in marriage is to help our spouse become like Christ. And that, of course, means cleaving.

How Do You Cleave?

Let's take a closer look at the specific aspects of cleaving. Cleaving involves two key components:

- ✦ Creating a marital identity out of two distinct personalities
- ✦ Bonding (or attaching) to your mate

Creating a Marital Identity

The marital journey is about pursuing a common goal of creating a Christ-centered marriage where you share His love and glorify Him. Both the husband and the wife have equal responsibility to create a great marriage that glorifies God.

Marriage is like the unity-candle display that many couples use in their weddings: three candles—two short ones on the outside representing the bride and groom as individuals, and a taller one in the center representing their marriage.

If you haven't seen the unity-candle ceremony, here's how it works. The three candles are placed at the front of the church. At a time early in the ceremony, someone lights the outside candles, leaving the one in the middle unlit. The two lit candles represent the bride and groom before the wedding. They walk into the church separately; they are still single. The moment the bride and groom say their vows before God, however, they're not single anymore. They're married. They're united. The two become one.

So after saying their vows, the husband and wife approach the three candles. They take the individual candles, and using the two separate flames, they light the center candle.

The symbolism is beautiful and obvious. No longer will their lights burn for themselves alone. No longer will they live as two single people. Instead, they will enjoy one brighter light, a light that represents the oneness of their marriage.

Few things are more beautiful than the flame of a unity candle burning brightly during a wedding ceremony. It pictures the truth that in marriage the two become one. Oneness is the strength of marriage, a safe harbor. It is the place where the couple becomes stronger than either partner separately.

If you plan on using the unity candle in your wedding, do you understand what you plan to do? Erin and I used it, but had no real idea of its enormous significance. Today, we believe that this simple candle ceremony suggests the secret of oneness: the ability to let go of our single status and join with each other for the rest of our lives.

The lack of oneness that causes many people to suffer in unrewarding and disheartening marriages occurs because one or both spouses remain more devoted to the flame of self than to the one flame of the union. If you remain more focused on yourself than on what's good for your upcoming marriage, then conflicts inevitably will arise—conflicts that can ultimately blow out your unity candle.

"Then quit!" I yelled at Erin. "I'm tired of hearing you complain about your job—just quit!" She sat across the room, giving me her best evil eye.

"Sure, it's easy for you to tell me to quit when you aren't the one working right now," she replied. She was steaming over how I spent my leisurely days with my friend, John, while John's wife, Julie, and Erin worked all day. We would go to one or two graduate classes per day and then decide how we wanted to fill our time until the ladies got home to make us dinner. Quite the life—basketball, movies, lunch buffets, naps, Nintendo.

Working as a labor-and-delivery nurse, Erin was dealing with life-and-death situations every moment. She happened to work on a high-risk unit where patients had so many other health issues that most had been told to never try having a baby. She had reached her maximum stress quota dealing with this new job and leaving her family, friends, and a city that she had called home for most of her life. She didn't know how to get around this new city, and she definitely didn't know how to deal with cold weather and snow.

And then her new husband, me, was out having a great time all day while she worked. How *dare* my only response be, "Then quit!"

She had no backrubs waiting for her when she returned home, no dinner on the table, no "let's go out tonight" or "you spend tomorrow out shopping while I do the laundry!" She felt hopeless with the whole situation. All she wanted was some compassion and understanding and sympathy. She got none.

From my point of view, of course, everything seemed to be working out just fine. I felt perfectly content with my luxurious lifestyle. "Hey, it's *you* with the problem," I reminded her. "*I'm* not the one complaining!"

When a short time later we visited our mentor couple to discuss our very different takes on our first few months of marital bliss, they gently reminded us that we both had remained more focused on ourselves than on what was good for our marriage.

The Bible says that when a husband and wife join as a couple, they become "one flesh," united into one (see Genesis 2:24; Matthew 19:5–6). The two become bonded together, woven together, blended together. *One.*

When you leave the church after the ceremony, you will no longer be single and separate. If you continue to function as separate people, your marriage will feel completely unsafe. The secret is learning how to *blend* the two in a way that will honor both partners and bring a heightened sense of unity.

The two single flames become one.

The husband and wife become one.

Let's use another image that may help you understand the importance of oneness, to better grasp the blending that must go on if two single people are to be united.

Picture the groom with his distinct personality, his uniqueness as a male, the issues and influence from his family of origin, his goals and dreams. Then assign a color to that unique blend of factors: let's say the color blue.

Next, picture the bride, with her own distinct personality, her uniqueness as a female, her own issues and influence from her family of origin, her own goals and dreams—and these may be very different from those of her groom. Assign a very different color to her: perhaps yellow.

Now go back to the unity candle. If the groom is represented by a blue candle, and the bride is represented by a yellow candle, then what color would their unity candle be? What color would represent their oneness? You're right: green. When these two people come together to become one, they take their separate lives (blue and yellow) and weave them together in a very special way to become one (green). The more they blend and weave their differences, the more intimacy and love they will feel. And the safer their home will be.

Now let us make a very important point. In every wedding we've been a part of, we have encouraged the couple not to blow out the flames of the individual candles after they have lit the center candle. Why? We want to continuously seed the fact that becoming one (green) does not mean both people have suddenly become exactly the same. Oneness does not mean sameness. You still are responsible for your blueness or yellowness; you are still responsible for becoming like Christ. You do not abandon your own individual journeys. This is why we don't like couples to blow out their single candles. Instead, we want the marriage candle to be larger than the two individual candles. Represented by this large, center candle, we want the couple to clearly realize that they are now also responsible for a third journey, the marriage. You are equally responsible for the health of your "green" marriage. It is both of your jobs to create a marriage that thrills you both.

And how do you accomplish this? It has everything to do with cleaving to your spouse.

Bonding to Your Mate

After your relationship with God, your marriage should be your top priority. Throughout the Bible, marriage is portrayed as a visible picture of Christ's love for the church. This begs the question: if marriage is such a high priority to God, then why do couples struggle with prioritizing their spouse and marriage?

Your wedding ceremony will not magically transform your relationship into a marriage—at least not the type of marriage God desires for you. The marriage ceremony is more like the first day of kindergarten than it is like a graduation ceremony. It's not the culmination, but the beginning.

Commit right now to putting your marriage first. Trust us, this is much more difficult than you may realize! We know that you can't wait to get married, to spend the rest of your lives together, loving each other. We know; we remember that feeling. We recall thinking the same thing: *there is nothing that will get in the way of our time together!*

But talk to older couples. Most will tell you that life just sneaks up on you, and then, all of a sudden, you feel as if you're married to your roommate. No one starts out with this as a goal! No one enters marriage thinking, *I can't wait for life to consume us to the point that I start to feel lonely in my marriage.* The Evil One wants nothing more than to snare you into the vicious trap of busyness. In fact, it's astonishing how many demands get placed on our time:

+ parents
+ extended family (in-laws, siblings, grandparents, etc.)
+ work
+ school
+ friends
+ church
+ hobbies
+ ministry opportunities
+ TV

The key is to remember that *your marriage is the most important relationship next to God* and needs to be put in front of all else. Unfortunately, many couples act like their relationship will magically grow stronger after the wedding with little or no effort on their part. That's like putting some expensive fish into a new aquarium and then doing nothing else to it. My six-year-old son, Garrison, just recently received several goldfish for his birthday. We set up the aquarium next to his bed. I then helped him spread out the colorful rocks, place the water plants, coral formations, and shark statues around the tank, and then we filled it with water. He was so excited to watch his fish swim and play. I'll never forget Garrison giving me the biggest hug and saying, "I love you so much . . . you're the best daddy ever!"

I'm sure this is how most newly wed couples start off, as well.

To be honest, I had no idea what these goldfish needed to thrive. I just thought, *How hard can it be? Just give them food, keep water in the tank, and everything should be fine.* Boy was I wrong.

Several weeks later, I found Garrison in his room crying. "Something is wrong with my fish!" When I inspected the tank, you could barely see the fish through the green slime and algae. Sadly, one of his fish had died as a result of living in a home no better than a cesspool.

Over the years, I have watched many marriages turn green and slimy as the result of being ignored. Ask yourself: How important will my marriage be to me? Do I put in the effort that shows this relationship with my fiancé is a top priority for me?

If you want to show your fiancée how valuable the relationship truly is to you, you must be willing right now, before the wedding, to put in the necessary time and energy to build a great relationship. Make a commitment to yourself that you will maintain a *whatever it takes* attitude for the rest of your life.

The reality is that marriage is difficult! All marriages experience peaks and valleys. Real-life marriage contains dreams that come true and dreams that go unfulfilled. Having a great, God-honoring marriage will take hard work. Make that your expectation. You will face a seemingly endless stream of choices, both small and large, that will dictate the health of your future marriage. Marriage is a balancing act of careers, kids, maintaining a home, paying bills, cooking meals, church, alone time, date nights, family, friends and in-laws. Sadly, for many couples, the one you're supposed to love "until death do you part" often gets lost in the chaos of life.

Start working now to put activities into your life *together* that will help you to enjoy and encourage each other as husband and wife, as well as to foster talking, learning, and growing together.

We reveal our priorities by our actions. Answer the following questions:

+ How do I spend my time?
+ How do I invest my money?
+ How do I use my energy?

Once you answer those three questions, you'll have the answer to, "What are my real priorities?"

Love: An Act of Will

Love is an act of will, both an intention and an action. The Bible says, "Let us not love with words or tongue but with actions and in truth" (1 John 3:18).

It takes both *saying* you love your future spouse and proving it by how *you live out what you say* to show what kind of love you truly have. Words are great, but words alone—even religious words, spiritual words, words of faith—have to be backed up with solid, loving action.

A young woman brought her fiancé home to meet her parents. After dinner, her mother told her father to find out about the young man. The father invited the fiancé to his study for a talk.

"So, what are your plans?" the father asked the young man.

"I am a biblical scholar," he replied.

"A biblical scholar. Hmmm," the father said. "Admirable, but what will you do to provide a nice house for my daughter to live in?"

"I will study," the young man replied, "and God will provide for us."

"And how will you buy her a beautiful engagement ring, such as she deserves?" asked the father.

"I will concentrate on my studies," the young man replied, "and God will provide for us."

"And children?" asked the father. "How will you support children?"

"Don't worry, sir, God will provide," replied the fiancé.

The conversation proceeded like that; each time the father questioned him, the young idealist insisted that God would provide.

Later, the mother asked, "How did it go, honey?"

"He has no job and no plans," the father replied, "and he thinks I'm God."

Real love, genuine love, takes both sincere words and practical action. If you want to cleave to your future spouse, then you will have to stock up on both.

Cleaving as a couple involves discovering and deeply understanding what you need from each other to feel loved. To encourage the process of genuine cleaving, you need to get familiar with each of your relational needs.

What Makes You Feel Loved?

To give you an idea what a relational need looks like, let me tell you about a time I almost drove my car into the Mississippi River.

One day Erin and I were driving from Springfield, Missouri, to Nashville, Tennessee, to attend a conference. In the days leading up to the trip, Erin had asked me to consult AAA about the best way to get to Nashville. As a guy, I resented her request and felt I could get us there as well as AAA could. I spent several hours diligently studying maps, and soon realized, unfortunately, that no road goes in a straight line from Springfield to Nashville. This was very painful for me. The only thing I remembered from high school math was the "shortest distance between two points is a straight line" principle. And how could I let Mr. Stark, my high-school geometry teacher, down?

So I continued to study the maps in order to draft as straight a route as I could. Finally, I was done. I had done the impossible! I had found a route that was basically a straight line. As I stood back to bask in the glory of my accomplishment, I knew that I had to share my success with "the boys." I knew Erin would not appreciate my route like my guy friends would, so I summoned some male friends. As each one held up my map, it was as if they were holding directions to the Holy Grail. Their eyes moved slowly up and down the page, while they uttered things like, "wow" . . . "unbelievable" . . . "impossible" . . . "you da man!"

I must admit, I had impressed myself.

When word of my accomplishment finally reached Erin, I did not receive praise or applause. No homage, not even simple adoration. *Nothing.*

To make matters worse, she begged and pleaded for me to have someone check out my route. Her suggestion deeply offended me. For guys all around the world, I was not going to cave in and ask for directions. At this point, I had much more riding on our trip than simply getting there. Men everywhere were counting on me to show my wife that I could find the way.

Several hours into the trip, I felt great. My route was *perfect*. We were thirty minutes ahead of AAA's schedule. I was king of the road!

But then disaster struck.

Erin and I were laughing and singing, just as the sun began to dip behind the scenery. We had a great view and miles back she had stopped asking if I really knew where we were. Then all of a sudden, Erin said, "Did you see that sign? I swear it read 'dead end.'"

"Nice try," I joked, "You just can't admit that I was right and you were wrong."

"I'm serious," she insisted, "I think this road dead ends."

"This road does *not* dead end," I shot back, "Don't worry. Trust me!"

Have you ever uttered something you wish you could take back? For me, "don't worry, trust me" remains one of those sayings.

We continued to drive for about an hour without either of us speaking a word, waiting for the truth to be revealed. The surrounding area began to be less and less populated until it became cornfields as far as the eye could see. And then it happened.

Dead end!

I barely stopped the truck in time to avoid crashing into a large "dead end" sign.

"That's impossible," I shouted in disbelief. "This wasn't on the map!"

The worst thing was that Erin didn't have to say anything. She just sat there with a look of disdain, shaking her head from side to side. So I did what any man would do in such a situation. I got out of the truck to survey the area. As I gazed down at the mighty Mississippi River, you could actually see my road form again on the other side.

"It's not my fault that the map didn't show that a bridge wasn't here!" I shouted back at the truck. Then I began to wonder what would happen if I drove around the barrier and . . .

Erin's voice interrupted my thoughts. "Don't you even *think* about it!" she snarled. "Take us back the way we came!"

As I reached to study the map, Erin quickly jerked it out of my hands. Defeated, I didn't even try to get it back. Sitting there, watching my wife attempt to determine our location, I began to notice how scary fields of corn look at night in the middle of nowhere. It didn't help that buzzards had begun circling overhead, squawking excitedly. I started to remember a movie about murderous children who lived in cornfields. We needed to leave. *Now!*

Driving back, Erin and I said nothing for quite some time. When she finally spoke, I felt certain she was going to give me a piece of her mind. I deserved it! But she didn't yell or tease me. She actually did the very thing you can do to unlock the most important relational needs of your future spouse.

"I believe we can learn a great deal about each other's relational needs by answering the statement: 'I feel loved when you . . .' " Erin said in a calm voice.

I gulped and nodded, grateful to have escaped what could have been well-deserved wrath. She began first.

"I feel loved when you ask AAA about our trip route."

Touché.

Top Relational Needs

My counseling office fills up with troubled people who sadly never understood or fulfilled their spouses' wants and needs. To better grasp what those needs might be, I spent a year doing a great deal of research on relational needs. I wanted to discover what people *really* want in a relationship.

I read countless studies and many books on "love languages" by noted authors, such as Gary Chapman. Eventually I constructed a list of almost fifty relational needs that repeatedly pop up in the literature. Then I put that list in front of more than ten thousand husbands and wives who attended various conferences. I asked each couple to rank these needs from most to least important. Finally, based on their responses, I came up with a top-ten list of the most important relational needs (we'll look at this list a little later).

My survey of relational needs led to an interesting conclusion: the list of common top *needs* for couples, when unmet, looks identical to the list that nationally known researchers have identified as the most common reasons why couples *argue*.

What does this mean? When needs do not get met, look out! Your marriage is at stake. Your mate will become overly defensive, argumentative, jealous, belligerent, withdrawn, or degrading. When your deepest relational needs go unmet, you tend to feel more irritated, discouraged, edgy, hypersensitive, and reactionary to "average" events that occur in a typical marriage.

Furthermore, the need for companionship in a long-lasting relationship is so strong that most men and women will go to any length to satisfy it. If marriage doesn't meet their needs, they may go outside the marriage and into an emotional or sexual affair. Or they will get these needs fulfilled at work, play, through relatives, friends, children, or in the community at large.

Why focus on relational needs? How are they important to the health of your future marriage? To answer this question, consider how some groups of surveyed couples answered another question: *What is the benefit of sharing relational needs?* Note what they said, in order of importance:

◆ *Increases positive communication.* Talking about relational needs fosters healthy communication by fulfilling the need to share wants and desires. The key is to focus on understanding and validation. This strengthens the relationship because a spouse is doing something that his or her mate perceives as important and positive. If one mate starts to degrade or dishonor the other's important needs, communication ultimately ceases. Therefore, husbands and wives must guard this sharing of needs as a priceless treasure. No one and nothing must be allowed to harm it.

✦ *Increases understanding.* When your mate shares a relational need, he or she reveals a deep part of himself or herself. You begin to deeply understand what he or she needs in order to feel cared for and loved. Understanding is knowledge, and knowledge is power.

✦ *Promotes action in the relationship.* Once you know your mate's needs, you can act upon that knowledge.

✦ *Fosters trust, security, and safety.* As you gain the right knowledge and take action to meet your mate's needs, you promote security and trust in the relationship.

✦ *Promotes conflict resolution.* Conflict in a marriage is inevitable. But if relational needs are getting met, then the conflict usually does not grow as intense as it might otherwise, and it gets resolved faster.

✦ *Increases honor in the relationship.* The essence of honor is making someone feel that his or her needs and wants are important and valuable.

Can you see how relational needs provide an important key to creating a safe home? If you try hard to understand and meet your future mate's relational needs, you can look forward to a long time of enjoying a deeply satisfying home life.

LOVE Is All You Need

One thing is certain: before you can begin meeting your future mate's deepest needs, you have to know what they are. Consider the first law of fulfilling needs: *Everyone's needs are different.* Relational needs are based on unique personalities, backgrounds, and expectations. Before anything else, you must learn to recognize your fiancée's or fiancé's individual needs (as well as your own).

My research with more than ten thousand couples helped me to uncover the top-ten relational needs. To help you remember them, I've listed them under the letters of a fabulous word: LOVE. The acronym stands for *Listen, Offer yourself, Value and honor, and Embrace.* I can find no better description of true love, and it plays strongly into the idea of relational needs.

L= Listen

To really listen means more than nodding at your fiancé while keeping one eye on an email or on the latest sports score. Active listening means being devoted not only to hearing your future spouse, but also to understanding him or her and responding in loving ways. Within this category I found the following needs:

1. Honesty and trustworthiness. In other words . . .

+ Remain open.
+ Be vulnerable.
+ Share details of your life, feelings, needs, opinions, and concerns as they come up.
+ Don't tell half-truths or "white lies."
+ Give your honest opinion, not what you think your loved one wants to hear.
+ Be genuine, be a person of integrity.
+ Never give your future spouse reason to doubt; avoid questionable situations.
+ Be faithful, both physically and emotionally.

2. Attention to my opinions, thoughts, and beliefs. In other words . . .

+ Listen honestly and without condemnation.

- ✦ Listen with your body through attentive eye contact and body language.
- ✦ Take your fiancée/fiancé seriously and never mock her or him.
- ✦ When you challenge your future spouse, do so with respect.
- ✦ Accept differences of opinion.
- ✦ Be a cheerleader and support your loved one.
- ✦ Don't disagree too often in public.
- ✦ Validate your mate-to-be by not interrupting while she or he is talking (that is, while sharing her/his feelings).
- ✦ Solicit your future spouse's opinion.
- ✦ Prayerfully consider issues together.

3. Readiness to resolve differences, conflicts, and arguments through love. In other words . . .

- ✦ Plan how to work out conflicts.
- ✦ Come to a resolution together.
- ✦ Work through problems and find a compromise.
- ✦ Be concerned with your future spouse's opinion when conflict arises.
- ✦ Try to understand your loved one's position, rather than insisting that he or she understand yours.
- ✦ Express your deeper feelings and concerns.
- ✦ Develop rules that include no put-downs, no yelling, no accusing, no defensive reactions, no going to bed angry, no comparing, no allowing anger to build.

O= Offer Yourself

Offering yourself goes to the heart of love. It means that you consider your fiancé's needs more important than your own (see Philippians 2:3). In this way you will offer yourself to your marriage. You will feel more concerned about meeting your future spouse's needs than whether yours are being met. This aspect of love includes the following relational needs:

4. Security that we'll stay together. In other words . . .

+ Make an unconditional commitment to each other: "No matter how we feel or what we do, we are committed to always be together."
+ Make plans for the future together.
+ Believe that divorce is not an option, and choose to never talk about it.
+ Take action in meeting your future spouse's needs.
+ Make your marriage the most important earthly relationship you have.
+ Express your love through hugs and surprises or whatever best meets your loved one's needs.
+ Be proactive in your relationship (seek counseling, read marriage books, attend marriage seminars, etc.).
+ Be available to your future spouse.

5. Unity regarding raising our children. In other words . . .

+ Offer yourself and your viewpoints to help form a childrearing plan.
+ Decide not to disagree about childrearing in front of the children.
+ As a couple, take in parenting seminars, classes, books, etc.
+ Be united in making decisions about the kids.
+ Avoid the nice-parent/mean-parent syndrome.
+ Discuss discipline and rules.
+ Pray together about the direction of your future children, and continue this forever.
+ Help each other be consistent parents.

V = Value and Honor

One of the greatest sets of relational needs involves feeling validated and honored. This will happen only when you take time to verbalize the reasons why you value and honor your fiancée. At the same time, you must act on these feelings. Let's look at some of these value-related needs.

6. Acceptance for who I am. In other words . . .

+ Let your future spouse know that you value his or her thoughts and opinions.
+ Make sure your loved one doesn't need your permission to be himself or herself.
+ Eliminate judgmental attitudes.
+ Encourage and praise your fiancée/fiancé.
+ Avoid excessive criticism.
+ Often tell your betrothed of your love.
+ Appropriately display your affection in public (PDA).
+ Unconditionally accept your future spouse's good and bad characteristics.
+ Show interest in your future mate's interests.
+ Spend time with your partner-to-be—get to know him or her.
+ Make sure your loved one is your top priority, after God.

7. Inclusion in most decisions that affect our upcoming marriage. In other words . . .

+ Develop a sense of togetherness and belonging.
+ Discuss in advance important issues, purchases, or decisions.
+ Make decisions that are best for both of you.
+ Commit to holding family meetings.
+ Work to be more inclusive with each other.
+ Don't make assumptions about your future spouse's thoughts or choices.

8. Acceptance for what I do. In other words . . .

+ Recognize and appreciate accomplishments or efforts.
+ Acknowledge the importance of your future spouse's work.

✦ Recognize that your future mate's work is part of who he or she is.

✦ Offer words of affirmation for your loved one's work or hobbies.

✦ Appreciate what your future spouse does.

✦ Include your fiancée in your work and other activities.

✦ Take an interest in your betrothed's work and activities.

E = Embrace

In order to maintain the oneness of marriage, it is crucial to connect with each other again and again. High on the list of relational needs lies the need for physical touch. Embracing also means to stay close to your future spouse, both emotionally and spiritually.

9. Feeling connected through physical touch and spending time together. In other words . . .

✦ Look for ways to add touch to your relationship.

✦ Hold hands more often.

✦ Give your future spouse a hug for no reason except that you love him or her.

✦ Enjoy the physical nearness of spending time together.

✦ Set aside time for each other on a regular basis.

✦ Spend time with your future spouse's activity of choice without complaining.

✦ Engage in activities you both enjoy.

✦ Realize that time together must be mutually fulfilling to cause a feeling of connectedness.

✦ Look for ways to make any moment together one of quality.

10. A mutually vibrant spiritual relationship. In other words . . .

✦ Pray together. As we've said, research has shown that couples who pray together every day have a divorce rate less than 0.1 percent (1 out of 1,152)![1]

✦ Study the Word individually and together.

✦ Faithfully attend church together.

✦ Get involved in church activities.

✦ Hold each other spiritually accountable.

✦ Maintain a Christ-centered relationship by seeking God's will, living by biblical principles, and making God your top priority.

✦ Discuss spiritual growth or ask spiritually challenging questions.

✦ Read spiritual books and seek other spiritual development.

Drawing Out Relational Needs

Because emotional safety within a relationship is so important, I asked couples attending our seminar: "On a scale of 0 to 10 (10 being completely secure), how secure do you feel in your relationship to share those needs?"

On average, respondents rated their degree of safety in the relationship at a 7. Keep in mind that because most seminar participants seek enrichment in their marriages, they generally feel more satisfied with their relationships than the average population. The respondents cited the following techniques as the most effective ways to draw out their spouse's needs:

✦ *Validate.* "I want to feel that you hear me and understand what I'm saying." This can be accomplished by repeating back what you hear. Remember the meaning of LOVE? Apply it to your upcoming marriage, and your future spouse will feel safe enough to share his or her needs.

✦ *Ask.* Although it's your betrothed's responsibility to share his or her needs, realize that at times you must take the initiative.

✦ *Focus on your future spouse's needs.* When your future spouse shares his or her needs, use your body language to show that you are listening.

+ *Create a positive environment.* People share their deepest needs when they feel free from distractions, both physically and emotionally.
+ *Reciprocate.* As you share your needs, your loved one will be more likely to share his or hers.
+ *Honor.* Help your future mate feel that you value his or her needs.
+ *Security.* Your betrothed needs to trust that the information he or she discloses will be protected not only from your ridicule, but also from that of others.
+ *Follow through.* Your future mate must trust that once he or she opens up and reveals relational needs, you will act upon them. It would feel discouraging if nothing changed after relational needs were disclosed.

Just Twenty Minutes Per Day!

Every person has unique relational needs. Now you need to develop the skill of finding out which needs are most important to your future mate. According to Dr. John Gottman, you can effectively do this *in only twenty minutes a day!*

Gottman's research revealed that the difference between a couple who divorces and one who stays together (but feels unhappy) is ten minutes a day of "turning toward" each other. By this, he means that a husband and wife must encourage and build up each other every day through positive words or affirmative interactions. Furthermore, Gottman found that happy couples who stay together "turn toward" each other an additional ten minutes each day.[2]

From these discoveries, we can safely declare that a total of twenty minutes a day of "turning toward each other" in substantial ways can make the difference between divorce and staying together in a happy, satisfying relationship. Just twenty minutes a day!

It's Your Turn

It's time for you to create your own top-ten list. What things need to happen in your upcoming marriage in order for you both to say, *I feel loved*?

And don't worry—it won't be as hard as you might think. For the most part, you'll be working from a list that we've developed over the years in our work with thousands of couples. Why a list? Because if you're at all like me, you need it.

If you were to ask me, "Greg, what do you really want or need in your relationship?" I'd more than likely say, "I don't know." I'm pretty laid-back and easygoing, and without a list, I tend to struggle. So use the list (with our blessings) to discover how to make your home the safest place on earth.

On a separate sheet of paper, both of you fill in the blank: *I feel loved or cared for when you_____*. Be sure to record all your responses. This information is a gold mine of relational material and will help to give you a clear picture of how to make your home safe.

In order to understand which of the following needs are most important to you, rank each one from one to ten. If you have any needs not listed, write them on the "other need" lines at the end of the list.

LITTLE IMPORTANCE   **EXTREME IMPORTANCE**

1   2   3   4   5   6   7   8   9   10

___ Feel connected through talking

___ Feel connected through sharing recreation/fun times together

___ Be touched nonsexually

___ Receive verbal tenderness

___ Receive physical tenderness

___ Support my desire to live by the laws of man

___ Support my desire to live by the laws of God

___ Know that we'll stay together and feel secure in love

___ Know we'll stay together and feel secure in finances

__ Feel accepted and valued for who I am

__ Feel accepted and valued for what I do

__ Feel safe when I share who I am

__ Be included in most decisions that affect our life or future marriage

__ Gain agreement and harmony in decision making

__ Know that you need me

__ Support my desire to give away money

__ Support my desire to give gifts to others

__ Support my desire to serve others

__ Receive genuine appreciation, praise, and affirmation

__ Support my desire to have alone time

__ Be physically attractive

__ Be honest and trustworthy

__ Support my desire to assist the younger generation in developing and leading useful lives

__ Receive gifts

__ Receive acts of service

__ Develop with me a plan for our future marriage

__ Develop complete faith in each other

__ Become emotionally healthy

__ Maintain a mutually vibrant spiritual relationship

__ Apologize and seek forgiveness

__ Resolve differences/conflicts/arguments

__ Provide mutually satisfying communication

__ Cope with crises and stress

__ Understand my personality and gender differences

__ Demonstrate a willingness to change (flexibility)

__ Agree on how to raise our future children

__ Be passionate and romantic

__ Socially connect with others

__ Maintain careful control over your expectations

__ Notice our positive relational history

___ Strive for mutuality and equality in our relationship
___ Share negative and positive feelings without delay
___ Accept my influence
___ Periodically update your knowledge of my greatest needs
___ Receive genuine appreciation for my service
___ *Other need:* _____.
___ *Other need:* _____.

From the preceding list, record your top-ten needs, in order of importance (with number 1 as your most important need).

1. _____

2. _____

3. _____

4. _____

5. _____

6. _____

7. _____

8. _____

9. _____

10. _____

In order for your future mate to completely understand your top-ten relational needs, it's necessary to explain what each need means to you. If one of your top needs is to "provide mutually satisfying communication," for example, then you must explain what that means to you. Moreover, if your future mate were to give you "satisfying communication," then what would he or she be doing? Make your explanation as specific as possible. Tell your future mate what specific behaviors would provide mutually satisfying communication. In the space below, define each top need.

1. _____

_____

_____

_____

2. _____

_____

_____

_____

3. _____

_____

4. _____

5. _____

6. _____

7. _____

_____

_____

8. _____

_____

_____

_____

9. _____

_____

_____

_____

10. _____

_____

_____

_____

A Word from Erin

(Since Greg has provided the main voice for this book—
even though both of us have worked together in producing the text—
we thought it was only fair that Erin should have the last word.
So here goes!)

This May, Greg and I will celebrate our fifteenth wedding anniversary. What a joy to realize how far we've come in those years!

During the creation of this book, Greg and I had to relive many painful experiences from early in our marriage. In fact, as we sat at our dining-room table, we actually "danced" as we discussed (and debated) some of our past issues and stories.

Our buttons definitely got pushed!

We still see many things very differently; for example, regarding the details of our breakup as told in chapter 1. Greg doesn't even want me to say that we broke up. He swears that he plainly and clearly said *only* that he wanted us to "slow down."

What can I say? I heard "break up." Slow down, break up—what's the difference? It pushed my *Rejected* button.

As we wrote the story for this book, we started debating what really happened and who was right and who was wrong—all of the things we told *you* are a waste of time! The next day, Greg and I were scheduled to speak at John Brown University's Valentine's Day chapel service on love and relationships. How ironic! We were actually at a good place relation-ally, until Greg asked all one thousand students to vote on whether we actually broke up, based on what he remembers telling me. Like *that's* real fair.

I must admit, he made a pretty compelling argument, and the stu-dents unanimously voted that he was right—we never broke up. But if that's true, then I was two-timing him with that other guy. Oh, well. Either way, I still win—I got what I wanted. I got my man!

(Still, I'd really like to set up a website and ask *you* to vote for whether we really broke up, and whether I was right after all. We wouldn't even have to tell Greg about it until all votes had been counted!)

Despite our occasional missteps, today we "dance" in a completely different way. I celebrate the revision. These days we work through our differences in a much healthier manner. Our interactions aren't always reaction free, and we don't always automatically respond in healthy ways—at times we still have the kind of dance I wouldn't recommend to others—but I can say quite truthfully that our typical interactions help us get to where we want to be relationally. We have definitely learned to care for our own hearts, and each other's hearts, in a whole new way. I feel *much* safer in my marriage. And to me, that is worth celebrating.

One of our greatest relational success stories happened almost two years ago, when we took a major fork in the road on our marital journey. In the past, the event would have been a separating force in our relation-ship; this time around, however, the opportunity drew us closer to each other and to the Lord. I still look back and smile as I think about it.

You have to understand that Greg is notorious for thinking out loud. You may know just how unsettling this can be for a woman who wants to feel secure. The bottom line is, Greg often spews these ideas that often make no sense to me whatsoever. Frankly, they scare me—especially if I follow his line of thinking. He has learned to preface and qualify his ideas with "Erin, I'm just thinking out loud—so don't freak out." I actu-ally love it when he says that!

Anyway, on this particular day, Greg came home from work and said, "I had the strangest phone call today. My mentor and dear friend, Dr. Gary Oliver, called and asked for some names to fill a job position he has open at the Center for Relationship Enrichment (CRE) on the campus of John Brown University. And the most amazing thing happened! As he described the job and the perfect candidate, I realized that the person he was describing was—*me!*"

He paused, then said gently, "So, Erin, what do you think about moving to a small town in Northwest Arkansas? It's in Wal-Mart country!" He said that last part in a way that he figured would make me more open to the idea, knowing that the university was near Wal-Mart's corporate headquarters.

He was wrong!

My mouth dropped open, but no words came out. Immediately, I had to soothe myself by remembering that Greg was probably just doing his typical thinking-out-loud thing, and in no way, shape, or form was he being serious. So I laughed and joined in the festivities of imagining what our life would be like in Arkansas. I said things like, "Actually, Garrison would fit right in, since he has only two teeth!"

(Speaking of teeth, the best Arkansas joke we've heard goes like this: "You know that the toothbrush was invented in Arkansas? Otherwise, it would have been called the teethbrush!" Sadly, we never realized that one state had so many jokes told about it until we moved to Arkansas. The truth is, Northwest Arkansas is a *beautiful* part of the country and has some of the smartest, most interesting people we've ever met.)

But I digress. After I had totally invalidated the idea in my mind, Greg stopped me and said, "Actually, Erin, I'm *serious*. There is something about this position that I feel drawn to, and I think I'd like to look at it a bit further."

My heart stopped in my chest. Only then did I realize he was no longer just thinking out loud.

Months passed, and we didn't talk much about this job opportunity in . . . *where* was it again? Arkansas? *Whatever.* I knew that, inevitably, we were going to have to talk about it. As we've all heard, talking is a requirement for a healthy marriage! In the end, I knew I had to prepare my case as to why this surely could not be a good idea. Clearly, it was not God's will.

The intervening time gave me an opportunity to practice what we've preached to you about taking care of yourself. One way I know I've matured is that I can identify what I'm feeling inside. I took some time to better understand what was going on in my heart. I worried about my kids having to leave their friends and start in a new school. I started grieving the possibility of leaving family, friends, and our dream home. We had lived in southwest Missouri for nearly eight years. This move—and even the *possibility* of moving—caused some deep feelings to surface.

In the past, I would have stuffed these feelings, judged them away, or tried to get Greg to validate them. Now, I handle my heart very differently. So instead of invalidating my feelings, I identified them and then embraced them with loving tenderness. I made it okay that I was feeling anxious and scared. I spent some time with the Lord, asking him to attend to my heart, as well. The bottom line is, I worked very hard to keep my heart open to the Lord, to Greg, and to this possibility.

As Greg and I approached the moment for *the* conversation, my heart had fully opened. I took the role of listener and worked to understand my husband. Mostly, I just listened as I heard Greg dream about what it would be like to be a university professor and work with Gary Oliver. I reflected, validated, and stretched myself to hear my husband's heart. And with the Lord's help, I was able to help him feel understood.

When he was nearly through dreaming out loud, he said, "Erin, I want you to remember that the only possible solution I will accept is something that feels great to both of us. This isn't just about me and my dreams! It has to be a win for both of us in order for our team to win."

I still find it amazing what happened next. I was in a pretty good place emotionally before the conversation, but to hear Greg say out loud that we both had to feel great about any decision caused me to feel completely safe with him. I know that we teach this concept all over the world, but it never ceases to amaze me when I experience its power for myself. It brought my heart great comfort to know that he wouldn't pack us up without my being fully on board. I felt safe knowing that I wouldn't be steamrolled, minimized, or told to submit.

But I also felt safe with *me*.

I had taken the time to attend to my heart. I also felt safe with the Lord, knowing that if He was in it, this would be a *great* decision.

Over the next several months, we talked often about this opportunity. Finally, we decided that we needed to visit Northwest Arkansas. We packed up the kids in our van and drove the two hours from Branson. I'll never forget how, as we approached the area, our kids started complaining about a strange odor in the air.

"Oh . . . yes," Greg explained, "that is the sweet aroma of the chicken farms."

The largest meat producer in America, Tyson Foods, has its corporate headquarters there. Again, I thought, *this is* so *not going to happen*. We spent the day in Siloam Springs and then headed back home.

Several days later, Greg asked me if I had an idea of what my wins would be if we were to move. I came up with quite a list: a house the same size as our home in Branson (which I knew could never happen, because the move would mean a pay cut); great schools; a new car—on and on I went.

He just smiled and encouraged me to keep praying.

I took to heart his challenge and spent many days talking to God about this possible move. And in all of my bitterness and disgust, I realized that the Lord was beginning to change my heart. *Isn't that so often the case?* I thought. *He would choose to change my heart on the one thing that I said "never" to.* But I continued to pray, in hopes that I was wrong about what God seemed to be saying to me.

Finally, the day came when Gary Oliver needed our final decision.

Again, I knew that Greg would want to talk about it. Being the mature person that I am, I got really busy with things outside the home and was unavailable.

As always happens, darkness fell upon the earth, and Greg came home from work. The time had come to talk, especially since I had run out of excuses and busywork. In the past, I realized, this conversation would not have gone well. We would have ended up dancing and ultimately disconnecting from each other. This time, however—even though I felt anxious—I had confidence that we would end up in a good place, both with the decision and relationally. I looked at Greg and boldly said, "You asked me what my win was several months ago, and I finally know the answer. My win is knowing that you feel God is calling us to Arkansas."

I wish I could have taken a picture of the look on Greg's face! In some ways, I think, he had geared up for a battle. Now he was in total shock. The best part was that he didn't hesitate one moment. Instead, he said confidently, "Then we are moving, because I know that God is calling us to Northwest Arkansas."

As strange as it all seemed, we had achieved unity in what could have been the most tragic decision-making process in our marital history. Rather than pushing us apart, it drew us closer to one another and to the Lord.

Six months later, we moved. Not a day went by that I didn't wonder if we had made a mistake! I loved calling Greg and saying, "I am just curious, but . . . today, do you feel like we could back out?"

He would laugh and say, "No way! God is calling us there, Erin." I do believe that by the fiftieth or sixtieth time, he could have just recorded a canned response for me to hear. But instead, each time he reassured me, gently and confidently. And by so doing he continued to make me feel safe.

To be completely honest, there were plenty of times when I felt anxious and fearful about the transition. Greg would always say, "Remember, Erin, the moment that moving doesn't feel like a win to you, all you have to do is tell me, and we will not move. We'll continue to talk and seek the Lord's will. I will *not* move our family until that decision feels great for both of us."

You know what? I have zero doubt that he really would have taken the move off the table the second he felt we had failed to reach a win-win.

Now that we are proud residents of Siloam Springs, Arkansas—and yes, our children wear actual shoes and still have all their teeth—we have experienced over and over again the confirmation that God, in fact, called us to Northwest Arkansas. And remember my original list of wins for moving? Well, I should never have doubted that God would provide.

We have found a great church; Greg and I have some amazing friends; Taylor and Maddy have made many wonderful girlfriends; we have a great house that we enjoy every bit as much as our Branson home; Garrison (who loves to fish more than anything else in life) has a pond right outside our back door that teems with bass, perch, carp, and catfish (his record so far is a four-pound bass he caught and landed all by himself); we *love* the school system and our precious teachers; we've gotten involved in the community; Greg and I get to minister together at CRE; I even got a new car—and the list goes on and on. There have been special blessings, too. As we write this book, God has blessed our center with a large federal grant to launch a healthy-marriage initiative in our community.

God is great!

Although this process may look different for the two of you, we pray that you can walk into your marriage prepared to function as teammates and that you can honor each other in the midst of differing opinions. Give each other grace when you make mistakes. Continue to gain insight into what is going on for you personally and when your buttons get pushed. Seek forgiveness when you blow it by reacting badly to each other.

We wish for you great success, by which we mean that you both become more like Christ and are thrilled with your marriage. And we hope that, in the end, your marriage will feel like the safest place on earth.

We are rooting for you! May you be able to look back as you approach your own fifteen-year anniversary and see how far your relationship has come. What a joy it will bring to our hearts to join you in that great celebration!

Self-Test to Discover Reactions That Hurt Your Relationship

Not sure how seriously your reactions may have hurt your relationship? Then take the following simple test to see to what extent these reactions have invaded your relationship. Read each of the statements below, and write down the number that best describes how often you feel you and your spouse experience what the statements describe. Use a three-point scale: 1 = almost never; 2 = once in a while; 3 = frequently. When you finish, total your score:

REACTION SCORE

1. When we argue, one of us withdraws—not wanting to talk about it anymore—or leaves the scene. _____
2. Little arguments escalate into ugly fights, with accusations, criticisms, name calling, or bringing up past hurts. _____
3. My partner criticizes or belittles my opinions, feelings, or desires. _____

REACTION SCORE

4. My partner seems to view my words or actions more negatively than I mean them to be. ____

5. When we have a problem to solve, it is as if we are on opposite teams. ____

6. I hold back from telling my partner what I really think and feel. ____

7. I think seriously about what it would be like to date or marry someone else. ____

8. I feel lonely in this relationship. ____

TOTAL ____

What Does This Mean?

These statements, aimed at identifying the communcation and conflict-management patterns that predict trouble in a relationship, are based on fifteen years of research completed at the University of Denver. Dr. Scott Stanley and Dr. Howard Markman conducted a nationwide random phone survey using these statements. The average score was 11; higher scores mean your relationship may be in even greater danger.[1]

GREEN LIGHT: SCORE OF 8 TO 12

If you scored in the 8 to 12 range, your relationship is probably in good or even great shape *at this time*. I emphasize "at this time" because relationships never stand still. In the next twelve months, you'll have either a stronger, happier relationship or one sliding in the other direction. If you scored in this range, think of it as a green light *for now* and keep moving forward to make your relationship all it can be.

YELLOW LIGHT: SCORE OF 13 TO 17

If you scored in the 13 to 17 range, think of it as a yellow caution light. While you may feel happy in your relationship, your score reveals warning signs, pointing to patterns you don't want to get worse. You ought to take action to protect and improve what you have. Spending time now to strengthen your relationship could be the best thing you could do for your future together.

RED LIGHT: SCORE OF 18 TO 24

If you scored in the 18 to 24 range, think of it as a red light. Stop and look at where the two of you are headed. Your score indicates the presence of patterns that could put your relationship at significant risk. You may be heading for trouble—or perhaps you're already there. But there is good news! You can stop *now* and learn ways to improve your relationship. If your dream is turning into a nightmare, don't just pull the sheets over your head. Wake up and take action!

What should you do if you notice the strong presence of one or more of these four reactions? Seek help and counsel at once.

NOTES

1
IF ONLY WE HAD KNOWN

1. Based on the Oklahoma Healthy Marriage Initiative's random phone survey of 3,344 adults in four states, www.okmarriage.org/oklahomamarriageinitiative.asp.
2. David H. Olson and Amy K. Olson, *Empowering Couples: Building on Your Strengths* (Minneapolis: Life Innovations, Inc., 2000).
3. Jason Carroll and William J. Doherty, "Evaluating the Effectiveness of Premarital Education Programs: A Meta-analytic Review," *Family Relations*, 53 (2003):105–118.
4. Genesis 2:24 NLT.
5. John M. Gottman and Nan Silver, *The Seven Principles for Making Marriage Work* (New York: Crown Publishing Group, 1999), 2.

2
HOW TO HAVE A "10" ENGAGEMENT

1. Stephen R. Covey, A. Roger Merrill, and Rebecca R. Merrill, *First Things First* (New York: Simon & Schuster, 1994), 265.
2. David H. Olson, John Defrain, Amy Olson, *Building Relationships: Developing Skills for Life* (Minneapolis: Life Innovations, Inc., 1999), 63.
3. Olson, Defrain, and Olson, *Building Relationships*, 57.
4. George Barna, "Born Again Christians Just As Likely to Divorce As Are Non-Christians," September 8, 2004, The Barna Group, Ventura, CA, www.barnagroup.org/FlexPage.as px?Page=BarnaUpdate&BarnaUpdateID=170.
5. 1997 Gallup Poll commissioned by the National Association of Marriage Enhancement in Phoenix, Arizona, www.galluppoll.com.
6. John Gottman, *Why Marriages Succeed or Fail . . . And How You Can Make Yours Last* (New York: Fireside, 1995).
7. Gottman and Silver, *The Seven Principles for Making Marriage Work*, 49.
8. Olson, Defrain, and Olson, *Building Relationships*.
9. Ibid., 57.
10. National Center for Health Statistics, "43 Percent of First Marriages Break Up Within 15 Years," May 24, 2001, news release, www.cdc.gov/nchs/pressroom/01news/first marr.htm.
11. Martin K. Whyte, *Dating, Mating, and Marriages* (New York: Aldine de Gruyter, 1990).

12. Lawrence A. Kurdek, "Marital Stability and Changes in Marital Quality in Newlywed Couples: A Test of the Contextual Model," *Journal of Social and Personal Relationships* 8 no. 1 (1991): 27–48.

13. Deborah Tannen, *You Just Don't Understand: Women and Men in Conversation* (New York: William Morrow, 1990).

14. Steven Nock, *Marriage in Men's Lives* (New York: Oxford University Press, 1998).

15. R. A. Lewis and G. B. Spanier, "Theorizing about the Quality and Stability of Marriage," in *Contemporary Theories about the Family,* Welsey R. Burr and others, eds., 1:268–94 (New York: Free Press, 1979).

16. M. Christian Green, *Marriage—Just a Piece of Paper? A Video Discussion Guide for Congregations and Communities.* The Religion, Culture, and Family Project, Divinity School of the University of Chicago, 2003.

17. Helen J. Raschke, "Divorce," in *Handbook of Marriage and the Family,* M. B. Sussman and S. K. Steimetz, eds. (New York: Plenum, 1987), 597–624.

18. Kelly J. Grover and others, "Mate Selection Processes and Marital Satisfaction," *Family Relations* 34 (1985): 383–86.

19. Lawrence A. Kurdek, "Predicting Marital Dissolution: A 5-Year Prospective Longitudinal Study of Newlywed Couples," *Journal of Personality and Social Psychology* 64 (1993): 221–42.

20. Stephen R. Covey, *The 7 Habits of Highly Effective People: Powerful Lessons in Personal Change* (New York: Simon & Schuster, 1989), 98.

3

GOD'S PURPOSE FOR MARRIAGE

1. C. S. Lewis, "Is Christianity Hard or Easy?" *Mere Christianity* (New York: HarperCollins, 1952), 195.

4

ARE YOU EXPECTING?

1. Jeffry H. Larson, "The Marriage Quiz: College Students' Beliefs in Selected Myths about Marriage," *Family Relations* 37, no. 1 (1988): 3–11.

2. David H. Olson, John DeFrain, and Amy K. Olson, *Building Relationships: Developing Skills for Life* (Minneapolis: Life Innovations, Inc., 1999), 53.

3. Olson, DeFrain, and Olson, *Building Relationships,* 57.

4. Mort Orman, "Are You Expecting?" (1995), www.stresscure.com/health/expecting.html.

5. H. Norman Wright, *So You're Getting Married* (Ventura, CA: Regal, 1985).

6. Ronald M. Sabatelli, "Exploring Relationship Satisfaction: A Social Exchange Perspective on the Interdependence Between Theory, Research, and Practice," *Family Relations* 37, no. 2 (1988): 219.

7. Ronald M. Sabatelli, "Exploring Relationship Satisfaction: A Social Exchange Perspective

on the Interdependance Between Theory, Research, and Practice," *Family Relations* 37, no. 2 (1988): 217–22.

8. J. D. Ball and L. H. Henning, "Rational Suggestions for Pre-Marital Counseling," *Journal of Marital and Family Therapy* 7, no. 1 (1981): 69–73.

9. Rachel R. Barich and Denise D. Bielby, "Rethinking Marriage: Change and Stability in Expectations, 1967–1994," *Journal of Family Issues* 17, no. 2 (1996): 139–69.

10. C. Hendrick and S. Hendrick, "A Theory and Method of Love," *Journal of Personality and Social Psychology* 50, no. 2 (1986): 392–402.

11. Barry Sinrod and Marlo Grey, *Just Married* (Kansas City, MO: Andrews McMeel, 1998).

12. Sinrod and Grey, *Just Married.*

13. Sinrod and Grey, *Just Married.*

14. Norman Epstein and Roy J. Eidelson, "Unrealistic Beliefs of Clinical Couples: Their Relationship to Expectations, Goals and Satisfaction," *American Journal of Family Therapy* 9, no. 4 (1981): 13–22.

15. M. Scott Peck, *The Road Less Traveled: A New Psychology of Love, Traditional Values and Spiritual Growth* (New York: Simon & Schuster, 1978), 84.

16. Virginia Satir, *Conjoint Family Therapy: A Guide to Theory and Technique* (Palo Alto, CA: Science and Behavior Books, 1967).

17. Howard J. Markman, Scott M. Stanley, and Susan L. Blumberg, *Fighting for Your Marriage* (San Francisco: Jossey-Bass, 2001), 148.

6
PERSONAL RESPONSIBILITY

1. The Serenity Prayer is attributed to mid-twentieth-century theologian Reinhold Niebuhr, who used it first in a sermon. It was later adopted by Alcoholics Anonymous and widely distributed in their pamphlets.

2. Gottman, *Why Marriages Succeed or Fail,* 177.

3. J. D. Mayer, M. T. DiPaolo, and P. Salovey, "Perceiving Affective Content in Ambiguous Visual Stimuli: A Component of Emotional Intelligence." *Journal of Personality Assessment* 54 (1990): 772–81.

4. Daniel Goleman, *Emotional Intelligence: Why It Can Matter More Than IQ* (New York: Bantam Books, 1995).

5. Travis Bradberry and Jean Greaves, *The Emotional Intelligence Quick Book: Everything You Need to Know to Put Your EQ to Work* (New York: Fireside, 1995), 48–49.

8
WILL YOU FORGIVE ME?

1. William A. Meninger, *The Process of Forgiveness,* (New York: Continuum International Publishing Group,1997), 33.

11
LEAVING

1. Presentation: "Separation-Individuation from Parents and Marital Adjustment in Newly-wed Couples," Wendy Amstutz-Haws, M.S., and Brent Mallinckrodt, Ph.D., University of Oregon, Session 1085, 11:00–11:50 AM, Friday, August 9, 1996, Metro Toronto Convention Centre, Exhibit Hall (B-13).
2. E. L. Kelly and J. J. Conley, "Personality and Compatibility: A Prospective Analysis of Marital Stability and Marital Satisfaction," *Journal of Personality and Social Psychology* 58 (1987): 27–40.
3. G. E. Vaillant, "Natural History of Male Psychological Health: VI. Correlates of Successful Marriage and Fatherhood," *American Journal of Psychiatry* 135 (1978): 653–59.
4. Erin Smalley and Carrie Oliver, *Grown-Up Girlfriends: Finding and Keeping Real Friends in the Real World* (Carol Stream, IL: Tyndale House Publishers, 2007).
5. S. E. Taylor et al., "Biobehavioral Responses to Stress in Females: Tend-and-Befriend, not Fight-or-Flight," *Psychological Review* 107, 3 (2002): 411–29.
6. "20 Questions for Guiding Opposite-Sex Friendships in Marriage" is used by permission of Dr. Todd Linaman, Relational Advantage, Inc.
7. Isaiah 61:3.
8. Al Janssen, ed., *Seven Promises of a Promise Keeper* (Colorado Springs, CO: Focus on the Family Publishing, 1994), 87.

12
CLEAVING

1. 1997 Gallup Poll by the National Association of Marriage Enhancement in Phoenix, Arizona, www.galluppoll.com.
2. Gottman and Silver, *The Seven Principles for Making Marriage Work*, 178.

APPENDIX
SELF-TEST TO DISCOVER REACTIONS THAT HURT YOUR RELATIONSHIP

1. This self-test and scale were created by Scott Stanley and Howard Markman. Used by permission.

ABOUT THE AUTHORS

Dr. Greg and Erin Smalley have been married for fifteen years. They have two daughters, Taylor and Maddy, and a son, Garrison. The Smalleys live in Siloam Springs, Arkansas, and work together at the Center for Relationship Enrichment on the campus of John Brown University. Together they share a passion to help men and women obtain the knowledge and skills to build satisfying, lifelong marriages where both people become conformed to the image of the Lord.

Dr. Greg Smalley earned his doctorate degree in clinical psychology from Rosemead School of Psychology at Biola University in Southern California. He also holds two master's degrees. One is in counseling psychology from Denver Seminary and one is in clinical psychology from Rosemead School of Psychology. He is the director of Marriage Ministries for the Center for Relationship Enrichment. He is also an assistant professor of marriage and family studies at John Brown University. Dr. Smalley also helps lead marriage seminars around the world and trains pastors, professionals, and lay leaders how to effectively work with married couples. He is the author or coauthor of nine books including *The DNA of Relationships for Couples*, *The Marriage You've Always Dreamed Of*, *The DNA of Relationships*, *The DNA of Parent-Teen Relationships*, *Men's Relational Toolbox*, *Life Lines: Communicating with Your Teen*, *Winning Your Wife Back Before It's Too Late*, and *Winning Your Husband Back Before It's Too Late*.

Erin Smalley earned her bachelor's degree in nursing from Grand Canyon University in Phoenix, Arizona. She worked for eight years as a labor and delivery nurse. Erin earned her master's degree in clinical psychology from Evangel University in Springfield, Missouri. She works at the

Center for Relationship Enrichment and enjoys working with Greg, writing and speaking on marital and parenting issues. Erin and Carrie Oliver have written a book for building healthy female friendships called *Grown-Up Girlfriends,* published by Focus on the Family.

WOULD YOU LIKE GREG AND ERIN TO SPEAK AT YOUR CHURCH OR MARRIAGE EVENT?

As a husband and wife team, Greg and Erin are well equipped to provide you with a fresh, fun, and honest way of looking at marriage and family relationships. They would love the opportunity to discuss your specific needs and customize a speaking event that will have maximum impact for you. If you are interested in scheduling the Smalleys, please visit their website, www.smalleymarriage.com or call 479-524-7105.

Dr. Greg and Erin Smalley
The Center for Relationship Enrichment
John Brown University
2000 West University Street
Siloam Springs, AR 72761
Email: greg@smalleymarriage.com & erin@smalleymarriage.com
Website: www.smalleymarriage.com
CRE website: www.liferelationships.com